Jean M. Baker, PhD

Family Secrets
Gay Sons—A Mother's Story

*Pre-publication
REVIEWS,
COMMENTARIES,
EVALUATIONS . . .*

"**T**his truly remarkable book manages to close the gap between the very personal experiences of a mother, as she learns that her sons are gay, and a psychologist's research perspective on the terrible stigma of homophobia.

In *Family Secrets* Jean Baker writes in her capacities as both a noted clinical psychologist and a deeply devoted mother. As such she is willing to share with us the heart-rending experiences of losing a brilliant son to AIDS along with a broad understanding of the psychological impact of growing up gay in today's world. Perhaps, best of all, she offers solid suggestions on ways to reduce prejudice and to offer emotional support to our youth whose predetermined sexual orientation is 'different.'

A suggested reading for all parents. A must read for parents of gays and for all professionals working with today's youth."

Rachel Burkholder, PhD
Clinical Child Psychologist
in private practice,
Tucson, AZ

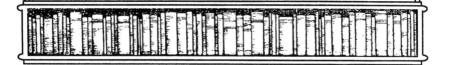

More pre-publication
REVIEWS, COMMENTARIES, EVALUATIONS . . .

"**A** refreshingly honest and moving portrait of a mother's love for her gay sons. Dr. Baker succinctly captures the emotional harm done, and the human toll taken, by keeping secrets. She also vividly depicts the horror a parent feels, as she describes the death of her youngest son from AIDS. Her brave personal exposé of the homophobia responsible for propagating shame in homosexuals and their parents serves as a poignant reminder of why our lesbian and gay youth take their own lives at a disproportionately high rate. This is a must read for every loving parent, for their family may also include a beautiful lesbian or gay child."

Alene Levine, MD
Staff Psychiatrist,
Department of Public Health,
San Francisco, CA

"**J**ean Baker has managed to capture the heart and soul of the struggles that surround the emergence of homosexuality and the devastation of AIDS, both from the gay man's as well as the parent's perspectives. I laughed with her as she described the joys of raising such exceptional boys, and cried with her as she described her anguish over Gary's struggles as an adolescent searching for answers regarding his sexuality and his futile battle with AIDS. The interspersions of Gary's journal and letters made the reader feel as if Gary were right there sharing his endless observations of his journeys. The inclusion of statements from various friends and teachers added still another perspective of Gary's life. I had the honor of knowing Gary and being with him near the end of his life. He truly was a special and gifted person. As a psychologist in private practice with Dr. Baker, I have also observed her growth as she endured the ecstasy and agony of watching her sons grow into such fine human beings. The amount of pain that Jean endured during such a short period of time was truly unbelievable. What a credit to her that she was willing to share her insights with us all.

This book is a must for all parents and educators, whether or not their children find themselves in the throes of this inner struggle. We all need to educate ourselves about society's homophobic tendencies. Only after we confront and counter the myths as so aptly done by Dr. Baker in this book, can we hope to overcome the prejudice against homosexuality."

Cheryl L. Karp, PhD
Licensed Psychologist
and author, private practice,
Tucson, AZ

More pre-publication
REVIEWS, COMMENTARIES, EVALUATIONS . . .

"**I**n *Family Secrets*, author Dr. Jean Baker deftly combines her professional expertise as a psychologist with her personal experiences as a mother of two homosexual sons to produce a comprehensive and compelling examination of growing up gay in America. She gently guides the reader on an intimate journey through the personal challenges of parenthood, the destructive effects of homophobia, and the tragedy of AIDS. Despite the personal sorrow, Dr. Baker leaves the reader with hope that society will one day accept, appreciate, and love all children regardless of their budding sexual orientation. Timely and clearly written, *Family Secrets* should be required reading for every parent, son, and daughter, as well as all who assume responsibility for shaping social policy regarding sexuality. Quite simply, this book should be read by everyone in America."

Larry A. Morris, PhD
Clinical Psychologist,
Tucson, AZ; Author,
The Male Heterosexual:
Lust in His Loins,
Sin in His Soul?

The Harrington Park Press
An Imprint of The Haworth Press, Inc.

Family Secrets
Gay Sons—A Mother's Story

HAWORTH Gay & Lesbian Studies
John P. De Cecco, PhD
Editor in Chief

Family Secrets
Gay Sons—A Mother's Story

Jean M. Baker, PhD

The Harrington Park Press
An Imprint of The Haworth Press, Inc.
New York • London

Published by

The Harrington Park Press, an imprint of The Haworth Press, Inc., 10 Alice Street, Binghamton, NY 13904-1580

Cover design by Marylouise E. Doyle.

The Library of Congress has catalogued the hardcover version of this book as:

Baker, Jean M.
    Family secrets : gay sons—a mother's story / Jean M. Baker.
       p.   cm.
    Includes bibliographical references and index.
    ISBN 0-7890-0248-5 (alk. paper)
    1. Baker, Gary. 2. Baker, Jean M. 3. Gay men—United States—Biography. 4. AIDS (Diseases)—Patients—United States—Biography. 5. Gay men—United States—Family relationships. 6. Parents of gays—United States. 7. Homophobia—United States—Psychological aspects. I. Title.
HQ75.8.B35A3 1998
305.38'9664'092
[B]—DC21
                                          97-18839
                                          CIP

To the memory of Gary Thomas Baker
and
with deepest gratitude
to my two dear sons
for teaching me about the many forms of love

ABOUT THE AUTHOR

Jean M. Baker, PhD, has been a licensed psychologist in private clinical practice in Tucson, Arizona, since 1970. Her practice has included individual psychotherapy with children and adults, family counseling, diagnostic evaluations, and forensic work. She has been the director of several nationally funded research projects, including a bilingual education project and a child abuse program evaluation project, and she has been a consultant to the State of Arizona in the field of child abuse and neglect since 1980. A past President of the Arizona Psychological Association and a former Social Issues Representative of its Governing Council, she is currently the Chair of its Gay/Lesbian/Bisexual Issues Committee. Dr. Baker has presented papers at numerous professional conferences and has presented recently on gay/lesbian topics at the American Psychological Association, of which she is a twenty-seven-year member. She has written book chapters and articles in the areas of child custody, child development, parent education, and lesbian/gay issues, including an article entitled "Breaking the Silence: Coming to Terms with Homosexuality and Bisexuality Among Our Youth."

CONTENTS

Preface

As a clinical psychologist who is also the mother of two gay children, I was professionally knowledgeable about homosexuality and believed I was more tolerant than most, but I was unprepared for coping with homosexuality in my own family.

In *Family Secrets* I have attempted to illustrate how societal attitudes about homosexuality encourage secrecy, preventing gay children from confiding in their parents and preventing parents from understanding or accepting homosexuality in their children. In this book I tell the story of how my own family was affected by homosexuality, and I trace the lives, from early childhood through young adulthood, of my two sons, Andy and Gary Baker—both of whom were to grow up to become accomplished adults, both of whom were to grow up to become gay. Secrecy made their father and me oblivious to our children's sexual orientation and secrecy made these two brothers each oblivious to the sexual orientation of the other.

In *Family Secrets* I have drawn upon research and scientific findings to attack the myths and stereotypes about homosexuality, those common beliefs that are so destructive to families with gay children and to the social and psychological development of gay youth. Accurate information is presented to help counter these myths and stereotypes, and practical suggestions are offered for parents, teachers, and others who work with youth.

Since we do not usually know which children will grow up to be gay, lesbian, or bisexual, the book suggests that all parents need to be informed about sexual orientation and that all schools should teach their students about sexual orientation and should promote tolerance and understanding of sexual minorities. The common fear that often prevents parents and schools from teaching children about sexual orientation is that such teaching will promote and encourage homosexuality. But children do not become gay or lesbian by hearing about or learning about homosexuality, and when schools and families talk openly about sexual orientation and encourage acceptance of sexual minorities, there are beneficial effects for both children who will grow up to be gay and for those who will not. Gay youth will no longer have to hide and be ashamed, and those who are not gay will learn that homophobia is another unacceptable form of prejudice.

Family Secrets also explores the tragic consequences of AIDS. Gary, the younger of my two sons, died from an AIDS-related illness at the age of twenty-seven. My book portrays Gary's life before and after his illness was diagnosed, the manner of his death, and how the stigma and tragedy of AIDS affected him and his family. Gary was a writer himself, and excerpts from some of his own writings have been included in the book to convey a sense of what he was like as a child, an adolescent, and a young adult.

Acknowledgments

I gratefully acknowledge two individuals, Genevieve Ginsburg and Randy Summerlin, who read early versions of my manuscript and whose feedback and comments were extremely valuable. I also thank Senior Production Editor Peg Marr for her astute and vigilant review and for her helpful suggestions. I am grateful to Dr. John DeCecco, Program Editor for The Haworth Press, who first read my book proposal and final manuscript and thought the book worthy of publication; to Susan Trzeciak Gibson, Administrative Editor, who expertly guided me through the many preliminary steps in the production of my book; and to Devon Murphy, Copywriter, who prepared the prepublication book announcement and who knows what else.

Chapter 1

Love Overcomes

My two sons, my only children, both grew up to be homosexual. Being a mother of gay children was not a role I had ever envisioned for myself, and as my sons grew through childhood and adolescence, the possibility that they might grow up to be gay was unthinkable. I was a clinical psychologist and I had also always considered myself less prejudiced than most, but a professional background in psychology and my supposed tolerance did nothing to shield me from the shock I felt when I first learned my younger son was gay.

The children who grow up to be gay are secretive because, from a very early age, these children—as do all children—learn from everything they hear, see, and read that homosexual feelings and attractions are wrong. Families contribute to the long legacy of secrecy by never mentioning to their children that homosexuality exists, by never considering that one of their own children might be gay, and by keeping it secret if they have a gay child. And so it is that children like my sons, unprepared and confused, with no one to guide or advise them, struggle alone with their feelings, afraid to reveal them to anyone, or often, even to admit the feelings to themselves.

Parents are also acutely aware of the shame and secrecy surrounding homosexuality, and so avoid thinking of the possibility that a child of theirs might grow up to be gay. Consequently, they are as unprepared as their children—children who are growing up gay in a heterosexual world. Parents have heard the same words their children have heard: "perverted," "abnormal," "deviant." Schools are silent on the topic. Churches label homosexuality as immoral. Politicians refuse to enact laws protecting the civil rights of gays and lesbians, and some speak publicly about the evils of homosexuality. Some mental health professionals even try to "cure" homosexuality. It is as though, if we are silent about homosexuals or if we condemn them or if we can cure them, there will be no homosexuals. How then can parents permit themselves to think that they might produce a child whom society will decree perverted and abnormal, unsuitable even for certain occupations or professions?

My husband, Jack, and I, like most parents, had never allowed ourselves to even imagine that we might have a gay child. A gay child was not among our hopes and dreams. But then our younger son Gary, when he was nineteen years old, told us what he had been secretly thinking of for some time: that he thought he was gay. My son, gay? Gary, a homosexual? Stunned, I wondered what I had done and what his father had done as parents to cause our child to be gay? At one level, as a psychologist, I realized this was probably not rational thinking, but as a mother, I was terrified and completely irrational, and I didn't want to believe that my son was a homosexual. Perhaps he really wasn't gay, perhaps he was just young and confused, or perhaps he was only rebelling against the conventional course in life.

My denial was damaging certainly to my son, but also to me, and it did not change the truth one iota. I would soon be forced to understand that Gary was truly gay; it was not just that he thought he might be gay. And beneath all my denial and shock and anguish, I knew instinctively that Gary was the same wonderful, beautiful son my husband and I had known and loved for nineteen years. The love we had for our son shook us into reality and overcame all the other chaotic emotions we were feeling. As parents, my husband and I had to learn to incorporate Gary's sexual orientation into our lives and into our view, our image of who he was as a person. We had to radically revise some of our expectations and dreams, to accept that they were only *our* expectations and dreams, not our son's. This is a lesson, of course, that many parents, not just those of gays, have to learn as their children grow up. We cannot impose our dreams upon our children. They will seek and find their own.

Andy, my older son, is also gay, but many years were to go by before he revealed his secret. Andy knew how much his father and I still loved and respected Gary, just as we always had before discovering he was gay, but nevertheless, Andy was afraid to confide in us that he, too, was gay. He had convinced himself that we would be terribly disappointed to know that our only two children were both gay. No weddings, no daughters-in-law, no grandchildren. He had been thoroughly and effectively indoctrinated, as most of us are, into believing that homosexuality is something to be, at least mildly, if not totally, ashamed of in oneself or in one's child. So Andy kept his secret. For a very long time he did not even tell his brother.

My contribution to the family secrecy was that I had never talked in any depth to my sons, while they were growing up, about homosexuality. I didn't tell them that normal people could grow up to be sexually attracted to people of the same sex. Did my silence contribute to my sons believing they could not mention their feelings to me? I believe that it did, and eventually I began trying to make amends for my silence, my reticence, by learning to accept and appreciate my sons for just exactly who they were, and by learning to understand at a very personal, not just a professional, level how false are the many myths and stereotypes about homosexuality.

And still something more threatening than my child's being gay lurked ominously in the background. It was the emergence of a frightening, newly recognized disease, which would eventually kill many gay men. The time was the early 1980s and the disease was called GRID (Gay-Related Immune Deficiency), as it was thought then to affect only male homosexuals. Because of the association of the illness with homosexuality, the general public barely reacted at first, and most of the medical community gave it scant attention. But the disease had a frightening meaning for me. Gary, by this time, was a student at Columbia University and living in New York City, one of the cities where the disease was most heavily concentrated. Was he in danger from a fatal disease, just because he was gay?

News began to spread widely about the disease, about its devastating effects, about how rapidly young men were dying. And those of us who had personal reasons to care, primarily gay men and the people who loved them, were becoming more and more frightened, though most people were still paying little attention. However, I clung to the belief, popular at the time, that only extremely promiscuous men were being affected, and reassured myself that Gary wasn't promiscuous. But what did I know of what promiscuity meant for a young gay man during that time period?

At first no one knew what was causing the mysterious disease. Moralists called it a punishment of "degenerates" because it seemed to affect only homosexuals and, later, heroin addicts. Then came the discovery that it was caused by a virus, was transmitted primarily through blood and semen, and could affect anyone. The virus was called HIV (Human Immunodeficiency Virus) and the disease was called AIDS (Acquired Immune Deficiency Syndrome). Organized medicine and government officials gradually woke up once it became evident that homosexuals and drug addicts were not the only persons who were at risk.

Although these alien words—gay disease, gay cancer, GRID, AIDS, HIV—hovered at the edge of my consciousness, they failed to arm me for the tragedy that was looming. But it came, on a bleak May day in 1987, a day engraved forever in my heart, when Gary's doctor informed him and he informed his family that he had AIDS. Stricken with the brutality and terror of my son's diagnosis, I survived only by clinging obstinately to the hope that somehow he could be saved, that somehow he would not die. But all of the love we had for Gary could not halt the inevitable. Gary did die, two years and two months after his diagnosis, and my hope was gone. I was a mother, left heartbroken and desolate, dwelling no longer in hope, but in memory.

I remembered Gary as a beautiful young boy, his blue eyes bright and shining, always excited, always so full of hopes and dreams and plans. I imagined his face and I remembered his little favored words and phrases, the expressions in his eyes, the sound of his voice, his laugh. And I remembered his thin, wasted body during the last weeks of his life and heard his tremulous voice whispering faintly, "Mother, I'm so sorry to cause you all this pain."

So many things reminded me of what my son would never experience or know again. Our beautiful Arizona sunsets became only sights that Gary would never see again. Listening to music only meant Gary would never hear his Todd Rundgren or his Roxy Music again. Birds on our patio and in the desert surrounding our house were reminders that Gary, an avid birdwatcher, would never again identify a new bird to add to his Life List. Gary's Macintosh computer, sitting silently on his desk in his room, was a haunting reminder that he would never write another story, another article, another book.

And in the weeks, months, and years after Gary died, the chillingly familiar words "died from complications related to AIDS," would leap out at me from news stories, articles, and obituaries, and sometimes I discerned them even when nothing explicit was written. The death of a man, particularly between the ages of about twenty-five and forty or possibly even older, who was unmarried; whose survivors included parents, siblings, nieces, and nephews, but no spouse and no children; whose death was unexplained; and who was often involved in some creative field, would immediately alert me to think that maybe this unknown person was gay, like my son, and maybe this person had died from AIDS, like my son.

I had a strange need, perhaps to confirm that I was not alone, which drew me unerringly to these stories and which led to my fevered imaginings, even when neither AIDS nor homosexuality was mentioned. When I sensed that the obituary was for someone who had died of AIDS, I would be reminded again of the stigma of the disease that had killed my son.

In this book I wish to tell the story of our family and of what we learned as we coped with homophobia, with AIDS, and with the shame and secrecy that are their consequences. The book will focus more upon Gary's life than upon Andy's because Andy can create his own story through the way he lives his life. Gary can no longer do that, and so through this book I have tried to create a lasting record of my younger son's life, before and after AIDS, a record to say he was here, a record to tell what he was like and how he died. Gary's own writing; my memories as his mother; the memories of his friends, his teachers, his lover, and his doctors will be used to document his short but full life and to convey the experiences of our family and of the other people who loved Gary as we journeyed with him through his illness.

Chapter 2

Childhood

Gary told me he was gay on an ordinary evening in the spring of 1980. We were in the kitchen together preparing dinner, and I made a casual, offhand remark about his new haircut, saying it might make people think he was gay. Gary seemed to hesitate for a moment and then, in a soft, almost apologetic voice, he said, "Mother, I think maybe I *am* gay." Much later he told me that since I was a clinical psychologist he thought I would be more understanding and accepting than the average parent would be about homosexuality. Gary was right in one sense. I was tolerant and accepting in the abstract, but Gary was very wrong about how I would react to knowing my own son was homosexual. I was devastated, frightened for my son and also for myself.

The night Gary told me he was gay was a turning point in my life. Suddenly and with no preparation, I was the mother of a gay son, an identity forcing me to see things in myself that I had somehow avoided recognizing. I had carried around this image of myself as tolerant and unprejudiced, but my gay son was to shatter the image. Though I had been accepting of homosexuality as a therapist, as a mother I desperately resisted accepting that my own child was gay. My so-called tolerance was obviously quite limited. It was also humbling to realize that my understanding of sexual orientation, despite my many years of professional training and experience as a psychologist, was quite shallow and inadequate. And I also had to admit just how oblivious I had managed to be to the pervasive homophobia in our society until it became my own son who was its target. In time I was able to overcome the prejudice, and through study and self-examination I was able to gain a deeper understanding of sexual orientation. But nothing I learned was to prepare me for the most difficult lesson of my life: the experience of learning to live with the grief of losing my dear son to AIDS.

It was after Gary's death and after discovering my older son, Andy, was also gay that I made the decision to write this book, a book to tell the story of my two children growing up to be gay, the story of their early lives, of the ways in which they were both like and unlike other children, the story of what it was like to be their mother, the story of a gifted young man living with AIDS, and finally the story of an ordinary family coping with unordinary circumstances.

The stories began with the birth of two sons, Andrew Jackson Baker, IV, and Gary Thomas Baker, to Jean and Jack Baker. My husband and I had never been quite certain that we wanted to be parents, but even in those days, the 1950s, biological clocks ticked away. We began to fear that we might wait too long to decide and then regret not having had a child. We had been married eight years, and I was thirty and Jack was thirty-six when our first child, Andy, was born. Gary was born almost four years later. Though it is not uncommon now for people to wait until their thirties and forties to have children, we were considered then to be quite ancient for becoming new parents.

Andy, my firstborn, taught me of the passionate intensity of mother love, that instantaneous bond which ties a mother irrevocably to her infant. I had never fully appreciated the intensity of the feelings a parent has for her child and I couldn't remember anyone ever having explained it to me. Perhaps it truly isn't explainable. Words are inadequate to convey the feelings you have holding your own tiny baby, listening to his little sounds and murmurs, feeling the softness and fragility of his body, realizing his helplessness and vulnerability. There are no other experiences like these, none to compare them with. I had never had the strong motivation to bear children, which most women of my generation seemed to have, and it was frightening to think that I could so easily have made a different decision and never known what it was to be a mother.

Our children brought Jack and me happiness we had never dreamed of, and we were totally infatuated parents. Madly in love with our faultless babies, we felt we were beholding a miracle as we watched them grow, blissfully admiring each little step in their development. How unthinkable that I could ever have been reluctant to have children; I was born to be a mother.

Since I had majored in psychology in college, I already knew a little about child development, but still I poured endlessly over books, articles, and manuals about infants and parenting. And while the children were still quite young, I returned to the university to enroll in a PhD program in clinical psychology and child development. I was eager to know everything I could to help me be a good mother; but none of what I was learning was preparing me to be the mother of homosexual children.

It was during the 1960s when I became a graduate student in psychology and when I was taught that what a child will become is primarily determined by the early experiences of life. At that time, biological and genetic factors were considered vastly less influential than the environment in shaping a child's personality. Nurture would prevail over nature. But theories changed over the years. Now most psychologists believe that a child's inborn characteristics may be as significant for development as are his or her experiences in life, and that the human personality is shaped by a complex interaction between these life experiences and the child's innate, biological predispositions. This interaction between biology and experience is thought to underlie sexual orientation just as it does so many other human characteristics.

And so when our children were young I was convinced, like so many other parents, that my husband and I would be totally responsible for the way they would turn out, for what they would grow up to be. This meant that each and every little thing we did as parents would have profound and lasting effects—a scary prospect. Mothers, especially then, and even now, were often blamed or given credit for their children's fates, for their shortcomings, for their accomplishments, for what they would become in life. Little wonder then I thought the job of being a mother was a serious calling, a complex, demanding endeavor.

Even as I took motherhood so seriously and was so completely enthralled with my children, I certainly made many mistakes as a parent. I can remember those individual moments of clumsiness and insensitivity, moments when the children wanted attention and I was impatient, moments when I was critical and they wanted affection and praise. Those moments stand out so vividly in my memory, so much more vividly than those times when I said or did just the right thing to show them how much they were loved and respected. I can also remember and feel the guilt about the tremendous amount of time and energy I devoted to my graduate studies and career, time and energy not devoted to the children. And I can remember the many conflicts between me and my husband. Certainly most parents, probably all, fail their children in an least minor ways and think back on their mistakes and regret them. However, when it turns out that one of your children, or in my case two, is homosexual, then you have even more reason to focus on your mistakes, your failures, and to believe that maybe those mistakes and failures were the very cause of your child growing up to be gay.

I no longer believe that the mistakes Jack and I made explain why Andy and Gary both turned out to be gay. I have come to believe that the question of why someone is homosexual is not a question that should even be asked since, first of all, it suggests that there is something wrong with being homosexual, and secondly, the question cannot really be answered. Does anyone ever ask parents why they think their child turned out to be heterosexual? Such a question is almost inconceivable. Heterosexuality is a given, it is assumed. But when the child is gay, the question seems always to be lurking around in the background, even when left unspoken. The underlying prejudice toward homosexuality is revealed in the very question itself, the implication being that you as a parent would certainly not want your child to be gay, and that, if you had just been a better parent or if you hadn't made some horrible mistakes, your child wouldn't be gay.

Jack and I didn't know, of course, that our two wonderful sons were both going to be homosexual. This was something we had never anticipated or imagined. We had no concern about our children's sexual orientation. We just took it for granted, as most parents do, that they would be heterosexual. But we did think about the goals we had for our children and the values we hoped they would learn. We wanted them to grow up to be self-confident, responsible, caring, and happy. We wanted them to be able to think for themselves and we wanted to give them the freedom to make their own decisions and discover what were their own special, innate talents.

But mainly we just loved our children, loved them with a strength never dreamed of during those many years of ambivalence about whether we should or should not have children.

Jack and I realized when our children were quite young that they were both extremely intelligent, even gifted. They seemed driven by an insatiable curiosity and a vast hunger for knowledge and they loved books even before they could say a single word. They were imaginative and creative, thinking up endless projects and activities and never complaining about being bored. Whether they were collecting bottle caps, building a city of blocks, studying the stars, or trying to identify all the birds in Arizona, they seemed always driven in their desire to learn about the world.

It was their intensity and persistence that sometimes made our children seem slightly different from other young children. Andy's driving passion was evident by the time he was four or five years old, when we first became aware of what was to be his lifelong infatuation with collecting and studying animals and of learning about endangered species. Andy's early ambition was to own a zoo when he grew up, and he began his own little childhood zoo by spending every free moment out in the desert areas around our home hunting for snakes, toads, lizards, frogs, and other small animals that he captured and kept in cages in his room. Money he received as gifts or allowances he inevitably used to purchase other more exotic animals or fish from local pet stores. Our home overflowed with his collections of gerbils, hamsters, rats, armadillos, iguanas, rabbits, chickens, tropical fish, snakes, and other animals that I have long since forgotten.

Gary greatly admired his older brother and so was easily infected with Andy's enthusiasms. He dutifully assisted his brother in his pursuits, helping catch, cage, and categorize the animals, and when Gary was old enough, Andy assigned him the task of telephoning the pet stores in town on a regular basis, inquiring about whether they had in stock certain rare fish, birds, or other animals that Andy wished to add to his collection. Gary became very adept as Andy's assistant and chief clerk. They were both endlessly engrossed in their obsession with animals and they had little time for anything else. Many of their friends became swept up in their zoomania and a few of them became almost as fanatical as Andy and Gary were.

Eventually, though, Gary began to find his own interests and to become less compliant with Andy's assignments. When Gary developed an interest, he wanted to know every detail about his subject. He read books, made phone contacts, investigated the materials and equipment he needed, and devised elaborate plans to persuade his unsuspecting parents of the absolute necessity of carrying out whatever his latest project might be.

One of Gary's first interests, separate from Andy's, was astronomy. He was just as dedicated to his study of astronomy as he had been to helping Andy with his animal projects. He made trips to the library and to book stores, he obtained catalogs of equipment, he estimated the costs. Finally, he located the telescope he wanted from an out-of-state company and he devised an elaborate plan for financing his purchase. This financial plan, of course, required assistance from the parents, a long-term loan that Gary would pay back with regular monthly installments out of his allowance and from the extra money he would earn from doing additional household chores. It all sounded eminently reasonable as his plans usually did, and, also, as usual, we agreed.

The telescope, after many mishaps, at last arrived, and Gary began long months of surveying the skies looking for various stellar and planetary objects, which he unfortunately could hardly ever locate. Each night he lugged his cumbersome telescope out into the backyard and peered into the sky for hours. He always made meticulous, rather sad notes of his activities.

> Plans: I plan to view the whirlpool galaxy (M51) in Canes Vanatici tonight. I also plan to look at M81, M82 in Ursa Major. I will try to look at the Andromeda Galaxy and the planetary nebula in Lyra if possible. I will also try to find M13 in Hercules. Results: Nothing.

Gary trudged dejectedly back into the house each night, his small shoulders sagging, dragging his telescope behind him, discouraged and disappointed because he had failed to find what he had been looking for. Still he persisted, desperately searching the skies for months, reading more books, examining more astronomical charts, devising new strategies for his searches, before finally giving up on astronomy and moving on to a new project.

Gary was always outrageously persuasive when he wanted something for one of his projects, and Jack and I could seldom resist his pleadings. Faced with his persistence, we found ourselves agreeing to his plans or purchases because his reasoning was so powerful or because his perseverance was superior to ours and he had worn us down. He produced elaborate written charts, notes, lists, and promises to substantiate his outrageous arguments. And when Gary fixed us with his big blue eyes and argued his points with relentless logic, neither Jack nor I had the heart to turn him down. Gary always had a way of winning us over. But that was never enough for Gary. He wanted more; he wanted enthusiasm and approval, not just agreement. He wanted us to say, "Oh yes, Gary, this is a wonderful plan. This new camera with better focusing (or whatever) is just what you need." Gary was not satisfied for his father and me to just acquiesce, to say "OK, go ahead; we're tired of listening."

Gary showed a talent and love for writing early in his life. He seemed to write because he had to write, because it was a compulsion. He wrote constantly about the little happenings of his daily life, and about his observations, ideas, opinions, feelings. He kept journals and diaries from the time he was about seven years old and he began writing a series of little mystery stories when he was around nine or ten. These stories always had a main character named Dr. Fabian. I have found at least twenty of these stories, carefully written on 4 x 6 index cards, with titles such as *The Case of the Camouflaged Hole, The Case of the Occult Expert, The Case of the Dead Archaeologist*, and *The Case of the Dedicated Violinist*.

Gary's somewhat idiosyncratic sense of humor was noticeable even in these early writings. He spent hours working on his stories and then forcing his parents, his best friend Gus, and his brother to listen as he read them aloud. Of course, his father and I didn't have to be forced. We admired everything Gary did, and to us his little stories were gems of wisdom and creativity. We were never able to be totally objective about either of our children.

Politics and social issues always interested Gary even when he was a very young child. Andy was mildly interested in politics, but his obsession with animals kept him too busy to become as excited as his brother about social problems and political figures and events. Gary was a nonconformist and liked to support controversial and unpopular viewpoints. He objected to the Vietnam War and wrote a school theme about it when he was in the sixth grade.

> I think that the Vietnam war is ridiculous. I don't think that the South Vietnamese even want us there. I don't see why President Nixon just can't take the troops out and leave it at that. I think it's kind of dumb to interfere in other countries' matters. And another thing is that there are millions of dollars spent on ammunition. And that money can be used on fighting pollution and other things. It all started out just that the United States interfered and now the United States is completely involved in a war. And the war kills many men. I don't see why we can't just stop the war. It's killing thousands of people and destroying a country. But they are finally coming home.

When Andy and Gary were young children, I don't believe they were aware that they were members of a minority group, even though it was a sexual minority; but I do think they had some sense of being different. In Gary's case, that sense may have helped account for his unusual childhood concerns about social injustice and discrimination against minorities. For example, when he was in the seventh grade, he wrote an editorial for his school newspaper, claiming that children were a discriminated-against minority.

> There has been much talk on liberation movements lately. Yet the most badly treated minority has not been heard from on equal rights. That group is kids. Take first, for example, school. Many teachers would paddle a child if he talked back to her or committed other "disrespectful acts" in such a way that if she did the same thing to another adult she could be sued for assault and battery. There are other discriminating acts against children, but there is not the time to mention them all. Of all acts in school, corporal punishment is the worst and should be abolished. Teachers may argue that [it] is the only way to control kids, but that is false. There are many ways to control kids that may be more effective.
> Now we come to how parents abuse their children. Parents can, and many do, psychologically abuse their kids. They can, within the laws, drive their kids to insanity. Of course, very

few parents do this, but there is nothing to legally protect children unless the child is physically beaten to the point of hospitalization. So children must unite to make their troubles heard and to encourage adults to promote programs to protect children's rights as people.

Andy and Gary were just vibrant little boys who were excited about life and who brought great joy and pleasure to their parents. Jack and I believed that, in some very strange and undeserved way, we had been granted a privilege to have become the parents of our two special children, and we frequently told one another how very fortunate we were to have these two wonderful sons. We were sensible enough that we didn't say anything to most other people about just how special we thought our children were, realizing that we would sound like the usual besotted parents bragging about their children. What we did not know then, of course, was that our children were going to be special in another way; they would both grow up to be gay.

I have thought back often to Andy's and Gary's childhoods, trying to recall whether there was anything that might have alerted us to their eventual sexual orientation. I remember so many things about them. They were children who were unusually absorbed in the world of words, ideas, and books. And I remember that they were never much interested in toy guns or in aggressive games. They loved blocks, Legos, Tinkertoys, binoculars, cameras, art and science materials, and they were fascinated with nature. I cannot remember either of them getting into physical fights with other boys, and they seldom got into the aggressive, rough-and-tumble play that many young boys seem to enjoy. They were not particularly interested in competitive sports like football, baseball, or basketball, but they did like tennis and swimming. If these were possible subtle indicators of their future sexual orientation, they did not make our children stand out as different and certainly not as abnormal.

I do not mean to give the impression that every young boy who is more interested in books and nature than in football and basketball will grow up to be gay. This is certainly not the case. However, many adult gay men, though not all, in remembering their childhoods, recall that they were less interested than average in typical "masculine" activities and games (Bell, Weinberg, and Hammer-smith, 1981). Nevertheless, boys who are not particularly interested in typical "masculine" games as children, who may prefer books and nature, are not destined to be gay; and many grow up to be heterosexual. On the other hand, there are boys who love typically masculine activities and aggressive, competitive sports, and yet who will be homosexual as adults. Many lesbian women also report that during their childhoods they were more interested in sports and were tomboyish (Bell, Weinberg, and Hammersmith, 1981).

The disapproval in our society of individuals who deviate in the slightest from the stereotyped male or female role contributes to a false view of homosexuality, that all gay men are effeminate and all lesbian women are masculine. What parents need to know is that most children who will eventually identify as homosexual are not noticeably different from other children. Parents will usually be unaware and unable to predict that their child will grow up to be gay or lesbian. Given the very strong societal prejudice toward homo-sexuality, and the lack of knowledge and understanding of sexual orientation by most parents, it is perhaps just as well that this is true. There is the substantial danger, given the present level of parental knowledge and the level of homophobia in society, that parents who suspect or fear (for whatever reason, right or wrong) that their child might grow up to be gay or lesbian, may try to suppress any pos-sible indicators of homosexuality. Parents sometimes believe they can prevent such a "horrible" outcome by punishing their boys for being "sissies" or trying to force their tomboyish girls to wear dresses and play with dolls. However, nothing the parents may do is likely to have an influence upon their child's eventual sexual orientation: Parents do not cause their child to be homosexual and cannot prevent him or her from being so. Efforts to prevent a child from becoming homosexual may result in psychological damage to the child while having no effects upon his or her sexual orientation.

As parents, we are simply never informed about the possibility that we might have a child who will grow up to be gay, and so we have no understanding, no basis for dealing with it should it happen. The result is that one of the more serious risks of growing up gay is that parents are not prepared for their gay child, have no knowledge about homosexuality, and have usually been indoctrinated throughout their lives with negative attitudes about homosexuals. The child has to face the sad fact that even his own parents may not accept him for who he is and will not understand what he is going through as he struggles with his sexual identity.

Regardless, however, of the common societal attitudes about homosexuality, there will always be children who will grow up to be gay or lesbian and there will always be parents of these children. All of the exhortations of the moral brigade about the immorality and perversity of homosexuality will not prevent one child from becoming homosexual nor give one parent the power to prevent homosexuality in his or her child. As parents and as a society, we all need to learn that homosexuality is not a pathological deviance, but is a particular way of being different. Parents need to know that there is a possibility that they may be raising a child who will grow up to be gay and that they often will be unaware. The little remarks that parents may make unthinkingly, remarks conveying dislike or even hatred of homosexuals, can have devastating effects upon a child who is beginning to recognize that he himself has those feelings which he hears his parents condemning or ridiculing, that he is one of those people whom his parents hate.

The habit of judging others whom you do not understand or who are different is strongly ingrained in humans, and it is this tendency which accounts for much of the hatred and fear of homosexuals: We do not understand homosexuality and so we judge it and condemn it. However, as more and more gays and lesbians come out openly to their families and loved ones, it becomes increasingly difficult to continue to label homosexuals as freaks or deviants. We learn that they are individuals whom we care about, individuals with the same range of good and bad qualities as heterosexuals, and we learn that sexual orientation has little or nothing to do with a person's character. There is no better way to learn this than by being the parent of a beloved child who turns out to be gay.

Chapter 3

Adolescence

Our sons grew from children into beautiful adolescents, tall, slender, good-looking boys, excited about life, energetic, witty, and funny. Jack and I were strangely oblivious to our children's flaws. Even though we were supersensitive to one another's faults, we tended to idealize our children and, somehow, were able to overlook characteristics that some might have thought less than wonderful. Jack and I felt blessed by our extraordinary children. To us, they were our life's greatest achievement.

Parents can certainly be overly accepting and uncritical, and when we erred it was probably in this direction. As a young adult speaking at his father's memorial service, Andy recalled that, as a child, he had not appreciated his father's unconditional positive regard because it seemed to him that it meant that his father didn't distinguish between his significant accomplishments and his inconsequential ones. Andy went on to say, however, that perhaps it was his father's unconditional regard during his childhood that had helped him grow up to be an adult who liked and respected himself.

I cannot help but wonder if we had known that our children might grow up to be gay, what would have been different in the way we treated them? Would we have loved them as unconditionally as we did or would we have been anxiously trying to shape their sexual orientation? Would we have looked upon some of their characteristics as less endearing? Would we have tried to force them to play football and basketball rather than spend their time reading and studying nature? What damage might we have done to their personalities, their emotional development, if we had known? These are all questions that cannot be answered but that call attention to the particular problems in child rearing that arise from antigay prejudice and parental ignorance about sexual orientation.

I came to realize that trying to influence a child's sexual orientation would be futile, and to realize also that I would have had no
right and no reason to do so. At the time, I had been led, like most
others growing up in our society, to think that it would be a tragedy,
or if not a tragedy, at the very least a terrible disappointment, to
have a gay child. So, much as I would like to believe I would have
been enlightened enough to know how to deal with knowing my
children might grow up to be gay, I think I may not have been. And
in all those parenting books I studied so assiduously, there was not
one word about the possibility of having a child who would be
homosexual, not one word of advice or guidance to the parents of
such a child. Parents, even those who prepare themselves in other
ways to be good parents, are truly unprepared for a gay child.

As our children grew into adolescence their infatuation with their
innumerable projects and hobbies continued. Neither of them ever
affected the blasé, disinterested attitude of many adolescents, and
they seemed sometimes still almost childlike in their enthusiasms,
while at the same time, unusually adultlike in their self-sufficiency
and self-motivation. Though they were four years apart in school
and so didn't attend Sabino High simultaneously, they, not unpre-
dictably, followed a similar pattern once there. They joined the
swimming team, the school orchestra, and the school newspaper;
took advanced classes; held offices; made close friendships; and were
still able to make straight As and finish high school as National
Merit finalists. Andy was even a Presidential Scholar, a national
honor awarded annually to only two students from each state, and
Gary was listed in Who's Who Among American High School
Students the year he graduated. We never had to encourage the boys
to do their homework or to study more. In fact, we sometimes
thought we should encourage them to try to slow down, to work a
little less. The one thing they didn't do much of was dating. Perhaps
that should have been a clue as to their sexual orientation, but I just
interpreted it as due instead to their being so preoccupied with their
studies, their hobbies, and their innumerable school activities.

Although their interests had gone in somewhat different direc-
tions over time, the one activity both our sons continued to be
obsessed with was birdwatching, more commonly called birding by
devotees. Gary originally became interested through Andy's inter-

est, but eventually he went on to become even more passionate about birding than his older brother had been. I had known nothing about this rather exotic hobby before my children exposed me to it, but I soon felt pressured to learn enough to be able to converse vaguely and imprecisely about yellow-bellied flycatchers, coppery-tailed trogans, harlequin ducks, rufous-sided towhees, and other enchantingly named birds.

Andy and Gary were fascinated with the fanaticism of the adult birders they came to know through the Audubon Society. Although they themselves were equally fanatic, they seemed to think that it was normal for them, but was quite eccentric for adults to be so obsessed. Sometimes it seemed they thought everything about adults was eccentric, not unlike the judgment of many adolescents I suppose.

There was a telephone system called the Bird Alert which notified the Audubon Society members that a rare bird species had been sighted. Whenever the Bird Alert call came in, if the children couldn't find an adult Audubon member to pick them up, Jack and I would receive impassioned phone calls trying to persuade us to drop anything we might be doing and race home to get them to their destination. They made heartrending emotional pleas insisting that they were going to miss the most important sighting of the year, of the decade, or whatever exaggeration they could think of to get us to comply. We were grateful when Andy reached his sixteenth birthday and was able to drive.

For years Andy and Gary were totally enamored of the endlessly fascinating birding world. The challenge, the competition, the excitement of finding a bird that was rare or difficult to identify were their obsessions. This was a hobby—actually it was much more like a calling—that fit in perfectly with their love of nature, their interest in science, and their boundless intellectual curiosity. They would come home from their birding adventures elated about some new bird to add to their increasingly long lists, Life Lists, Arizona Lists, and on and on. To see my children with interests that occupied them so compellingly was deeply satisfying to me, and I thought perhaps it was one reason why they didn't get into the trouble with sex, alcohol, and drugs, which so many adolescents did. Of course, had they been more interested in girls maybe they would have been less interested in birds, but that thought never occurred to me.

Gary was only fourteen when Andy graduated from high school and left home to attend Stanford University in Palo Alto, California. We thought perhaps Gary might become depressed after Andy left and might lose interest in the activity that had so united them. However, that didn't happen, and he became such a birding expert that he began to be asked to lead birding trips for the Audubon Society. The adult birders were sometimes startled when they learned that this young adolescent, who couldn't even drive yet, was the assigned leader of their expedition.

Gary's ongoing passion for birding carried over into his letters to his brother, letters that he filled with the details of his latest birding exploits, often to the exclusion of any other topics. Here is one of the letters Gary wrote to Andy in 1976, when he was fifteen years old.

Dear Andy,

In the realm of birding all goes very well. Today I went to the sewage ponds and on arriving found many teal and scaup (as well as many of the lovely coot) on the ponds in the plant. On strolling about I discovered a Prairie Falcon flapping over the fields. This made me quite happy. When I arrived back at the big pond, I found many ducks including Canvasback, Pintail and Shoveler.

I then walked back down the road to rendezvous with Mother at the plant. I again met a person who I saw at the pond. While before he was devoid of any news of exciting birds, this time he informed me, "There's a Barn Owl over there." Seeing my trembling he consented to show me exactly where it was. He brought me to the edge of a tank and pointed out a particularly leafy tree. "There it is." he said. "Where?" I shouted, for I could not see it and I was quite angry. I finally spotted it, and my friend quickly departed, grumbling. It was quite pleasant and I was able to see the pale, lovely, heart-shaped, glowing, beautiful face.

That brings my lists to 325 and 262. Your brother.

Craving adventure and excitement led our sons, while in high school, to join a group called Amigos de las Americas, a national program that trained young volunteers, mostly adolescents, to provide health-related services such as immunizations, dental care, and the building of wells to isolated communities in Central and South America. When Andy was in the program, the summer after his junior year in high school, he had been sent to South America where he and a small group of volunteers gave immunizations to children living in villages along the Vaupés River in Colombia. Gary was sent to a village in Honduras where his assignment was to teach the villagers how to build wells to ensure a safe water supply. In one of his letters from Honduras, written when he was sixteen years old, he described how he and his Amigos partner, another teenager, struggled to motivate the Honduran villagers to help with building the wells.

Dear M., D., and A:

I know you're probably worried that I haven't written until now, but I really have not had time. I'm stationed in Quemado in the Department of Yoro and it's really fantastic. My partner and I are staying in a small house with a dirt floor and a palm frond roof. We eat at a nearby house with a hilarious old lady who cooks for us. I already have hordes of Honduran friends and every night they come to the house and we chat and joke for a few hours.

As for the construction of the wells, things are not going well. There were two Amigos here before us and they had dug three wells, the deepest to 23 feet. We couldn't work on the deepest one at first because we needed to get all the water out and it began to look impossible. Then the problems really started. The mayor of the town began getting drunk every day and wasn't telling the people to work and he is the only one they listen to. As it turned out only one or two men showed up every day and we (my partner and I) were doing all the work and believe me, it's hard work. Today only one person showed up, so we just decided not to work. That's why I have time to write this letter. This afternoon I'm organizing a town meeting to lay the law down. The people know I'm mad.

Andy, I haven't had any time for birding except occasionally sitting under a tree in town with my binos. I've gotten a few lifers, some pretty good. I'll keep you in suspense until I get home. One [bird] tidbit . . . Citreoline Trogan. Love, Gary

The Sabino High School newspaper, *Cat Tracks*, was a focal point of Andy and Gary's high school years. Andy was a reporter and feature writer for all four years, and Gary held numerous positions during his first two years, finally becoming editor during his junior and senior years. Gary brought his passion and intensity to his job as editor of the paper, frequently tackling controversial topics that he seemed to deliberately choose in order to elicit strong reactions from either the students or from the teachers and administrators. His enthusiasms sometimes had to be curbed by Ms. Jones, the faculty advisor, though he strongly resisted her efforts. In one of his editorials he attacked the high school curriculum, claiming that it was narrow, out of date, and did nothing to dispel prejudices:

> This June, the class of '79 will receive their diplomas. Seemingly this would indicate a sound academic background, but most will leave the walls of Sabino with a huge gap in their education. They will be oblivious to the world around them, a fault that will hurt them more and more in our constantly shrinking planet. The prejudices that these graduates have, due to their ignorance of other cultures, should be considered an embarrassment to our educational system.
>
> Despite the fact that those in charge are distressed by their students' obvious void in world affairs, nothing is done to remedy the situation. Instead, they continue to require such courses as Free Enterprise, a class about an archaic economic system that has not existed since the beginning of the industrial era. The fact that this class is given preference over a class such as Geography and World Affairs, where substantial and current problems are dealt with, defies logic.

In another editorial titled *Killer Queens Are Dangerous*, Gary writes a bizarre parody of the annual homecoming queen elections. He always liked to ridicule social pretensions, which he does here, but in *Killer Queens*, he seems also to be revealing a singular lack of appreciation of female beauty and charm, perhaps a hint of a budding gay sensibility.

> Every fall, Sabino students are subjected to a hellish ritual euphemistically called Homecoming Queen Elections. Each year this warped cult custom is carried out with horrible regularity, punishing the other students with the constant smiles, perfect hair and perpetual pleasantness of the candidates.
>
> When the administration began the tradition seven years ago, it had no idea it would escalate to the strange rites that exist today at Sabino. "I shudder when I think of those creatures with the red roses out on the football field," moaned Principal John Mallamo.
>
> The only way to halt this bizarre form of entertainment is to go to its roots. Students must hunt down all past and present queens and hopelessly damage their self-confidence so that they prematurely become the dumpy, alcoholic housewives they are destined to be. But even more importantly, students must detect future queens before they hatch. Experts say that the typical field marks of potential queens are uncalled for kindness, big chests, and what experts call "beauty." Only with these procedures will Sabino be free from this hideous threat.

Gary's forceful personality was becoming more evident during his high school years. He was rebellious, nonconforming, and questioning of authority. He challenged and perplexed his parents and sometimes his teachers. But Gary also had a stable, steady side. He seemed to know just how far he could go in his rebellion. With Jack and me, he was never overtly defiant. Instead, he used logic and persuasion to bring us around to his point of view. He conformed to just the extent necessary so that he seldom got in trouble with either his parents or his teachers. He continued in high school to be academically outstanding just as Andy had. At times, though, there was an aura of melancholy about Gary, underlying his almost insatiable drive and energy and his sense of humor. This underlying sadness arose perhaps from a sense of alienation, of feeling different, both because he was extremely intellectual in a high school culture not particularly respectful of intellectuals, and perhaps, too, because of a developing awareness of his sexual orientation. Making fun of the high school cliques and status symbols may have been a way of compensating for feeling different, for feeling unaccepted.

After Gary died and as part of the process of writing this book, I talked with a number of people who had known him throughout his life. I hoped to learn about facets of his life that he may not have revealed to me, and I was curious about whether I was alone in being ignorant of his sexual orientation. His high school teachers remembered him well, and none of them knew or suspected that he was gay.

Ms. Judy Kolb, who was Gary's honors English teacher, said the following:

> I enjoyed Gary a good deal, but there was always a streak of rebellion in him. For example, he and Gus were seniors when they decided to start a Communist Club. They talked to Molly Baker, one of the teachers who finally said that she would sponsor the club, but that they should think of the possible ramifications. It really caused outrage at the school. It's like that's what they wanted; they wanted to shake everybody up. They were sure the Student Council would turn it down, and I think they wanted to then take the refusal and make a big thing out of it, maybe write it up in the school newspaper. However, they eventually dropped the idea.
>
> There was never anything evident in high school to suggest Gary was gay. In all of the honors classes, he was very much accepted. Among the really sharp kids, they admired him and looked up to him. The more average kids may have been intimidated by his intelligence.

Ms. Charlotte Jones was the advisor of the high school newspaper during all four years Gary worked on the paper, so she knew Gary quite intimately, and said the following:

> Gary was smart, verbal and witty. He had a lot of fun with his mind. Any teacher who had him got to see that. Gary was also very compassionate, dependable and truthful. He had lots of integrity and discretion. Gary was definitely a leader. The other kids liked him more than he realized, but his wit could be

sharp and they didn't want to be the victims. They were afraid of his wit. I didn't know that he was gay. I don't think Gary knew. In retrospect there could have been a few little things which could have been cues. I never heard anyone make remarks about Gary being gay.

Ms. Carol Schmidt, the Sabino High School yearbook advisor, also knew Gary fairly well because of the close association between the staffs of the yearbook and the newspaper. She said the following:

Gary was gentle and sensitive and he was always respected because he was incredibly bright. I didn't know he was gay and I don't think the other kids did. However, I do think he got the message that he was out of the mainstream. The kids at Sabino put a lot of emphasis on clothes, cars, and money. There was a level of intolerance toward any kind of difference. Gary may have felt some negative energy because he challenged the popular kids and the stereotypes. He did not accept the status seeking that was going on and he cut out a role for himself that maybe made other kids resentful or uncomfortable.

Andy and Gary, during their high school years, both seemed to have had some sense of being different, of not quite fitting in, even though they were both well liked and always had close friends. They certainly would have been acutely aware of societal views about homosexuality, aware that they might be shamed and ridiculed if their sexual orientation became known. The fear of rejection or humiliation by their peers compels many gay youth, probably most, even today, to be secretive about their sexual orientation while they are in high school. Students who are openly gay or whom others suspect may be gay are frequently subject to harassment, verbal abuse, and even physical assault by their peers. Numerous researchers (D'Augelli, 1996; Hunter, 1990; Remafedi, 1987; Remafedi, Farrow, and Deisher, 1991) have reported on the prevalence of verbal and physical harassment that gay youths experience as a result of their sexual orientation. D'Augelli (1996) even found that 23 percent of his sample of gay youth reported verbal harassment from teachers.

Andy and Gary were no different from many young gays in feeling compelled to be secretive about their orientation while they were in high school. Having to be secretive about their feelings and growing up with a sense of being different, may actually have fueled Gary's need to write, to create, and to achieve, and similarly Andy's very strong achievement motivation and sense of purpose. There have been an extraordinary number of important homosexual writers and artists who have written or spoken of their sense of isolation and alienation during their youth, their feelings of not being part of the mainstream, and of how these experiences led them to rely upon their imaginations and inner lives.

Lou Porcelli, Andy's best friend in high school, who also grew up to be gay, told me after Gary's death that he thought the exceptional achievements of many gays were because homosexuality is so looked down upon that homosexuals feel they have to excel at something in order to compensate. Here are Lou's words:

> Since homosexuality is so often seen as a deviance, gay men feel they have to excel in what they do and thereby maintain their dignity. If you are a homosexual and not a success, then you are a total failure. You're a double loser. The few gay role models we have are those who are so incredibly successful that society accepts them, like Oscar Wilde, Truman Capote, Lewis Carroll, etc. Heterosexuals have all these diversions and maybe they don't have as much of the motivation to prove themselves.

I came to believe, as I read and studied about sexual orientation and learned about the difficulties that young gays experience growing up, that the energy and time which most adolescents devote to sexual and romantic interests may, at least for some gay youth, be channeled into intellectual and creative pursuits as they suppress and sublimate the sexual interests they are afraid to reveal to anyone, even sometimes to themselves. Homosexuality may then, at least for some, as Lou suggested, actually stimulate their ambition and creativity.

Andy and Gary both seemed to either sublimate or deny their sexuality during their high school years. They did both date occasionally, and each one had a girlfriend for a short period of time, perhaps in an effort to fit in, to be "normal," but they were never preoccupied with girls in the way that heterosexual adolescent males usually are. And both of them told me later that they had no actual sexual experiences with males or females during their high school years.

Andy told me many years later that he realized he was sexually attracted to other males by the time he was in junior high, but at the time he thought the feelings would eventually go away, that they were just temporary. He said that he hadn't believed he could live a normal life if he continued to have such feelings. And even though Lou, his best friend, was also gay, neither one had acknowledged his homosexuality to the other and neither suspected that his best friend was gay also. Andy told me that he thought he was the only person in his high school who had such feelings, that he was totally alone. Gary was somewhat older; I think it was possibly during his last years of high school before he recognized that he might be gay.

The invisibility of gay and lesbian youth in the school setting and the absolute silence on the part of teachers and school administrators condemn these young people to secrecy and shame. They don't want anyone to know and they worry that someone will find out. They have no one to talk to and they cannot even identify each other.

We, as parents, had been of absolutely no help to our children with their growing up gay. It would have been so simple if, at times during their childhood and adolescence, we had only known enough just to have explained homosexuality to our children, to have told them that some people fall in love with people of the same sex, and that it isn't a sickness or a deviance, it is just the way some people are. We could have told them that if they should grow up to be gay, it wouldn't mean they couldn't have a normal life. Teachers could have told them. But, sadly, my husband and I never told them any of those things and neither did their teachers.

As parents, we weren't informed enough and we weren't understanding enough. We had been mainly silent about the topic, although we must have mentioned it because Andy, much later, told me that he remembered hearing me and his father speak of homosexuality, at least occasionally, in a way that helped him know that, at least, we didn't think of it as evil or immoral.

During their high school years, both Andy and Gary were each fortunate in having a close friendship that lasted into their adult years. Strangely, their best friends were brothers. Lou Porcelli was Andy's best friend. Gus Porcelli, Lou's younger brother, was Gary's best friend during junior high and high school, and they remained so until Gary's death. Gus was not gay and he did not know Gary was gay until after their first year of college. The two of them were intensely close and almost inseparable during their high school years. They worked on the school newspaper together and were both on the Indian Ridge Swim Team. Gus spent many hours in our home and was like a third son to Jack and me. Despite the closeness of their relationship, Gary did not reveal his homosexuality to Gus during their high school years.

After Gary died, Gus told me often how important Gary had been to him throughout his life and how deeply he mourned the loss of his friend. He acknowledged that when he first learned Gary was gay it had complicated their friendship, but that he came to the conclusion that having a best friend who turned out to be gay and having a brother who also turned out to be gay had been liberating and enlightening for him as a heterosexual man. In a conversation with me, some months after Gary's death, Gus said the following about their long relationship.

> I didn't know Gary was gay in high school, but looking back, maybe it should have been obvious. It always put a strain on our friendship when I had girlfriends. He never wanted to talk about girls and I remember thinking, it will be great when he gets interested in girls. We can double date, etc. Occasionally in high school someone might call Gary a fag and I would get very defensive.
>
> The last year of high school was our closest time. We spent so much time together. The school newspaper and everything. All the people in our circle of friends looked up to Gary. I had brought him into this group. He would tell us which books to read, which movies to see. I'm glad I didn't go to college with him. I learned from him, but when he was around, I was too dependent. He took on responsibility. If he was enamored of

you, he took care of you. I was so depressed after he left for college. I remember crying that night.

At times, with Gary, everyone would be the subject of scorn. It was just this point of view and it meant attacking everything else and everybody, including you and Jack and Andy. I remember the period when we were the only two people. I loved it. It was really nice, especially at that age. I mean it was really nurturing. We could talk about everything. It was such a clear understanding. I can't say that I have ever had that same sense of being able to communicate something and know that the other person understood thoroughly and totally.

And later, there was a lot of what, in the years after he told me about the homosexual thing, was a lot of nostalgia for that period, almost like a tribute to that period. Whenever we were able really to recapture that time period for a moment, we kind of found ourselves just laughing like that again. We would always say, "Yeah, you never make friends like that . . . like the friends of your youth."

I don't think Gary was having real sexual feelings for me when we were in high school. It was a very close relationship but it was asexual. Maybe there was a point when he was really admitting his homosexuality to himself that he thought about me this way. It must be such a conflicted thing. I don't know if homosexuals fantasize about men in their waking hours when they are adolescents, or maybe just on a nocturnal basis. I have no idea.

But I think I owe a great debt to Gary and to my brother Lou because they forced me to have intense, close relationships with other men and because they, being homosexual, made me confront the idea of it, and yet still feel heterosexually secure. In both these ways I owe them. It was just fortuitous, they weren't really trying to do that.

The intimate personal relationship that Gus had with Gary—that of a straight person with a gay—is an example of one of the best ways to reduce homophobia and antigay prejudice. Through knowing and caring for someone gay, the heterosexual learns that gays can be normal and likeable, that they do not need to be hated or feared. And I believe that my gay son was extremely fortunate to have had a best friend who was heterosexual, one who was not threatened by learning his friend was gay. Gus took Gary's homosexuality in stride and never wavered in his devotion and loyalty to him. Then later, when Gus found out Gary had AIDS, he remained steadfast in his love and concern for his best friend. Gus was always there, always faithful, never judgmental, never worried about what other people might think because he was the best friend of a gay man dying from AIDS.

Gary continued to have the support and friendship that meant so much to him during his adolescence and young adulthood, and Gus had a close, intimate relationship with another male, something that is very difficult for heterosexual men to experience. Many heterosexual men are reluctant to form close emotional relationships with other men, even more so with gay men, and the relationship between Gary and Gus was unusual. Prejudice toward homosexuality and the fear of being suspected of being gay are major barriers to such male/male relationships.

As Gary and Gus were completing high school at Sabino, Andy was completing college at Stanford. Andy graduated with honors and was elected to Phi Beta Kappa. Jack and I were extremely proud of him. While in college he had seemingly lived the life of a typical heterosexual male, joining a fraternity, dating at least occasionally, and going to school dances and parties. He always told us he loved Stanford, and Jack and I never had a hint of any conflicts or problems. When Andy came home for summers and holidays, he looked wonderful and seemed very happy. He was excited about his studies and college life and he had no dearth of friends, either male or female. Andy had apparently made the decision simply not to deal with his sexual orientation, to remain closeted during his school years, perhaps at some emotional cost to himself. However, an argument can be made that this was not necessarily an unwise decision because he may have not been psychologically ready to deal with the consequences of fully accepting his homosexuality. Andy's experiences do not differ from those of a vast majority of gay and lesbian individuals who tend not to openly come out as homosexual until early adulthood when their personal strengths are greater. Bruce Bawer, in his book *A Place at the Table* (1993), expressed this well when he pointed out that the individual should only come out when he is prepared socially, psychologically, and financially to face the consequences.

The entire time Andy was in high school and college he had never hinted to a single person that he might be gay, and Jack and I, at this time, were still totally ignorant of both his and Gary's homosexuality. I look back over those years with deep regret. I wish we could have helped our children to understand homosexuality and could have shown them that we understood and loved them just the way they were. I wish we could have helped them know they did not need to be secretive and did not need to be ashamed. But we would have had to have been much wiser than we were then. I can only hope that a new generation of parents will be more informed, less prejudiced, and better able to be supportive of the new generation of gay children.

Chapter 4

A Son Comes Out

Gary's high school graduation approached, the end of an era of his life. Parents are often ambivalent about their adolescents growing up and leaving home They want to hold onto their child even though, at the same time, they know they should let them go. So I was ambivalent about my younger child graduating from high school and going away to college, but Gary had no ambivalence. Eager and excited, he feverishly made his plans. He could easily have attended the University of Arizona right in our hometown of Tucson, but he had never seriously considered any school other than Stanford. Stanford was the school of his dreams, dreams created in his fertile imagination from the bits and pieces he had gleaned from his brother's descriptions of college life.

Gary sent his meticulously prepared application to Stanford during the final semester of his senior year in high school, and being confident he would be accepted, he sent applications to no other schools. His confidence was probably not unrealistic given his impressive array of accomplishments throughout high school. In addition to having been editor in chief of his school newspaper, his grades had been almost straight As, he had top scores on the SATs, he had been an officer in the National Honor Society, he had been a Boys State delegate, and he had been one of only four students in his school selected for a special arts program for gifted students. Jack and I, biased as we tended to be about our sons, were confident that Gary, like his brother before him, would be accepted at the school of his choice.

Gary was accepted at Stanford and enrolled in the fall of 1979. He wrote to us frequently, long amusing letters about his classes, the books he was reading, his uncertainty about a career, his inter-

ests in new wave and avant-garde music, and his observations on
the eccentricities of his professors. He never mentioned girls or
dating, but I guess, if we thought about it at all, we thought he was
just too busy for dating.

In the beginning, Gary seemed happy and contented as a student
at Stanford, but after the first few months, we noticed vague hints of
gloom and discontent. He began to complain about the atmosphere
of class consciousness and elitism at Stanford, perhaps again a
subtle sign of his feeling like an outsider, of not fitting in. Then, in a
letter written in January 1980, he expressed his reservations much
more directly.

> Dear Mother:
>
> I'm quite happy here, but I still am not satisfied. On the bus
> home from the airport, I heard someone say that Stanford was
> a rich kid's country club college. I no longer hold my Marxist
> beliefs really, but I still realize he was right. People are very
> elitist here. It really and truly does not appeal to me . . . I just
> don't like an atmosphere where people blithely talk on about
> how great they are for getting here, ignoring their fantastic
> advantages. And it's not so much an unintellectual atmosphere
> here, I think I could handle that, but almost an anti-intellectual
> one. I would say it's worse than Sabino High School. My two
> roommates (who I still get along well with, by the way) don't
> seem to have read a book for pleasure in their lives.
>
> Also, (I remember Andy saying this) many people here
> have no deep interests. The students here are the future finan-
> cially elite, the doctors, the businessmen, the lawyers, but not
> the future thinkers. Of course, not everyone is that way, but the
> climate of the university is. It's self-satisfied and stagnant. I
> know this is very bombastic, but (along with a certain amount
> of my natural theatric exaggeration) it is what I think. Well, at
> any rate, I am not satisfied with Stanford and, though I will be
> open-minded and wait until the end of the year to decide, I
> think I'll transfer.

Up until the time Gary went away to college, neither Jack nor I
suspected the secret side to each of our children. We still did not
know Gary was gay, we still did not know Andy was gay, neither

Andy nor Gary knew the other was gay. Our children, not revealing their hidden secrets, allowed Jack and me to remain blissfully ignorant and unsuspecting.

But during his first year of college, while Jack and I remained oblivious, Gary himself started coming to terms with his sexual orientation, at the same time as he was coping with the normal, but difficult, tasks of adolescent development, figuring out who he was, what he wanted to become and do in his life, trying to establish his autonomy from his parents. These normal adolescent tasks of growing up and becoming an adult were complicated for Gary, as for most gay youth, by his struggle to understand and accept his homosexuality and by the frightening feelings of difference that were tending to isolate and separate him from his peers.

Much later I learned that Gary, sometime during that freshman year at Stanford, had found someone to confide in. It was Lou Porcelli, Andy's best friend from high school, who was now attending the Manhattan School of Music. Each of them had somehow learned that the other was also gay and, although Lou was living in New York City, through letters and phone calls, Gary reached out to the one person he thought might understand him and relate to what he was going through. Lou was four years older than Gary and he became a mentor to his younger friend and remained so throughout their lives.

After Gary died, Lou told me his own thoughts about what Gary was experiencing during those first months at Stanford:

> The crisis for Gary came during his freshman year in college at Stanford. This is a time of crisis for almost everyone. Your childhood has come to an end. For gay men it can be especially difficult. In college you're expected to be sexually active. Your friends are all going out with girls.
>
> Gary was alone at a school where he didn't know many people and didn't have many friends. He started doing an incredible amount of pot because he didn't see how he was going to fit in at Stanford. He started writing to me in New York about his unhappiness. He was having night terrors. His roommates would find him wandering around in the hall. He thought that Stanford was very conservative, very judgmental.

I got hints of suicidal thoughts. He was reading Sartre, Dostoevesky, Burroughs. Then he decided that insanity was genius. To be an artistic genius, you had to achieve insanity. But then later he wrote a letter to Gus saying that he had realized the folly of drugs and how they distort the truth. He told Gus that when he was in Tucson for Christmas, he saw how Gus was acting and he realized that they were both falling apart. Gary decided then to stop taking drugs and he never took any again.

I was completely unaware of how troubled Gary had been during those first months at Stanford as he tried to deal with his sexuality and with growing up. Looking back over that time I have regretted not knowing enough and not having been sensitive enough to have recognized Gary's turmoil and been able to be more helpful to him. Unfortunately, because they are so unprepared and unknowing, parents are seldom able to be supportive to their young gay children. The children are usually afraid to reveal their secret longings to their parents, and, even if they were to do so, few parents are educated enough about homosexuality or understanding and tolerant enough to provide the emotional support their child needs. I was no different from most.

Gary's letters to the family never revealed this darker side, his experimentation with drugs, or his inner confusion throughout that first year at Stanford. He later described some of his experiences in a story he wrote after he left Stanford, while in a class with Spalding Gray at Columbia University. Although the story may be partly fictionalized, I think it does reveal something about Gary's sometimes tortured adolescence and his feelings of being an outsider. In the story, he writes about trying to fit in with certain cliques at Stanford, about experimenting with drugs, and about his fascination with madness and eccentricity. Gary had a vivid imagination and wanted to experience everything life had to offer, but he also had an inner stability that helped balance his wilder side and pull him back from the brink to which his imagination and daring sometimes propelled him. Some of these conflicting doubts and desires of his adolescence and the ways he dealt with them are hinted at in the story he titled *The Aberrant Nighthawks*.

My friend L. and I were talking the other day at the Body Center, and we decided everyone we know is crazy. Everyone, that is, but my older brother, A. J. By crazy, we didn't mean eccentric. We meant real modern madness, where the victim doesn't know what he is doing. We like to use the word "aberrant" which is usually used to describe an animal whose instincts have gone bad . . . like a nighthawk who begins flying during the day.

Then I thought about myself. I went to Stanford for a year, and during the first semester I was smoking a huge amount of marijuana. Somehow, I forced myself in with some Grateful Dead fans, who are the most dedicated drug-takers in the San Francisco area. Even though they were very different from me, I was determined to work myself into their group and I did.

After that I started to see another group of people, people who were very casual about smoking the huge amount of pot they did. I wasn't that way. I didn't enjoy smoking it, and I didn't do it casually. To me, it was a very serious business, like scientific research. I felt smoking this much pot was something everyone had to do whether they liked it or not. I had a picture of Timothy Leary and Allen Ginsberg, with their arms around each other, hanging on my wall. I also had a poster on my wall from the Aleph Gallery in San Francisco. An aleph is a point in space, like a grain of sand, where the entire world is contained.

I was having all sorts of visions and aberrations around this time. Every evening I would pad down the dormitory hall to my room and look at myself in the mirror, thinking I was Jesus Christ and that there was this ring of light about my head.

At the same time, I became very interested in schizophrenia. I began reading romantic books about madness, like "Reflections" by R. D. Laing. They made it sound interesting, and I began looking at more clinical books, searching for evidence that I was schizophrenic too. I was getting to the point where I was pretty certain I was, and I felt rather pleased and exceptional and daring like R. D. Laing said.

It came time, at the height of this interest, to fly home to Arizona for Christmas. Once home I looked up my best friend that I had left behind in Arizona. G. was acting strangely. At a Christmas party that one of my mother's business associates gave, G. began to get very drunk. I began to perceive that it was not simply drunkenness, but that it was the beginnings of schizophrenia. I began to have doubts about the honor of being schizophrenic. I was a little scared and I didn't hold schizophrenics in such high regard anymore, even if they were my friends.

When I went back to Stanford after the vacation was over, I took down my poster of Timothy Leary and Allen Ginsberg, and took down the Aleph Gallery poster. I put up a poster from the Fourth Annual Endangered Species Conference that my brother had given me . . . my brother who wasn't crazy, who never took LSD or smoked pot, and who thought schizophrenia was just self-indulgence.

Gary completed his freshman year at Stanford in June of 1980 with an outstanding academic record despite his first semester of using drugs and the crisis of dealing with his sexuality. By the end of the school year, his father and I had realized that Gary was terribly unhappy at Stanford, and he told us he was certain he didn't want to return. He wanted to come home for the summer and talk about his plans for the future.

Immediately upon arriving back in Tucson, Gary began to carry out his strategic plan, which consisted first of convincing us beyond any doubt that Stanford was not the school for him. He spoke disdainfully about Stanford, telling us it was only "a high class trade school," a perfect school for people who wanted a career in medicine, law, or engineering, but not the school for those who wanted intellectual challenges. Exaggerating and dramatizing to make his point, this blanket condemnation of Stanford was used to prove to himself and to Jack and me that it wasn't the right school for him. This is how he justified his decision to leave.

Having partially prepared us for what us to come, Gary presented his next bombshell. He didn't plan to transfer to another college; he planned to stay out of school for a year and go backpacking in Europe. With extravagant assurances that he would surely complete college after his year off, and even stronger assurances that he did not expect his parents to pay for his trip, that he would earn every penny himself, he carried out his usual bombardment against any parental resistance. Jack and I knew Gary wouldn't change his mind about his decision, but, as always, he wanted his parents' blessing and approval, which we half-heartedly gave even though we had our misgivings.

Within days after he got back to Tucson, Gary began a job search so that he could earn the money to finance his trip. He was incredibly persistent and very quickly found three part-time jobs—as a sales clerk at both the Broadway Department Store and at Walden Books, and as a maintenance man at the Indian Ridge Pool, the neighborhood pool where he and Andy had been swim team members and lifeguards for many years during their childhood and adolescence.

Gary's schedule was hectic and demanding. He often worked ten to twelve hours a day and for twenty to thirty days straight without a day off. He had practically no social life. He toiled night and day and on the weekends as well, but this backbreaking schedule didn't appear to bother him. He was totally obsessed with earning enough money as quickly as he could. Gary's obsessiveness didn't surprise me. When Gary had a goal, he had always committed himself absolutely, everything else in his life became subordinate.

It was actually during this same time period I learned Gary was gay. I still recall the night so vividly. Gary was helping me with dinner, which he occasionally did. He had just gotten a new haircut and immediately I hated it. I still don't know exactly why, because it had never occurred to me that Gary might be gay, but for some reason I said to him, "With that haircut people will think you're gay." He hesitated for a moment and then, looking directly at me, he said, "I think maybe I am."

I stared at my son, totally speechless, stunned, momentarily unable to react. Then I started crying and found myself talking incoherently about the tragedy of being gay. I tried to persuade Gary to say he wasn't sure and when I persisted, he said, perhaps to appease me, that, no, he wasn't sure and that he hadn't yet had a sexual experience with either another male or with a female. I rambled on senselessly about homosexuality as an adolescent phase, something people can grow out of, something that may be just a rebellion, a way of being unconventional and daring. Gary listened patiently to my incoherent ramblings and never tried to contradict me.

Knowing what I now know about homosexuality and having examined my own feelings and attitudes, I think my reactions that night were deplorable. My son deserved to hear immediately that I respected him for his honesty and his courage. What he heard instead was that his mother thought being homosexual was a tragedy. Wasn't this telling him that what he was was unacceptable to me? Gary was a troubled adolescent, dealing with what was certain to be a very difficult adjustment. I was an adult, a psychologist, and a mother who failed her son at a crucial moment in his life.

Jack and I were living apart at the time and I was desperate to talk to him. Early the next morning, after crying most of the night, I went to his apartment. Jack took one look at me and knew immediately something was terribly wrong. Frantic, he pleaded with me to try to tell him what it was. When I could finally talk and tell him that Gary thought he might be gay, Jack, perhaps from sheer relief, gave a perfect answer. He said, "Is that all? I was afraid you were going to tell me one of the children had been hurt or killed." Jack always seemed less troubled than I by the idea that Gary was gay, or maybe, hearing the news in a context that forced him to consider the possibility that one of our children might have died helped him to immediately put the issue into clearer perspective than I had so far been able to do.

Although I had, of course, heard of the term "coming out"—a shortened version of the term "coming out of the closet" of hidden homosexuality—I had never expected it to be something that would affect my family. My son coming out to me as a homosexual? I didn't want to believe it; the very word homosexual did not fit with my image of who my son was, of what I wanted him to be, of what I dreamed of him being. As I think about my reactions that first night and during subsequent days and nights, I am still ashamed of what I learned about myself as a mother dealing with my child's homosexuality. Instead of thinking first about how I could help my son cope with what he might have to face in a society so condemning of homosexuals, I focused on how I felt. I tried to convince myself that my reactions were only because I feared the prejudice and stigma Gary would have to face in his life, but this was, at least to some extent, self-deception. Though I didn't want to admit it, I was concerned also about the prejudice and stigma I myself might have to face.

It had always been so easy to be a good mother to two children who met every expectation a parent could possibly have, children who were outstanding students, were motivated and ambitious, were good looking, responsible, intelligent, witty. I had never had to cope with the problems that many parents of adolescents have to deal with. Then, at the first sign of what our society deems imperfection, I failed the test . . . no longer that perfect mother. It seemed I was only a perfect mother for perfect children.

In the immediate aftermath of Gary's devastating announcement, I cried every day. I was truly grieving, something I tried to conceal from Gary, probably not very successfully. Jack and I both loved Gary so deeply and he knew this without any doubt, but I am, to this day, regretful that I gave him a message that I was terribly unhappy about his homosexuality.

As the weeks went by, I thought more and more about the prejudice and the bigotry, the sneering and snide remarks that might confront Gary throughout his life if he were truly gay. I was in anguish that my beautiful son might be ridiculed, shamed, or even physically attacked. I thought about his career and how being gay might interfere. I thought about what other people would think if they knew. Would he be rejected, would he be an outcast? How would he be able to live a normal life? Was he always to be viewed as a "second class citizen"? Unable to concentrate on anything else, I obsessed on and on about Gary, about his future, about the problems he might have to face in his life because he was gay.

Even as I focused so obsessively on Gary's homosexuality, he and I didn't talk a lot about it. Neither of us seemed to know exactly what to say to one another. Ashamed and guilty about my initial overwrought reaction to Gary's coming out, I tried to conceal my depression and to let him know how much Jack and I loved and cared for him. Foolishly, however, I would occasionally ask him if he were sure he was gay and whether he wouldn't like to see a therapist to help him sort out his feelings. I think he understood this was somewhat of a ploy and that my hope was that a therapist might help him realize he wasn't really gay. I think too, as Gary realized how painful it was for me to accept his being gay, he decided to allow me to believe that he really wasn't sure, that perhaps it truly was "just a phase."

I'm certain also that Gary wanted to protect me from knowing how much turmoil he was going through himself in growing up gay and dealing with his sexual identity. And to complicate things even further, Gary still wanted, as he always had, his parents' admiration and approval. Now that he had revealed to his parents something they might not admire or approve of, wasn't he wondering, do they still think I'm so wonderful?

Jack did not seem to agonize as I did in the days after we learned about Gary's homosexuality. He had never been homophobic, and I had always thought of him as unprejudiced and tolerant. He loved his son deeply, and Gary's homosexuality didn't lead him to question himself as a parent in the way it did me. In fact, Jack was highly resistant to my endless ruminations about what we might have done wrong as parents, even when I couldn't stop reminding him of our unending marital conflicts mostly revolving around his alcohol abuse. Some might argue that marital conflict, a father who abused alcohol, a mother highly involved in a professional career could have created homosexual children. But dysfunctional family histories, much more dysfunctional than ours, occur in the lives of many heterosexuals, and no one attributes their sexual orientations to their dysfunctional families. I came to understand that parents, whether functional or dysfunctional, are unlikely to have the power to determine their children's sexual orientation.

Despite our constant discussions over whether we had played a part in our son's sexual orientation, Jack and I were united in our mutual concern and love for our son and we were brought closer together again as we thought of how much he would need us both to help him through whatever he might have to face in his future.

Myself, I was at the beginning of a long, painful process of adjusting to my son's sexual orientation, a process that would involve learning to understand and appreciate exactly how my son's sexual orientation was going to affect his life and also what it would mean in my life. But it had been my spontaneous reaction to my son's revealing that he thought he was gay which made me realize my own underlying homophobia. I knew immediately that I did not want my son to be a homosexual, and this knowledge compelled me to face that heretofore hidden prejudice. Though my prejudice was perhaps not the blatant, overt prejudice of some, it was there, even if in a more subtle form, and it was exposed openly by my emotional reaction to Gary's announcement.

My limited and even erroneous understanding of homosexuality was paradoxically related, at least in part, to my training as a psychologist. Up until the early 1970s, homosexuality was considered by most psychiatrists and psychologists to be a psychiatric disorder. It was listed as a disorder in the American Psychiatric Association's *Diagnostic and Statistical Manual*, and was viewed as a sexual deviance that needed to be corrected or cured. Homosexuals were considered deviant simply because they weren't heterosexual.

During my own training as a clinical psychologist in the 1960s, the deviance view of homosexuality was the predominant view in my profession. In those days, as a psychologist in training, I was taught the approaches then in vogue for treating homosexuality, treatments aimed at eliminating homosexual arousal and behavior and helping patients learn "appropriate" heterosexual behavior—in other words learn how to change their sexual orientation. Treatment models included psychoanalysis and other forms of psychotherapy to help resolve unconscious childhood conflicts or family dysfunctions that had supposedly caused the "deviance" and even the use of aversive conditioning techniques such as electric shock or nausea-inducing drugs to decrease homosexual arousal.

However, as early as the 1950s, research was beginning to emerge that contradicted the popular and professional beliefs that homosexuality was a psychiatric disorder and that homosexuals were all psychologically maladjusted. Dr. Evelyn Hooker, a young psychologist, conducted a now famous study (1957), in which she demonstrated that homosexual males were no different from heterosexual males in terms of psychopathology or psychological adjustment. Dr. Hooker administered a battery of psychological tests to an equal number of homosexual and heterosexual males and then had these test results scored and interpreted by an outside panel of well-known and respected psychologists who did not know the identities or the sexual orientation of the subjects.

To their own and even to Dr. Hooker's astonishment, the psychological experts were unable to distinguish the test results of the heterosexuals from those of the homosexuals. Dr. Hooker concluded that homosexuality as a clinical disorder did not exist. Numerous studies since then have resulted in the same findings and have drawn the same conclusions. Reviews of these studies can be found in John Gonsiorek (1977, 1982, 1991) and Bernard Reiss (1980).

Dr. Hooker's research findings were not, however, incorporated into most professional training programs for many years, and it was not until 1973 that the American Psychiatric Association acted to remove homosexuality from its list of mental disorders. It was not until 1975 that the American Psychological Association adopted a similar policy position, stating that homosexuality per se implied no impairment in judgment, stability, or general social and vocational capabilities. This policy statement also urged psychologists to take the lead in helping to remove the label of mental illness that had long been associated with homosexuality.

Most mental health professionals who have carefully examined the scientific research about homosexuality now believe that sexual orientation is established very early in life; that it is not a pathological condition, but is a normal variant of human sexuality; and that attempts to change an individual's sexual orientation are misguided, unprofessional, and most likely doomed to failure. Unfortunately, societal attitudes, popular opinion, and even the attitudes of some mental health professionals have been slow to reflect these more enlightened views. There is still a relatively large group of these professionals who practice what is called "conversion therapy," in which they attempt to change homosexuals into heterosexuals in the belief that, if an individual is unhappy about being gay and has come voluntarily for therapy, the therapist has the obligation to help him change his orientation. Unfortunately, these therapists do not seem to realize that the source of their patients' unhappiness is not their sexual orientation per se, but their shame—shame resulting from society's condemnation of homosexuality. As Charles Silverstein (1972) said in a presentation at the American Association of

Behavior Therapy, "What brings them into counseling is guilt, shame, and loneliness about their secret."

So it was that prior to my learning my younger son was gay, I had not only been influenced by the general social prejudice toward homosexuals, but in my training as a psychologist I had been taught that homosexuality was a personality defect, a clinical disorder. It was only much later that I became aware of the scientific studies contradicting this position, and gradually began to modify my views. However, I believe that at the time I learned of Gary's homosexuality, I was still under the influence of my earlier training and also, certainly, strongly affected by the general social stigma associated with homosexuality.

As a mother, I just had chaotic feelings of confusion, desperation, and fear. This was my own beloved child now, not a patient, not a diagnosis, not a theory, and I found that I was terrified to think that my child was a homosexual.

It was shortly after Gary came out to me that he also came out to his friend Gus. He and Gus had gone on a trip together to California, on one of the rare weekends when Gary was not working. In the car during the trip Gus told Gary he had just found out that his brother Lou was gay, something which Gary already knew. Gus was overwhelmed from learning about his brother's sexual orientation, and apparently Gary decided he couldn't keep quiet about himself, so he told Gus in the same manner he had told me, that he thought he might be gay too.

Gus was later to tell me that he was extremely shocked because it had just never occurred to him that Gary might be homosexual. Gus and Gary didn't talk much about it at the time, and on the surface there was no observable damage to their relationship. Gus reacted in somewhat the way I had done, in that he latched on to the "I think I may be gay" as uncertainty and a possible indication that Gary was just being unconventional by trying out homosexuality.

Although at first Gus was vaguely uneasy about the idea of Gary's homosexuality, it was only later, after Gary actually had a boyfriend, and Gus met the boyfriend, that he had to more directly confront the reality and deal with the fact that his best friend was actually, not just possibly, a homosexual. It was not without some pain and confusion that he was slowly able to do so.

Gus told me that during the years after Gary had openly acknowledged that he was gay the relationships within their old circle of
friends from high school had been very much affected. Gus sometimes felt that he had to protect Gary in this group, and said the
following:

> In our group of friends, they all admired Gary, but they were
> scared of him because he was gay. The rest of us just thought
> about doing the things he did . . . going to Europe, going to
> New York, writing books. There was always tension when
> Gary would come back to town and was around us. Gary was
> always in control, what are we going to do, how are we going
> to think. Gary would flourish in those situations.

All through this same time period, while Gary had been a student
at Stanford and after he returned to Tucson to work and save money
for his European sojourn, Andy was working at the Los Angeles
Zoo as an animal keeper, working especially with golden lion tamarins, a species of small monkeys. Although he hadn't actually fulfilled his childhood ambition to "own a zoo," this job was a good
approximation and Andy loved his work. When I occasionally mentioned to him that he had abilities and education beyond being an
animal keeper, his response was, "How many people do you know
who love their work as much as I do?" This was difficult to argue
with, and Jack and I were truly very happy for Andy. When we
visited him or he us, we could tell he was totally engrossed with his
job and seemed happy and contented. We could hardly be dis-
pleased.

Andy didn't seem to have a regular girlfriend, but he did have
numerous female friends, mostly other zoo employees, and he spent
a lot of his time with these women, both at work and outside of
work hours. When we visited him in Los Angeles we met several of
these women, and he brought one young woman home with him
over a holiday, but we could sense that none of these were really
romantic relationships. I remember asking him about girlfriends,
about getting married, and his answer was always, "I guess I'm just
too picky." Somehow it never occurred to me that Andy might also
be gay. I was blind to the few clues that might have been there.

I noticed at this time that Gary, not knowing then that Andy was also gay, and worried that Andy might be judgmental about homo-sexuality, began to pull away from his brother somewhat. After seeing the way I had reacted to his coming out, he may have not wanted to take a chance on his family again.

Our two sons, though similar in so many ways, differed significantly in how they dealt with their sexual orientation. Gary decided at a relatively early age to confront his homosexuality head on, to suffer through whatever he had to suffer, to deal with it. Andy chose a more cautious approach and postponed the confrontation until he was more mature and better able to cope. Or was it, perhaps, not caution, but just a young man desiring his last fling as an unfettered, unburdened youth without having to deal with the difficulties he knew he would experience as a homosexual adult? Or was it that he had always been looked up to and put on a pedestal in the family and by his friends, and that coming out might tumble him off his pedestal? Whatever reasons Andy had, he told no one he was gay, no friend, no family member. He was coping totally alone.

Chapter 5

Coming of Age

Driven by the strength and intensity of his dream to backpack through Europe and knowing he had to finance it himself, kept Gary toiling unceasingly at his three jobs, trudging dutifully from one to the other, often to all three in a single day. He was not excited by any of the jobs, they were just a means of achieving his dream and certainly showed his father and me how motivated he was. If we had offered to help him financially we would never have known just how important the trip was for him. We were reminded of his childhood projects where once his decision was made nothing could deter him from his goal—not hard work, not parental resistance, not logical arguments about the difficulty of the task, nothing.

It seemed also as I watched him that this trip meant much more to Gary than just a vacation from school and responsibility, and I wondered why he felt so strongly that he had to make this trip alone, at the young age of nineteen, and why he wasn't willing to wait awhile, at least until he graduated from college. Aside from his natural impatience and drive, I think there were other motives. During his year at Stanford he had had to live a life of secrecy, facing alone, with no social support and no role models, the emotional quandaries that came with the recognition of his sexual desires for other men. Perhaps he longed for a dramatic change in his life, an escape from his loneliness and his feelings of being an outsider, and a time in which to confront his sexuality, to think about how he would live his life as a gay man.

Then too, Gary had always been fascinated by literature, art, architecture, museums, and other cultures. And he was perhaps eager to prove to himself that he could survive on his own, far from home, with no parents, no friends for support. Perhaps it was as his friend Lou said: gay men have to prove themselves in order to make up for what they have been told is a deficiency, a flaw, and have to find new ways of being themselves since they do not fit the molds society has laid out. So Gary's trip could satisfy his youthful artistic interests and also provide a means of proving something to himself.

After seven months of hard work Gary had succeeded in earning enough money for both the trip and an additional $500 to set aside toward his future college tuition, a stipulation of his parents, perhaps in the vain hope of deterring him. He set off in February 1981, for New York City, the first leg of his journey, where he planned to visit his friend Lou before departing for London. He stayed on in New York for several weeks, and it was during this time that Gary first had close contact with a group of openly gay young people, mostly Lou's friends, who were almost all dancers or musicians. I believe this was also the time of his beginning to fully accept his sexuality and openly acknowledge it to others who were also gay, a time for him to emerge further from the closet.

These experiences, the enchantment and magic of the city, and the supportive atmosphere of being accepted by a large gay community persuaded Gary that when he returned from Europe he wanted to live in New York. I think he realized he had reached a turning point in his life. Those feelings of exclusion, of being an outsider, did not have to last forever. There were others like himself, he could fit in somewhere, he could be accepted for who and what he was. It must have been a tremendous relief to him.

Gary kept a journal throughout his trip and he wrote home frequently. Excerpts from his journal and his letters have helped me reconstruct his experiences. His first letter home was written from Oxford, where he was spending a few days with the Eisner family, friends from Tucson, who were living there during Dr. Sig Eisner's sabbatical as an English professor from the University of Arizona. The Eisners were parents of six children, several of whom were close in age to Andy and Gary, and they took him in as if he were one of their own children.

Dear M. & D:
A quick note from Eisner manor in Oxford. I'm having a great time and already dread leaving. I arrived in London with

no problems, found a little hotel and saw the city in a rather jet lagged state. After a few nights, I moved to a beautiful youth hostel . . . a castle with flocks of exotic birds . . . where I met numbers of similar travelers. Despite constant rain, London has charm and I saw much of it. Everything is old (very).

I then zoomed up to Oxford to quickly visit the Eisners and they generously took me in and fed me. They're very entertaining. Patrick showed me around Oxford, Halley and Cassie took me to a pub and today took me to Stonehenge and the countryside, and Sig entertains with numberless stories and facts. I'm really enjoying it and may stay another day or two. I'm having very few troubles. Hope you are well. I'll write again soon. Love, Gary.

When we next heard from Gary, he was in Italy, where he had contacted his cousin Nan, who lived in Scandicci, just outside Florence, with her husband and their three daughters, all close in age to Gary. Nan had married an Italian man while living in Italy as a student from Stanford, and she had remained there ever since. Gary spent several days with his relatives before launching off totally on his own. While in Florence, in one of his journal entries, he writes of how he has made his adjustment to being gay and of his satisfaction in knowing that he may have a commonality with famous artists from the past and that homoeroticism was not unknown in previous eras.

May 30, 1981, Florence, Scandicci—Rose late, spoke with Nan over breakfast. I decided to go into town. There I saw the Barghello Museum . . . a fairly uninteresting collection of sculpture. But I do have a better appreciation of the Renaissance now. It seems strange that the two periods of art that are most admired . . . the Renaissance and Classic Grecian . . . are dominated by gays or at least by the spirit of homoeroticism. Michaelangelo was as gay as they come, I'm sure. It's very odd or perhaps it's not. I'm now on an anti-straight binge. I have almost a Jamesian attitude. I'm really much happier than I've been in years.

After the museum I met Andy K. (a fellow student from Stanford) on the street. Had a brief talk. He's rather a sad creature, an example of the destructive effect being gay can have. Perhaps he's not as broken down as he appears, but his voice and posture sure seem to attest to it. I'm glad I've finally made my peace with my brother, who was a sort of symbol of my own homophobia. (At the time of this journal entry Gary did not yet know that his brother was also gay.)

After leaving the security of visiting friends and relatives, Gary's next stop was Athens. He writes in his journal of other young travelers he has joined up with, mostly students like himself. He stayed at a placed called Apollo House, some sort of youth hostel where he slept on a concrete roof because there were no rooms. In one of his journal entries, Gary writes of the tremendous emotional impact he felt when he viewed the Parthenon:

June 7, Athens—Got up. Wanted to go to Acropolis. Made my way there after parting with short Australian boy. I was soon there with tens of thousands of other people. Despite all the tourists, the Parthenon was inspiring. It did not disappoint me. It was a blazing hot day. Everything seemed bleached . . . even the sky's blue was paled. The pillars rose up in difficulty, some damaged, all of them straining. The Parthenon is man . . . man divorced from nature, man divorcing himself from nature. It is man's struggle in the realization and acceptance of original sin. The Parthenon is man's tragedy in a form.

After Athens, Gary went on to the Greek island of Mykonos where he was fascinated by the decadence. In a letter to Gus, he wrote about falling in love at first sight with some beautiful man whom he saw about town and danced with once.

June 14, Mykonos—Dear Gus: How long has it been since I've written to you? One can never be sure with the mail service in Europe. I'm currently beached on the Greek island Mykenos . . . a place that is almost impossible to describe. It is an unreal, decadent place . . . like a miniature New York City. I have had an incredibly good time here . . . I can see myself slipping into this spectacular decadence very easily.

I'm leaving today for Santorini to meet my friends from Colgate University, a boy and girl, David and Margaret, that I met here. I've become very good friends with them. But I also think I've fallen in love with someone here. This may all seem a little bizarre. Let me go on to tell you things more clearly. I'm staying in a room of a private house. Margaret and David are staying below me in a separate room. They are a charming pair who had been studying in France and are now traveling. We immediately hit it off and soon I discovered David was gay. Though very regal, I didn't find David attractive, so we are a very platonic trio.

During the day we've gone to the famous Super Paradise nude beach and at night we've gone to various discos. The disco scene is really wild. I'll recount a typical night: After a pleasant dinner of octopus and swordfish, Margaret, David and I drift about to various shops. At about 11:30, we waft into the MedClub . . . a new wave disco which always seems empty. We dance briefly and then on to another disco where the trendies are to be currently found. We observe a chic drag queen . . . Eunice Deutsche I call her . . . she drifts toward us and she swings a string of pearls in my face.

On to yet another disco, where we dance endlessly. Here I meet a man I've exchanged smiles with at various places about town. We dance and it gets very intense. But then suddenly he must leave with a middle aged man he's always with. I am devastated. He says, "I'll see you later in the week." I don't know what to make of this. I feel utterly drained. Since then, he has possessed my thoughts like nothing else ever has . . . I'm in love. I have since seen him about town, always with the older man, and he smiles at me but doesn't talk to me. Your friend, Gary.

Gary's youthful yearnings about this man made me think about the difficulties young gays experience as they go through the adolescent stages of social and sexual development. Because young gays and lesbians may suppress their sexual feelings during their growing-up years, they may not have the same opportunities for the sexual exploration, the romantic attractions, the dating that are typical of early and middle adolescence. When they finally acknowledge their attractions, it is often only then that they begin to go through the stages of experimentation that heterosexual youth have usually done at a much earlier age. Gary's enchantment with a man he didn't even get to know seems to me, in some ways, more like that of an early adolescent of perhaps fourteen or fifteen, rather than a nineteen, almost twenty-year-old man. Perhaps, though, I am wrong about the nature of Gary's feelings about this man, having only his journals to help me understand.

In his letters to the family, Gary wrote not of sexual awakenings and romance, but of the usual travel experiences: sightseeing, the museums, the architecture, and the people he had met. Gary's letters helped me continue to avoid identification of my son as truly homosexual, allowed me to keep picturing him as a youthful, asexual student and traveler.

There are many long and detailed daily entries in Gary's journals describing the rest of his stay in Mykonos, the intriguing travelers he met, and various other equally brief encounters with the beautiful stranger. After a trip to Santorini, which he described as a blown-out volcano with sheer cliffs and black volcanic rocks, Gary decided to go back to Athens with Margaret and David, despite no apparent culmination of his tentative "affair" with the man of his fantasies.

In Athens, Gary separated from Margaret and David and went on to Corfu. Corfu has a special significance for Gary since it was the place where Andy's idol and role model, Gerald Durrell, naturalist and author, spent his childhood. It was Andy's reading of Durrell's books, especially *My Family and Other Animals*, which had been so influential in the development of his fascination with animals and his lifelong ambition to "own a zoo." Gary had made Andy a promise that he would visit Corfu and he sent us a postcard from there in which he wrote about visiting several villas where Durrell and his family had formerly lived.

From Corfu, Gary went back to Florence for a few entertaining days with his relatives, "Nan, and her enchanting daughters." His next stops were in Venice and Marseilles. He loved Venice, which he thought magical and romantic. He visited the museums and cathedrals, sat in the Piazza San Marco, and discovered the Bridge of Sighs. He was entranced with the Peggy Guggenheim former palazzo, which had become a museum, and wrote this description:

This was a really entertaining museum. Set in, what was until recently, Peggy's pallazo, it is absolutely beautiful. Among the paintings were a Malevich, an El Lissitzky, a Marcel Duchamp (sad young man on a train), a good Picasso. Also, there was a series of photos depicting Peggy around and about . . . "Peggy in her Brancusi designer bat sunglasses," "Peggy in her Fiorello quilt on her gondola in front of her palazzo," "Peggy in her famous Tiepolo evening gown sitting in her byzantine marble throne," "Peggy in her Cardin fur leaning against Giacometti's 'Tall Women'." What a dilettente. She looks like Di Hosley. I enjoyed the photos more than the rest of the museum.

In Marseilles, Gary visited Le Corbusier's Unité de Habitación and wrote in his journal:

July 3, Marseilles—When I first glimpsed the Unité de Habitación, I was absolutely astounded by it . . . it's certainly the most extraordinary thing I've ever seen. The building proper is a study in rationality . . . supremely organized, yet with incomprehensible and irrational features. Perhaps if I understood the Modular, I would perceive a system in the building's facade. The pilotis are perhaps the basis of the Unité's brilliance. . . . their power exceeds that of any sculpture. Le Corbusier can take a simple pillar and mold it into poetry.

But these features I had apprehended in photos (of course it was much more impressive), it was how the Unité fit into its surroundings, and the grounds around the Unité. The building is surrounded by lush grounds and the contrast . . . the way the building stands above it, is reminiscent of the Parthenon. The Unité is utterly divorced of its natural surroundings and intends to be. Again, this is a man against nature statement (re: Acropolis). The building is conscious man and his tragedy. But perhaps Le Corbusier is more optimistic, no, I think not. I could not get inside the Unité and eventually left, absolutely amazed. Only the Acropolis rivals this on my trip. I know now Le Corbusier is the most important architect since whoever designed the Parthenon.

I really liked Marseilles. I've never seen more deformed people in any one place. It was fascinating. Seedy, yet friendly. I felt at home.

From Marseilles, Gary traveled to Switzerland where he climbed the Eiger and was fascinated by the spectacular glaciers and alpine meadows. He left Switzerland and proceeded by Eurorail to Paris where he planned to spend his twentieth birthday, July 7, 1981. His journal indicated that Paris was disappointing except for a visit to the Pompidou Centre, which he thought a remarkable building, "the epitome of post-modernism."

He left Paris and took a train to Amsterdam where he wandered through the Red Light district. In his journal he describes his reactions:

July 9, Holland—Soon I was in Amsterdam and wandering the town, which turned out to be quite charming. There were several pedestrian shopping streets with avant-garde clothes shops, bars and food places. All types . . . hippies, drug dealers, imaginative punks were there. I ate at McDonalds and got in a conversation with a lovely Puerto Rican couple. This was the first time I spoke Spanish on my trip.

Then I made my way by steps to the Red Light district. I soon found myself in an area with lots of porno and accessory shops . . . really bizarre, some of them. Then I began to notice the whores sitting about. Between the porno movie houses and bars, they would sit in front of tiny rooms furnished only with beds, flimsy curtains on the windows to mask the action within. Some were in classic whore drag, some were drab-like housewives. Very few were classy. A few cooed at me or said a few words.

I was fascinated by the scene and wandered all the streets in the area, even the ones where the pimps gathered, eyeing me suspiciously as I walked by. I felt a strange kinship, this is the only word I can think of, with these girls. I thought of Lou. It was all very Mardi Gras. It didn't seem real. It's hard to believe it goes on every day. I felt that it was somehow a special festival or show just put on for this one night. I'm not sure why it's so open here . . . the residents don't seem to mind.

Gary's next days were spent in London and then Edinburgh. From Edinburgh, he went back to Oxford to visit the Eisners, grateful, no doubt, to have a secure place to go to recover from his wandering, homeless state. On July 19, Gary left Oxford to go to London to meet Andy, who was also fulfilling a childhood dream and completing an internship on the Isle of Jersey at Gerald Durrell's zoo. In the following excerpt from his journal, Gary describes himself and Andy seeing the sights in London, meeting Sig Eisner at the British Museum, then on to Paris:

July 22, London—We arose fairly early, left for Buckingham Palace. We peered out of the Green Park underground station, and seeing it was pouring, left for the Tate Gallery instead. It wasn't that great and Andy and I quarreled.

We walked from the Tate along the Thames, past Parliament and to Westminister Abbey. We found Charles Darwin's burial plot in the floor and we stood reverently over it. From there we zoomed to McDonald's and then to the British Museum to meet Sig. Sig was in his element. He greeted us sleepily, guided us authoritatively to the manuscripts. He discoursed on these, then led us to the Greek section. Unfortunately, he only had a little while and had to leave. He pronounced Andy "exactly the same" as he had always been. It was classic Sig in Bloomsbury. In general the British Museum was spectacular, and the thought of Sig pouring over ancient, yellowed parchments in some tiny back room inspired us to new heights of appreciation.

From London, the two departed for Paris where they visited the Louvre, the Jardin des Tuilleries, the Champs Élysées, the Arc de Triomphe, and the Galerie de Paris. It was sometime during this little sojourn in London and Paris that Andy told Gary he was gay, which Gary, like Jack and I, had not known. Gary made a brief note in his journal saying that he was shocked, but he didn't write anything more at the time.

Later on, while the two were in Paris, Gary wrote in his journal about an attempt the two of them made to explore gay bars and a bit about their conversations. Gary noted that he hoped Andy was happy. Although Andy told Gary that being gay didn't bother him like it did Gary, Gary wonderd why he, himself, was more open about being gay than Andy. This issue didn't get resolved. Gary expressed disappointment that Andy didn't enjoy going to the gay bars. Andy, much later, was to tell me that he and Gary laughed about the fact both of them had been gay and neither one had known about the other. For some reason, still inexplicable to me, they found this amusing. Also, it was apparently agreed between the two of them that Gary would not reveal to the family that Andy was gay, as Andy was still not ready to have us know.

Following their excursion in Paris, Gary went back with Andy to the Isle of Jersey for a couple of days and then returned to Tucson for a brief stay prior to leaving for New York, where he had been accepted to start his sophomore year at Columbia University.

I remember so well the day Gary returned home to Tucson from Europe. I hadn't known exactly when he was arriving, not even the day, so when I walked into the house after being gone all day and found him lying asleep on the living room sofa, I was deliriously happy. I had no thought of gay or straight. This was my beloved son, home once more. To this day, every time I leave the house and look over at that sofa, I imagine my son lying there and myself so happy, ignorant of what the future was to bring.

Chapter 6

Columbia Years: 1981-1984

The years of his Columbia education were wonderful years for Gary. He loved Columbia and he loved living in New York. He wrote home proclaiming his classes inspiring, his teachers brilliant, and he never complained that college was only a high-class trade school. To Gary, Columbia was a place where there was respect for ideas and critical thinking and where the students were excited about literature, art, history, and philosophy. And New York City was a center of gay life, a city tolerant of all kinds of diversity, a city where a young gay man could feel at home. Gary had sought liberation and acceptance and he found them in the city and in the university. His search for a new life, a place where he could establish his identity as a gay man, where he could be who he was without pretense, had ended. Now, in an environment tolerant of homosexuality and supportive of his literary and intellectual interests, he seemed happier than he had been in a long time. And my own anxieties about gay bashing, about bigotry and hatred of homosexuals were, at least partially, put to rest as I realized how happy he was.

An excerpt from a letter Gary wrote in October 1981, shortly after he started his classes, is an example of how he felt about his new life:

> Dear Mother and Daddy:
> . . . I sincerely believe that the environment in New York is as educational as the school itself. Thus, any extra expense in comparison to Stanford is repaid with 100% interest. And Columbia is truly a great school. I am obsessed with my studies. My classes are inspiring; many times I become distraught over the fact I can't take more units. I love Columbia, I love New York; I am happy here.

The new apartment is a cheerful, spacious (relatively) place. Its price is a bargain; if I don't get in a dorm you'll learn to appreciate its cost by the end of my Columbia career. I truly appreciate your supporting me while I am in college . . . never doubt this. But I am a truly thrifty person in a profligate city. In regards to furniture, a futon bed seems the best choice. It will cost about $100. I will dredge up a desk and a bookcase at a secondhand store. Lamps I will purchase as cheaply as possible. Remember: these are one-time expenses. The apartment will be in top shape for your spring visit!

My essential points are:

1. New York and Columbia are worth paying extra for.
2. I am thrifty. You have not deprived me of money by any means though.
3. I will be famous someday and will pay you back for the bed and my education. Love, Gary.

I had loved this letter, but in reading it again after Gary died, I was immensely saddened, especially by number 3 in his little list of "essential points." Gary never got the chance to be famous or to pay his parents back for the bed or for his education—not that we had ever asked or expected to be repaid.

In Gary's letters and in our phone conversations he told us about his classes, his impressions of New York and Columbia, the books he was reading, his views about the theatre and art, what he hoped for his future. Although he was majoring in English, he was also still fascinated with art, architecture, philosophy, and psychology, and he wrote impassioned letters about what he was learning and how he was growing up and changing. He never spoke or wrote about any difficulties concerning his sexual orientation. I am sorry to admit that I also remained strangely silent on the topic. It was so much more comfortable just to communicate with Gary about his studies, about his vast interests, about his getting to know the city, than it would have been to talk about how he was adjusting to coming out as gay, whether he had lovers or boyfriends, whether he had encountered any prejudice, how I was proceeding in my own adjustment to his sexual orientation. If I had only been able to adapt more quickly to Gary's homosexuality I think I could have been a much better mother to him during that time. Fortunately, Gary still had the support of his dear friend and mentor, Lou Porcelli, and they saw each other frequently.

Living in New York, Gary was exposed to outstanding theatre, music, and dance, and he was especially intrigued with the avant-garde and the experimental. He liked the Wooster Group, Merce Cunningham, Brian Eno, John Cage, and the younger performance artists in Manhattan. In his journal in May 1982, he wrote in his exaggerated and overly dramatic manner about this particular group of musicians, artists, and performers and their influence on his thinking.

> . . . Great god . . . I've skipped the most important event in my recent life . . . my artistic conversion from melancholic/doomy/ individualist romantic to sanguinary/collectivist/Duchampian. Mondrian, Malevich, early Corbusier are out. Cage, Duchamp, Cunningham, Wooster group are what is important. I don't have the energy to describe it all in detail, but it is a profound, positive change.

Gary's journals were filled with sentimental broodings about life and sex and art, but his sometimes tragic view of life was more evident in his journals than in his mainly optimistic and cheerful letters to Jack and me. His occasional journal entries about death, disease, and plagues seemed almost as if he had a sense of his doomed future.

> October 18, 1981—The crisis . . . life has become too human-ized in one way, too dehumanized in another. The latter is obvious; the former: life has too many opportunities, we are left confused like Hamlet. The fight against disease is absurd and even obscene . . . we should all be under peril of death at all times. It would make me more confident I know. Roles, classes should exist. Humanism is a sham . . . I've had it with obligatory emotions. What we need is a good nuclear holo-caust or plague to set us arights. People become so indignant when their lives are threatened.

During Gary's Columbia years, Andy had also gone back to school as a graduate student working for a PhD in zoology and animal behavior at the University of Maryland near Washington, DC. I was overjoyed by Andy's decision to go to graduate school and also that our two sons would be living so close to one another. They were now able to spend more time together than they had in recent years, and they seemed to be regaining the closeness of their relationship. I think this happened, at least partly, because each now knew that the other was gay; though, of course, I was still in the dark about Andy and not aware of the special commonality they now had.

At the beginning of Gary's Columbia years, I was still despairing about his homosexuality and still in a state of partial denial. I was almost totally in the closet, not acknowledging to most other people that my son thought he was gay, telling myself that he wasn't sure and that he was still young enough to change. I simply did not want to confront the truth. But even as I denied and avoided, at another level I was gradually learning to accept that Gary was truly gay. I was reading everything I could find about sexual orientation: scientific studies, personal stories by gays and parents of gays, and the ever-increasing news stories about homosexuality and gay rights. I was accumulating vast amounts of knowledge about sexual orientation and realizing that Gary was happy and productive and just as ambitious and motivated as he had always been. Being a homosexual was obviously only a part of who he was. And, of course, gay or straight, I loved him dearly

It was while Gary was in his first year at Columbia that he met Darryl, a fellow student from South Carolina, who was to become the only true romantic love of his life. Jack and I didn't know he had a lover until months after Darryl had become important in Gary's life—due, no doubt, to our reluctance to deal openly with his sexuality. In his journal, though, Gary was writing endlessly about his infatuation, an infatuation which was to turn into a passionate and obsessive love affair. His first journal entry about Darryl was the following:

> November 29, 1981 . . . . After talking with Darryl tonight at the library I am obsessed with him. But he is crafty and I don't trust him. Darryl, Darryl, Darryl, Darryl . . . there that should do it. Romance gives way to corrective behavior mod.

Lou and I visited the Whitney Museum and got along well, though I waxed pedantic. I do know a lot about modern art. I'm reading Ulysses. It is brilliant and alien. It seems a fragment from some lost, advanced culture. One certainly sees where the absurdists got their lingo and style. I like my English professor now that I said something clever about Proust and got an A- on my last paper. Pettiness? Of course. I really like Columbia.

Gary's journal entries during this time are filled with his increasing preoccupation with Darryl, and from them it is obvious that he had fallen deeply in love. But he seemed tortured by Darryl's quixotic ways and demanding nature and was filled with ambivalence and confusion about the relationship, about whether he should end it.

April 15, 1982—Discussion with Lou about Darryl last night. I was a little fed up with the way Darryl was treating me. I can intellectualize and thus forgive his rudenesses and failings due to his understandable insecurity, but only so far. After awhile I want some genuine affection and simple niceness. With Darryl I continually refer to the existentialist idea that your actions define you, although he claims he thinks differently than he acts. . . . I do deserve more than he gives me. But I don't know if I can end it with him. I realize how much Darryl has reduced my self-esteem for his own ends. How can that be good? I simply cannot understand the profundity of Darryl's neurosis . . . well, no, I can. But why can't he break through it when I give him as much love as I do? I was willing to wait and see if Darryl would let some sort of real humanity creep out towards me, but he really hasn't. I deserve a mutual respect, not a stunted, one-way attachment. I must still have a great deal of self-hatred to be stuck in this.

April 24/25, 1982—Of course, it's over with Darryl. I won't bother with the tedium of detail; suffice it to say that the boy is deeply misguided, has elaborate delusions of grandeur. I can intellectualize all this, but it still has me in a state. I know Darryl is not good for me/not good enough for me, but I am still obsessed with him.

May 5, 1982 . . . . Darryl was beginning to kill my self-esteem with his hands. I may still sleep with him from time to time. I am willing if he is, even though I know it isn't a good idea. The crisis he has put me through, I am certain, was good for me. I have learned I must support myself, that I do have things to be satisfied within and of myself. I do not need another person to verify my existence and I must not let myself slip into that situation. . . . If I believed Darryl, I am an ugly, stupid, slow, incompetent bourgeois who no one likes. In fact, I am a reasonably attractive, intelligent, quick, horribly competent, independent person whom Darryl's friends like much more than they do him.

Gary completed his sophomore year at Columbia with top grades and wrote us just before school was out about his feelings of accomplishment and told us he had stopped romanticizing the city quite so much.

Dear Parents:
. . . I'm in the library trying to study. I finished all my papers, after which I felt a huge release. Now, though, I can't accept the fact that I still have finals, four of them. I only have a week left though. I've looked back over my sophomore year at Columbia and am quite pleased. I've accomplished a lot in school; I've made friends (not an easy task for me) and have matured through the suffering New York and its attitudes force upon one. New York is not the paradise I once said it was (or did I ever say it?); in many ways it is evil. Materialism, cynicism, and all types of superficiality are the fashion in all sectors of life . . . even in the arts to an extent. One has to be rigidly independent here to survive with one's originality intact. But, I'm becoming grave again. Still New York is loads of fun, no end of things to do. The big new Broadway play is *Medea* by my favorite, Euripedes. If you come this summer, we must see it. Love, Gary.

Gary had decided to stay in New York and work during the summer after his sophomore year, and Andy would be busy during the summer with his graduate program in DC. Jack and I missed our children and, since they couldn't come home, we planned a trip to New York to celebrate Gary's twenty-first birthday. Andy would meet us there.

It was then, in July 1982, that we first came to know about Darryl. Though Gary had been writing constantly in his journal about their relationship, in his letters to us he had only mentioned Darryl casually along with names of many others. We were introduced to Darryl within hours after our arrival in New York. Darryl was very attractive, charming, intelligent, and black. I was still slowly adjusting to Gary's being gay, but an actual lover was something I had not yet allowed myself to think about. And not only an actual lover, a black actual lover. I was not much affected by Darryl's race, what overwhelmed me was just the fact that he existed, that Gary truly had a lover. Darryl made Gary's gayness much more real to Jack and me.

Jack and I could see why Gary was so entranced with Darryl, but we could also tell that they had a troubled relationship. Right away Darryl began to establish his reputation as a creator of chaos. As an example, Jack and I had planned a birthday party for Gary and his friends at a New York restaurant, but Darryl became very coy about whether or not he would attend the party. Gary was in a terrible state and was making hourly phone calls to Darryl. He couldn't conceal his despair, and I felt so sorry for him. Darryl did finally decide to come to the dinner, but it seemed to Jack and me that he had been needlessly cruel to Gary. We realized that perhaps we were being unduly protective of our son and biased in our judgment, but we couldn't quite let ourselves believe that Darryl would be good for our son. I did secretly wonder at the time, however, if I had allowed myself to be overly influenced by the fact that this was a gay relationship and whether I would have noticed every little flaw quite so readily if it had been a girl Gary was falling in love with. So many things I have come to regret over the years, things like this that I may not have handled well simply because of my difficulty in dealing with the fact that my son was gay.

Because I was still struggling with my feelings about Gary's homosexuality, the reality of my son actually having a sexual relationship was an experience I had tried to avoid thinking about. But now Gary was romantically and sexually involved with a real per-

son. Darryl was Gary's lover. It was now impossible to keep pretending that he might not really be gay. When there was no partner,
or at least when I had not known there was a partner, it was much
easier just not to think about Gary's sexual orientation. However,
even after meeting Darryl, knowing he was Gary's lover, a lingering
self-delusion enabled me to think that maybe this was just an adolescent infatuation. I couldn't begin to imagine then that Gary's and
Darryl's destinies were going to be forever locked together.

Toward the middle of his junior year at Columbia Gary began to
think more about his future and how he would support himself after
he graduated with only a major in English. He knew he needed to do
something drastic to prepare himself for the job market and he made
the decision to add a second major in computer science. He wrote us
about this in February 1983.

> Dear Mother and Daddy:
>   . . . I've been researching the various routes I have open to
> me for computer science. Graduate school, it seems, is open
> only to those that were undergraduate majors in computers.
> This makes it imperative that I get an undergraduate degree in
> computers. This is only a backup career. My main aim right
> now is writing for TV. But these days, one has to be career
> mobile. An English/Computer Science double major, I am
> told, would be quite sought after in the job market. So few
> computer people know how to write, much less have degrees
> in English from Columbia.

Gary was now under tremendous pressure because he had to earn
an additional twenty-four hours of credit in computer sciences and,
at the same time, continue with his arduous English major. He was
working day and night, with his usual dedication and self-disci-
pline, going to summer school and taking excess units of credit
during the regular semesters. But he sounded excited and happy.
Gary had always seemed to thrive under pressure, deadlines, and
crises of major or minor proportions. It may have been partially this
need for excitement, drama, and crisis which even fueled his obsession with Darryl. Darryl never allowed Gary to relax his vigilance
for more than a moment.

Gary remained enthralled with Darryl as his journal clearly reflects. He brooded about their seemingly irreconcilable differences, their repetitive breakups and reunifications, and Darryl's impossibly difficult temperament. He seemed disillusioned about the possibility of ever finding real happiness with his lover. However, he eventually began to blame Darryl less, to take his own share of responsibility for their problems, and to predict that the relationship was destined to end badly.

> March 14, 1984 . . . Darryl wants people, people, people. All gay men are that way, or so it seems. Maybe I just don't feel adequate to participate in that sphere. I really wish Darryl could love me alone, but he can't, and I don't blame him, really, for it. Maybe I should. Anger at him might be good.

> March 22, 1984 . . . Darryl never promised much, but I continually tried to collect on an unsigned contract. I was wrong in a real way. I really was. Darryl is difficult, but it is my attitude that is the problem too. I'm finally realizing this. Maybe I can get over it, and Darryl and I actually will have a good relationship some day. Even if we never met again, and this is more likely than I can admit, I have learned a valuable lesson from Darryl. I gave him too little credit. Perhaps he has cured, or begun to cure, me of my arrogance.
>
> It really is over, how odd. Two years of my life, most of my emotion, used on Darryl, is gone. This is self-pity, but I hope therapeutic. Probably not. Perhaps it's just to pass the time. I have so much time now.

In another journal entry around this same time, toward the end of his senior year at Columbia, Gary wrote a poem of sorts about death and decay. The poem doesn't refer to AIDS directly, but since reading it after Gary's death, I have wondered if it discloses a developing fear of AIDS, a foreboding of his own future.

Death, said the doctor. Death. What does it mean? What does it say?
The doctor said:
Think of me as a critic
A good critic, I might add

In fact, think of me as artist/critic
I read a patient for a disease
A theme to the random letters, pages, symptoms
A trend, an idea, a resonance
It is these I seek
It is also these I create
I will read you like a book
I will pour over passages, sections,
I will examine your text
I will find resonances, structures
I will diagnose a disease

Death came very briefly to T.
It alighted, it seared.
With a touch, it reduced
Stripping away the ailments
The diseases of life
He watched silently as the change came
Watched the malignancies, the infections, the parasites
Watched the penis, the skin, the bones
All fled, all gone
He could only nod.
For death is health
And health, death.

Gary's writings remind me of my own anxiety at that time about AIDS. The ever-growing references in the media to this harrowing disease plaguing gay men alarmed me, but I tried desperately to pretend they could not possibly have anything to do with my child. The unavoidable connection between homosexuality and this frightening disease was thrusting homosexuality into the public eye, ripping away some of the secrecy surrounding it, making homosexuality much more visible. Unfortunate that the trigger to this greater openness was a ravaging epidemic.

Gary had completed his work at Columbia and was to graduate in May of 1984. Jack and I planned to go to New York for the graduation, and Andy would meet us there. The graduation coincided with Andy's return from Brazil where he was doing field research for his PhD dissertation, studying the social behavior of small monkeys known as golden lion tamarins. My sister June and her husband Leonard were also going with us to the graduation. No longer so secretive about Gary's homosexuality, I had revealed to June and Leonard that their nephew was gay. Neither of them had intimately known anyone they knew for certain was gay and they were a bit shocked when I announced it, but they didn't seem at all judgmental. Knowing they would be meeting Darryl, who was also graduating, I had also forewarned them about the relationship.

Gary's college career had been highly successful. He graduated with honors, had been elected to Phi Beta Kappa, and had been awarded two very prestigious literary prizes for his short stories. At the graduation, Jack and I were filled with pride and love watching our son, tall and handsome in his graduation cap and gown, receiving his honors and watching our two sons together, best friends and companions still as in their childhoods. Following the graduation ceremony we celebrated with a dinner for Gary and Darryl at the Ginger Man, a restaurant on Columbus Avenue. Darryl's mother, Gary's proud brother, of course, and many of Darryl's and Gary's gay and straight friends were there. How happy, how unknowing we all were.

Columbia and New York had had a tremendous influence on Gary, and the prizes he had received for his writing had given him the confidence to believe that he could truly become a writer. Jack and I foresaw a brilliant future for our son and we again reminded ourselves of how very lucky we were to be the parents of both of our wonderful sons.

Chapter 7

A Mother's Coming Out

Those years while Gary was a student at Columbia coming out as a gay man were the same years I was struggling to adjust to the reality that my younger son was truly homosexual. Stricken with terror when Gary first told me he thought he was gay, I couldn't then begin to fathom that his announcement would be the beginning of a long and sometimes painful process of my learning how to be the mother of a gay child. Just as my son had to come out of the closet of hidden homosexuality, I would learn that I, too, must come out of the closet. However, it took me a long time to realize this because the knowledge and understanding which I needed as a mother and which would have enabled me to help rather than hinder my child's adjustment to being gay were denied me for a number of reasons, all primarily revolving around the stigmatization of homosexuality. Until this stigmatization ends, parents will continue to fail their gay children.

When parents discover they have a gay or lesbian child they eventually discover also that they have a significant choice to make in their lives—the choice of whether to conceal their child's sexual orientation, even to pretend to themselves that their child is not really gay, or to come out of the closet, to acknowledge first to themselves and then to others that, yes, they do have a child who is gay.

If the parents of a gay child make the choice to come out, they will learn that their child isn't going to fit the usual molds, isn't going to meet certain of their expectations. They will learn to reconcile opposing views of who their child is, reconciling who they thought he was with who he actually is. If the parents choose to avoid the perils of coming out and choose instead the safety and comfort of the closet, they will choose also a life of secrecy, a life of emotional and often physical distance from their child, a life in which they may never really know their child. But secrecy is the choice many parents make and for compelling reasons.

The dynamics leading to the pattern of secrecy are the same for both homosexuals and for their families. Both know of the frightening prejudices that exist toward homosexuals, and both are fearful of rejection and blame by whomever might find out the dreadful truth, that one is gay or that one's child is gay. To leave the secrecy of the closet is not a decision made lightly or without some agonizing about the possible consequences.

Writers have often described the coming out process for gays and lesbians as a series of stages (Cass, 1979, 1984; Coleman, 1982; Gonsiorek and Rudolph, 1991; and Troiden, 1979, 1988). The word stages suggests well-defined, discrete events, but in reality the stages are aspects of an evolving process with starts, stops, and regressions. Many think of coming out as only the public acknowledgment to others that one is homosexual, but public acknowledgment is only a later part of the coming-out process. Self-awareness is the beginning. The awareness that one may be homosexual does not usually come suddenly or with certainty. Just as almost no one wakes up one morning and says, "Oh, I believe I must be heterosexual," so almost no one who is gay achieves this kind of sudden insight about his or her sexual orientation. An awareness of your sexual and romantic attractions, whether they be to the same or to the opposite sex, is a process, a development, that evolves over time throughout childhood, adolescence, and young adulthood. The process, in most ways, is the same for homosexuals as for heterosexuals.

However, there is a major difference for homosexuals. When a young homosexual begins to be aware that he is attracted to persons of the same sex, there are compelling reasons to deny or block the feelings. A child growing up soon learns that such feelings are thought by others to be perverted and abnormal. This message is sent in many ways, through casual remarks made or not made by parents and peers, through the news media, through television and movies, through pronouncements of elected officials, through religious teachings, through schools that fail to ever mention the word homosexuality. It should not be surprising then that most youth who grow up to be gay or lesbian are afraid to admit, to acknowledge even to themselves, that they have sexual feelings that are condemned so strongly by society.

Struggling to overcome the shame and stigma of their identity, young gays and lesbians may internalize the homophobia of society and begin to hate that part of themselves, their sexual attractions, that society seems to hate. When this happens there may be years of denying their homosexuality to themselves. However, when the feelings persist, at some point, usually during adolescence or young adulthood, most eventually acknowledge honestly, at least to themselves, that sexual feelings for the opposite sex are either absent or weak.

Telling someone else that one is gay is, of course, a crucial stage in the process of coming out as a homosexual. With some, many years may elapse between self-acknowledgment and the decision to reveal to even one other person. Even though today more and more gays are coming out of the closet, there is still a great range of openness. Some individuals are very selective and cautious and only tell a few other people while some have an active social life with other gays, but remain in the closet professionally or at work. Many never tell their own families. However, there is an increasingly large number of gays and lesbians who, tired of living in secrecy and resenting the necessity to do so, are completely out of the closet and open with almost everyone they know. Recent changes in our society, including media attention and the strong gay rights movement, are making it somewhat easier for gays to come out of the closet. The particular circumstances, however, under which gays live often make a critical difference in how open they feel they can be. In certain professions and in certain geographical locations there is, of course, much more freedom to be open than in others.

Coming out for most gays and lesbians who have decided to do so is a process that never ends, primarily because of the implicit assumption in our society that everyone is heterosexual. The heterosexual doesn't need to keep telling people that he is straight; it is totally unnecessary. The homosexual is always having to either pretend to be straight or to announce deliberately that he isn't. This is an often awkward thing to do. Every small social encounter can represent decisions to be made, to tell or not to tell, when to tell, how to tell. The decision to disclose one's homosexual orientation to other people always requires a realistic assessment of the benefits and risks of doing so in any given social situation or context.

The coming-out process for parents and families of gays can be very similar to the coming-out process for gays. However, this is true only if the parents are open to actually going through the pain and the drastic changes in viewpoint and attitude that are required in coming out. This phenomenon of parental coming out has been referred to in several books written by parents of gay or lesbian children (Dew, 1994; Fairchild and Hayward, 1989; Griffin, Wirth, and Wirth, 1986).

As it is for many, maybe most, parents, adjusting to my son's homosexuality was a complicated and often distressing experience, though eventually I realized that I had been personally enriched by it. Being a psychologist didn't seem to help me at all. In fact, there were ways in which it made the experience more difficult. First and foremost, there was the shame that came with recognizing my own hidden homophobia. Although my formal training as a psychologist had first instilled in me the conviction that homosexuality was a deviance, was pathological, I had, in subsequent years, learned more about sexual orientation and I believed that I had conquered any remaining antigay prejudice. I viewed homosexuality in my patients as normal for them. However, when it was my own son, all of my latent prejudice emerged. I did not want to believe that my son was gay. It was not normal for him to be gay and it was not normal for me to have a gay son. Having to acknowledge my own homophobia damaged my self-esteem as a psychologist and made me question myself as a professional.

And there were other reasons why my professional identity hindered me in being able to deal with my son's sexual orientation. All of those guilt feelings about not having been a good enough parent and perhaps fitting that blameworthy stereotype "controlling, smothering mother" were intensified since I was a psychologist and should have been able to do a better than average job as a parent. Hadn't I tried to apply everything I learned as a psychologist to the task of being a mother? But then, if I were a good mother how did my child turn out to be gay? Had I caused him to be gay through clumsiness, lack of awareness, ignorance, or loving him too much? Also, being a psychologist, I was especially ashamed of my unsympathetic reaction to Gary at that first moment when he told me he thought he was gay. Instead of compassion toward my son when he had the courage and the honesty to tell me the truth, I was just a disappointed mother, stunned, disbelieving, frightened and totally unprepared to accept that my child was homosexual. Crying and talking about tragedy was insensitive and even cruel, and I feel fortunate that my son was wise enough to understand and that he never blamed me. It must, though, have been a terrible blow to Gary to have his own mother tell him that she thought his being what he was was a tragedy.

The first step in my coming out as the mother of a gay child was, however, barely a step at all, because it consisted mainly of just shock and denial. I wouldn't believe that my son was gay and I tried to convince myself that he was just being rebellious, that he wanted to be unique and different. When I suggested this strange concept to Gary, he laughed and said that he didn't think being gay was a choice and if he just wanted to rebel or be different there would probably be better ways that trying to become homosexual. This approach not having worked, I began telling myself that he was too young to know whether he was gay—how could he possibly tell since he was only nineteen and was sexually inexperienced?

Then I went through a long period of blaming myself and feeling guilty, thinking that somehow Jack and I had shaped Gary's sexuality by having done something terribly wrong as parents. Despite the body of scientific literature suggesting that family factors alone are unlikely to create homosexual children, I still wondered if family issues might not somehow be responsible for Gary growing up to be gay. My husband and I had a close emotional relationship, but we had a conflicted and often unhappy marriage. Our conflicts were almost never about the children or how to raise them. Jack and I were entranced with our children and had always agreed that they were wonderful and that we were fortunate beyond belief to be their parents. But Jack's alcohol abuse and my intense anger and resentment about his drinking created ongoing conflict and unhappiness in our own relationship. We had tried not to let our marital problems affect our children, but, of course, had not been successful. So I had ample reason to indulge my already guilt-ridden nature. But Jack simply would not agree that our marital conflicts had anything to do with our son's homosexuality, and I came to believe that he was probably right. But at the time, I blamed myself and blamed Jack.

I have sometimes imagined that parents of gay children, who have idyllic, perfect marriages, might have less guilt initially than I did. But perhaps that is not true since almost all parents, even in the best of marriages, can look back and recognize many mistakes they made as parents and wonder whether these mistakes contributed to their child becoming homosexual.

In agonizing over what I may have done or not done as a parent to contribute to Gary's being gay, I had this nagging thought that because I had raised my children to question authority and to think for themselves I had taught them also that it was acceptable to be different, and certainly being homosexual in our society is a dramatic way of being different. Openness to experience and a willingness to challenge conventional wisdom seem to characterize the personalities of many gay persons, and our children were brought up in a way that allowed them to be different, to question, to challenge.

I don't wish to give the impression that I think either of our sons made a conscious decision to experiment with homosexuality—to try it out, so to speak—but rather that, in the development of their personalities, there may have been an openness to experience that made homosexuality less fearsome. However, I think what is more likely is that being raised to think for themselves, to question, simply made it a little easier for our children to acknowledge to themselves the existence of feelings that are so socially unacceptable, and perhaps also helped them adjust somewhat less painfully to their sexual orientation.

While I was still partially in my state of disbelief, I knew that I needed to find out more about sexual orientation and began compulsively seeking out books just as I had earlier sought out books about infant and child development. Here is where being a psychologist was a great asset. I knew where and how to look for information, I knew how to interpret scientific research, and I was able to maintain a level of objectivity. I began learning much more about sexual orientation than I had ever learned during my professional education. Of course, it must be remembered my basic training as a psychologist took place in the 1960s, a time when professional knowledge about homosexuality was much more limited. But as I read more up-to-date findings, I came to believe that although experiential and psychological factors may play some part in determining sexual orientation, there is probably in each individual a predisposition to either homosexuality or heterosexuality, a predisposition arising from genetic or other inborn biological factors. There are numerous research studies, to be described later in the book, that provide some support for this viewpoint.

But sexual orientation, like many other human characteristics, is an exceedingly complex phenomenon, and the final explanation for why one is homosexual, heterosexual, or bisexual isn't yet known and may never be known. It is most unlikely that there is a single cause or single factor that fully accounts for a person's sexual orientation. What is generally accepted by those who have examined the research, and are able to remain objective, is that homosexuality is not a conscious choice and that sexual orientation is established early in life and is not generally susceptible to change.

As I gained knowledge and understanding about homosexuality, I became better able to overcome my denial and confront the reality of my son's sexual orientation. But confronting the reality did not help to minimize my concerns and fears about how he might be treated because he was gay, how his career and his life might be affected. And I grieved because I loved Gary so much; the thought that he would be discriminated against and treated as inferior was a constant torment.

I couldn't bring myself to tell anyone else that Gary was gay for a long time because I hadn't truly been able to believe it or accept it myself. However, as time went by and as I learned more about sexual orientation and about gay culture, I came to truly accept my son's homosexuality. I saw that he didn't view being gay as a tragedy as I had been doing. He was just living his life as he always had, a productive meaningful life. I was finally able to say with all honesty to myself, "Gary is gay, he is a homosexual, he is always going to be a homosexual." The very words . . . homosexual, gay . . . can provoke anxiety and unease. As the mother of a gay child, I had to learn to be comfortable just saying those words about my son. It was only after I was able to say these words in this very specific way, and believe them, that I was able to start acknowledging Gary's homosexuality to other people.

Telling other people "My son is gay" was the next critical step in my coming out. There were so many different reactions. Some said practically nothing or looked puzzled. Some, I thought, seemed to feel sorry for me and felt they should sympathize. Some, most often other psychologists, were extremely accepting and nonjudgmental. Each time I told someone new, I found it easier to do; it was a process of gradual desensitization. At times I became quite compulsive about announcing it, doing so in situations where it might have seemed strangely inappropriate or unnecessary. But looking back, I am not proud to admit that for a long time, even as I became more open, I still worried about people's reactions, about what what they really thought of Gary and of me. Still worrying about myself— isn't that truly absurd and self-centered?

Around this same time, July 1982, Jack and I had gone to New York for Gary's twenty-first birthday and first met Darryl. As I mentioned earlier, meeting Darryl, Gary's actual lover, was a monumental step in my coming-out process. Homosexuality was not abstract any longer, there was a lover. Then, later that year, at Christmastime, Gary asked if he could bring Darryl to Tucson for the holidays. Now Jack and I knew that Darryl was not just a casual lover or boyfriend, this was a significant relationship. Our close friends all came to our annual Christmas Eve party and met Darryl. We were partially coming out, but we had not quite reached the point where we could say, "This is Gary's lover." On the other hand, we didn't try to hide it either. We still had a long way to go. We could say our son is gay, but we still didn't want to say, "This is our son's lover."

During Gary's three years at Columbia, we visited him a number of times and he came home for holidays, sometimes bringing Darryl and sometimes not. As we spent more and more time with Gary and his gay friends, we became increasingly able to view homosexuality as perfectly normal for our own child. Our New York experiences— seeing theatre productions such as *La Cage Aux Folles* and *Torch Song Trilogy*, where gay relationships were portrayed in positive and loving ways; going to museums and galleries where gay artists displayed their work; attending the ballet, which had always had many gay male dancers; reading novels with gay characters—all helped move us along the process of acceptance and appreciation of gays and of our own particular gay child.

I have become convinced that a significant factor in the process, whereby parents become able to accept their child's homosexuality and maintain a healthy relationship with him, is the parents' learning to view the child's sexual orientation as normal for that particular child. Some parents are unable or unwilling ever to do this, largely because of the social stigma and the false myths and stereotypes associated with homosexuality and often also religious beliefs. As long as the parents truly believe that their child is abnormal or inferior in some way, the relationship cannot be healthy and communication will be limited, even if the parents insist that the child is still loved.

The coming-out process continued and as I talked to others about Gary and as I learned more about sexual orientation, I eventually came to realize that acknowledgement and acceptance were only beginning steps in coming out of the closet. Coming out goes far beyond admitting and accepting, it requires appreciation of the gayness itself. When you love a child fully, if possible you want to love everything about him, and in Gary's case that had to include his sexual orientation. I began to understand that Gary's homosexuality was an essential part of his nature, that he would not be the Gary I knew and loved if he were not gay. I knew then that I would never want to change my son. I would never want to turn him into someone different from who he was, to change him into a heterosexual. He was a creative, imaginative, productive human being, and his homosexuality was an essential and integral part of who he was. If I had done something to contribute to his being gay, then I must also have contributed to his becoming the outstanding person that he was. I was intensely proud of my son just the way he was, and his homosexuality no longer seemed to be just an undesirable or unfortunate characteristic.

I also realized I had stopped thinking and worrying about why Gary was gay and instead was remembering just how grateful I had always been to be the mother of my two extraordinary sons. Gary just needed, as do all young people, parents who supported him and who loved him for who he truly was, not for what they wanted him to be.

Distressing and difficult as it was to go through the process of coming out as a mother of a gay child, there were many rewards. I believe that parents who are able to work through this process will find that it can strengthen the relationship between them and their child and can result in a deeper understanding of love in its many forms.

There is an organization that has helped many parents in the coming-out process. The organization is the Federation of Parents, Families and Friends of Lesbians and Gays, known as PFLAG.* The national office is based in Washington DC, and there are chapters located throughout the United States. This organization has helped thousands of families learn more about homosexuality and has helped them adjust to having a gay family member. PFLAG provides encouragement and support to parents and families of gays, advocates for gay rights, and helps to educate the public about homosexuality. This is an invaluable resource to families who are willing to deal honestly and openly with their child's homosexual orientation, and many families have come to view their child's homosexuality in positive, affirming ways and have been helped to maintain family love and cohesiveness through their participation in PFLAG support groups. I myself benefitted greatly from attendance at these groups, although unfortunately I only discovered PFLAG after I had gone through the most difficult period of my adjustment to learning Gary was gay. Another outstanding contribution that PFLAG has made to families of gays is its wonderful newsletter, published by the national office, which conveys to parents of a gay or lesbian child that there is a whole group of parents and families out there with whom they have a kinship and a commonality.

---

*Parents, Families and Friends of Lesbians and Gays (PFLAG), 1101 14th Street, NW, Suite 1030, Washington, DC 20005, (202) 638-4200, (202) 638-0243 (fax).

Chapter 8

Becoming a Writer

With his graduation from Columbia, the freedom of college life had ended for Gary and the adult world made its demands. Getting a job and becoming self-supporting loomed ahead of him. He wasted no time basking in his accomplishments and within days of his graduation found a job with a computer consulting firm in New York. But the things Gary craved—excitement, challenges, being in charge—were singularly lacking in his job. Driven to succeed in his new life and hesitant to admit to himself how unsatisfying the job was, Gary struggled desperately to generate enthusiasm, struggled to fit into a job that never matched his personality or his talents. He didn't complain about his work to Jack and me, but he never sounded excited about it either. For Gary not to be excited about what he was doing was totally unlike him. I sensed something was amiss.

His relationship with Darryl, its dramatic conflicts notwithstanding, continued after they graduated, and still being a couple of sorts, they decided to establish a home together. They located a large apartment, but being unable to afford the substantial rent, they subleased out two of the rooms. A series of renters—all friends or semifriends, all of whom were described by Gary as quite eccentric—came and went over time, with Gary designated as a sort of treasurer, the reliable one who had to make sure the rent and other bills were paid. He had found himself in the unwanted and demanding role of managing a strange and tumultuous household.

In one of his letters in late 1984, Gary wrote of the hated role he had to play in running the apartment and also of his feelings about being a writer. He described a short story he was working on at the time, titled "The Museum."

Dear Mother:

Everything here is as usual . . . in a state of flux. Darryl remains in the apartment, but Dante (yet another roommate, a

Peruvian trying to be a theatre director) and he are at each
other's throats. George and Darryl want Dante out, Dante wants
Darryl out, and I'm just trying to get the various checks I'm
forced to collect from them all. I don't enjoy being a landlord.

My writing is progressing, but it takes such a toll. I worry
all the time that I don't have talent, a completely unproductive
concern. I've just completed a story that started off being
about Patte Scott (that old college friend of yours). It turned
into a strange daydream of a woman whose husband is perhaps
unfaithful, and who is herself perhaps unfaithful. She moves
about in an art gallery in her daydream and the art works
reflect her identification with the mythological Medea and
Clytemnestra, one of whom dealt with her husband's infidelity
by killing their children, one by killing her husband. The epi-
logue has her finally connect with her daydream and do greatly
watered down versions of what both Medea and Clytemnestra
did. It sounds odd, and it is. I keep thinking, "Perhaps I should
write more normal things." I despair sometimes. Love, Gary.

Around this same time, in a letter to Gus, Gary revealed to his
friend how frightened he was about AIDS and he wrote of how the
fear of AIDS had affected his feelings about sex. By now gay men
knew how the disease was transmitted and had realized the dangers
of HIV infection from unprotected sex. Here is an excerpt from this
letter:

Dear Gus:
    . . . One of our friends, Jorge, is suddenly convinced he has
AIDS. He has a swollen gland in his armpit and he's saying,
"If I have it, I want to know." We're all (Darryl, Jorge, and
me) getting checked at the Sloan-Kettering Blood Center.
They'll give us extensive tests to see how our immune systems
are doing. It's all fairly frightening. It's a very bad situation . .
. it makes the thought of sex, even with your lover, repulsive.
You've just got to be extremely careful until they come up
with a vaccine.

Gary's unsatisfying job, his haunting fears about AIDS, and the
unhappiness and turmoil in his relationship with Darryl all took

their toll. He often sounded despondent, but when Jack or I tried to question him, he attributed his mood solely to his job. He said nothing to us of being worried about AIDS, enabling us to continue in our ignorance, and he said very little about Darryl. Always protective of Darryl, Gary didn't like to complain about him and he never spoke of how troubled the relationship was, although we certainly got vague hints. But he did, at last, confess his desperate unhappiness with his job and said that he was thinking of quitting.

In early April 1985, Gary made a decision. He phoned to ask whether he could come live with us in Tucson for a few months, a plan which would allow him to devote full time to his writing. He had a definite goal, to write a romance novel and try to get it published so that he could earn enough money to support himself while he worked on a more ambitious, serious novel. Jack and I believed in Gary's talent as a writer and I, at least, had always hoped that writing would be his ultimate career. Of course we said yes; we loved the idea of Gary being at home.

Gary had also written to Gus, still living in Tucson and attending law school at the University of Arizona, telling of his dissatisfaction and frustration with life in New York.

Dear Gus:

Well, I quit my job yesterday. I was planning on quitting effective April 26, but I've been going mad here! So, I've compromised. I'm quitting in two weeks. I'm not leaving here a minute too soon. The pall of failure is what I'm leaving. New York churns out failures and then imprisons them here to endlessly toil at making their failure even more wretched. I have a success-oriented personality. You know that. Despite my neuroses, I am basically sane.

. . . I've spoken to Andy and we plan to drive home arriving on May 15 or so. Driving home should be fun and a good transition between New York and Tucson. Here's a rough map of these United States. The dotted line is the route Andy and I will follow. Note how we will stay near the border. That's where the most birds are. This trip should be fun. We'll imagine ourselves to be "On the Road." There's something defi-

nitely mythic about driving across country, don't you think?
Your friend, Gary.

Andy and Gary arrived together back in Tucson following their
"mythic" cross-country auto trip. The two brothers had used the
trip as an opportunity for numerous stops along the way for birding
expeditions, a pursuit they were both still impassioned about, happily adding new species to their myriad lists and, now as when they
were children, excitedly describing their discoveries to Jack and me
almost from the moment they walked into the house.

Andy was with us for only a few days, as he was leaving the
country again, to return to Brazil and continue research for his PhD
dissertation. Our two children were extremely excited about their
plans for the future, Gary about his writing and Andy about his
research with golden lion tamarins, and they seemed, even now as
young adults, filled with the same passion and commitment that they
had always brought to their childhood hobbies and projects. For each
of them, his childhood impulses seemed to have been, through some
mysterious mechanism, transformed into an adult passion.

All these years had gone by and still I had not the slightest
suspicion of Andy's homosexuality. Although he was now twenty-
seven years old and didn't have a girlfriend, I naively attributed his
lack of involvement with women to his commitment to his studies
and his isolation in Brazil where he had little opportunity to meet
women. Gary, on the other hand, was completely open about his
involvement with Darryl and thought Andy was making a serious
mistake in not telling me that he was gay. I learned of Gary's
thoughts about Andy's secrecy in a letter he wrote right around this
time to a friend who lived in New Orleans, someone I never met.

> . . . I just think that Andy's excuse that he doesn't want to hurt
> our mother (she really freaked out when I told her) by telling
> her he's gay is bullshit. Her first question when I told her (I
> was 19 and hadn't even had sex yet) was, "Why didn't you tell
> me sooner?" She'll feel like she hasn't even known him for all
> these years. This is sure to hurt her more than the fact that he's
> gay. It's been an ongoing feud between Andy and me, but I've
> just given up.

As Gary guessed, I was terribly hurt when I finally discovered that Andy had hidden his homosexuality from me for so many years. But, at the same time, I understood Andy's reluctance and understood why he might have felt that he had failed his family by being gay. Having seen my struggle in dealing with Gary's homosexuality, he had every reason to believe that learning I had two homosexual sons might just be too much for me to handle.

Almost immediately upon his arrival back in Tucson, Gary began working on his book. Highly disciplined and energetic, working on a very strict schedule, he spent hours every day hunched over his Macintosh computer. It was during this time that Gary really began to believe in himself as a writer and to think of himself as a writer. He wrote incessantly and with an all-consuming commitment. In addition to working on his book, he wrote letters, he wrote in his journal, he worked on short stories. He never seemed to stop, translating and transforming his life into words, words, words.

Gary spent, not just a few months, but a little over a year in Tucson feverishly working on his writing. During that year, he actually completed two romance novels and one more ambitious novel. I now think that Gary suspected then that he was infected with the AIDS virus, though he had not actually been tested other than the immune system tests he mentioned in his letter to Gus. However, at the time it was a common belief that not everyone who was infected would necessarily develop AIDS. It was also a common belief that if persons who had contracted the virus took care of their health; ate well; exercised; avoided alcohol, cigarettes, and drugs; and had a positive, life-affirming attitude, they might never get sick. Certainly, while Gary lived with us in Tucson, he followed a very strict health promoting regime. He went to the gym almost every day to work out, he was careful about his diet, he didn't smoke or use drugs, and he seldom used alcohol except for an occasional beer.

He was also trying hard to gain weight, and he actually got up to more than 180 pounds, his usual weight being about 160. Gaining weight may have been Gary's way of trying to ward off AIDS, but a way also of avoiding looking anything like the gaunt, wasted image of people who were sick with the disease. For myself, seeing how healthy and productive Gary was enabled me to push aside my vague apprehension about AIDS. Gary still said nothing to us of AIDS anxiety, probably in an effort to protect Jack and me from what he hoped was needless worry.

Gary's computer clacked away at all hours of the day and night as, with all his energy and zeal, he devoted himself to yet another project. The idea of Gary as a writer appealed strongly to me both because that is where I always thought his talents lay, and also because I thought it was a field where he was not as likely to be discriminated against as he might be in many other lines of work. The arts community has always been unusually tolerant of gays, and if Gary were a writer, homophobia would likely have less of a negative impact upon him than if he were in a more conventional profession.

In his letters to Darryl and to his friend Lou, Gary described his frenzied, almost manic approach to his writing. Here are some excerpts:

July 2, 1985
Dear Lou:

My book continues at an admirable pace. I go at the rate of one chapter per day. There must be some obscure mathematical formula I can work this into that would prove I have approximately 1200 novels in me if I live to age 70.

. . . People don't understand . . . life is as much art as is any canvas or poem. Live it so that it's beautiful and tragic and absurd and wretched and banal, and don't regret it for a moment. (This seems a bit overblown now that I look back over it).

July, 1985
Dear Darryl:

Sorry I haven't written for so long. I've been writing on my book in a mad fever, 10 or 12 hours a day. This book will have taken a total of about 3½ weeks. I hope to compress my next one into the space of 10 days. What a life, to make a handsome living off of 20 or 30 days of work a year. Of course, I have great plans for more ambitious projects.

Strange, but the *New Yorker* ideal of writing, those bland, post-modernist stories about normalized people, seem so bor-

ing to me. Come on, let's face it. Glamour and excitement and
bizarre and wonderful characters are what we really like. I
don't aspire to be a Jackie Collins, but I don't want to write
about boring, suburban people either. I have a great, exciting
novel already in planning. In retrospect, this sounds so overblown, and you're no doubt saying to yourself, "I like/hate
Gary's youthful opinings." Love, Gary.

Not too long after these expansive and overly confident letters
about his writing, Gary seems to come to his senses and writes
again to Darryl:

July 29, 1985
Dear Darryl:
    I've decided that I am being very impatient about my writ-
ing. Ideally, I would like to get one of my little gems published
right away so that I'll have money to support myself in NYC
and write my chosen novel (I can't say "real" novel. I don't
like to look down on what I'm doing now). However, that
could be a bit of fantasy. I must be prepared for rejection, but I
am so anxious to begin work on my chosen novel.

In late August, Gary made a short trip back to New York where
he and Darryl supposedly broke off their romance, their loving
truce having been short circuited by the conflict that always arose
when they were together. In subsequent letters to Darryl, Gary
seems to feel hopeless about their flawed and unhappy love affair
and even about his writing.

September 10, 1985
Dear Darryl:
    . . . Life here is distinctly depressing, as all my supports
vanish before my eyes. No more letters from you, no more
amorous phone calls, no Gus, no hope that every word I write
will be an instant Romance success. Of course, *Last Dance*
[title of his first book] is washed up. I'm undertaking a complete rewrite that will leave it a totally different novel. I'm
immersing myself in reading romance novels, trying to
become a romance writer in spirit as well as deed. I can't tell

you what a help your suggestions were in that long phone conversation we had before I left. You remain far and away my best critic.

I went to see *Kiss of the Spider Woman* with my mother last night. I loved it. I can't say how much. I thought about you a lot. I think about you all the time. I can't help it. I'll never forget you. I'll always love you. And I'm not going to tell you at any time that these words are anything but the complete truth. Never lie to me again.

. . . It's all so sad. The movie has made me so pensive. So many things remind me of you. You, if not I, have outgrown the relationship I guess. We have too much bad history, too many bad habits, too many assumptions. You've changed and it's hard for me to completely accept it. I'm trying. Don't cross me off your list at any rate, and keep that support for my writing, it's very valuable to me.

September 30, 1985
Dear Darryl:
. . . I certainly hope you're not having sex, at least not gay sex. Doesn't that term sound horrible? It's good enough reason to become celibate. But then heterosexual sex sounds even worse. At any rate, after your preaching to me, you better not be. We really shouldn't have sex with anyone else until the cure for AIDS comes anyway.

I've thought of a word for my writing that is inspirational. "Accretion." It's just so hard for me to adjust to the gradual process . . . accretion . . . that creates a book. I want to get it all done in one day and have it xeroxed and mailed by that evening. But there's something of a limbo in writing a book. Everything is suspended and you feel as if you're waiting to hear the verdict from a hung jury all the time. How could one possibly work on a book for ten years? Yet that's my ambition. Once I work on writing a book for ten years, my impatience will be vanquished. With my past books, "major revisions" were unthinkable. Accretion. I think I'll be rather proud of the book I intend to write. If it errs, it will do so on the side of over-seriousness.

Gary was always eager to acknowledge that Darryl was the inspiration for his writing and tells him so in many of his letters as, for example, in the following:

Dear Darryl:
. . . You must know that you are my main inspiration in my writing. You are a muse of the modern age, hardly serene, but endlessly, morbidly energetic in your crashing, murderous search for self. You won't object if you are a character in one of my books will you? How can I ask? Of course you won't! Perhaps together we can dredge up that revelation, the one Justine in the *Alexandrian Quartet* talks about . . . her search in life for a revelation that will demonstrate to her her true self. You're quite incredible. A normal person would regret his involvement with you, but I don't. But really, we're all looking for revelations, I know I am. I find minor ones in novels, my own work, a piece of music, a conversation, a mountainscape.

By January 1986, Gary had completed his two Romance novels, *Last Dance* and *Love Restored*, and had obtained a literary agent in New York in an effort to find a publisher. He immediately began work on his "serious" novel, *Performance Piece,* and wrote about his progress on the book to Darryl. Darryl was Gary's sounding board, the one person to whom he expressed his deepest longings and doubts. Their openness with one another, even when the revelations were painful, seemed to be at least partly what fueled the relationship and kept them together.

February 9, 1986
Dear Darryl:
I'm having fun writing this book, but as usual, I lapse into periods of depression and second thoughts, convincing myself suddenly that I'm writing something that is either brilliant but unpublishable, is pointlessly obscure, or is just complete pretentious junk. I really believe though, even through my failures of confidence, that this is the book I was meant to write. It is a true expression of what I want to do, want to say, want to accomplish.

I was saying to my mother the other night that I wonder sometimes if I have the strength to handle my own vision. For, as I write this book, I find that what naturally emerges from my mind is something so offbeat, so convoluted and exaggerated that I sometimes lose my nerve in presenting it to the world. I'm not like a James Joyce who has complete confidence that what he writes is brilliant, no matter how absurdly obscure it is. I don't have that confidence. Perhaps because what I write isn't brilliant.

I don't mean to trumpet on about myself, but you're the only one I can tell these things to. I'm sick of being modest . . . writing is one thing I'm good at and I'm not going to deny it. Also, this self-aggrandizement helps my confidence for my novel writing. You're the one who is responsible for me writing these books to begin with. I'm not sure I would've ever gotten around to writing anything if it weren't for you.

As Gary neared the completion of *Performance Piece*, he wrote to Darryl about what it meant to him to have written this book, the sense of fulfillment it gave him. In one particular sentence he writes, as if with ominous foreknowledge, that even if he were to die he would be satisfied as long as he has finished his novel.

May 6, 1986
Dear Darryl:
    . . . Standing in the bar the other night, it occurred to me: for so long I had idolized all these avant-garde artists, writers, composers, etc., hoping (but not really believing) that one day I would do what they were doing. I realized, as I approach the end of this substantial novel, that I am finally doing on a grand scale what I always dreamed of doing. I'm really doing it, really producing an intriguing, beautiful and strange work that I can be proud of, that I can truly say represents me and my ideas. That's an accomplishment. For once I felt somehow fulfilled, felt that even if I discovered I was to die soon that as long as I finished this novel I would be satisfied that I had led a decent, productive life. Self-expression is a powerful elixir

against despair. Despair is a camp joke to me . . . a good, long high camp joke.

May 21-27, 1986
Dear Darryl:

. . . Darryl, the book is four days from being done. I quake! Of course, there's some serious rewriting to do before I even begin the editing process, but the main bulk nears completion. A life's goal! It occurs to me at moments that this is really a wonderful thing I've done, even if the book fails as a novel.

By June of 1986, Gary had spent over a year at home writing novels and attempting to get them published without success. He was disappointed but not in despair, and he made the decision to return to live in New York. He told Jack and me that, even though he hadn't accomplished his goal of becoming self-supporting through his writing, he simply couldn't continue being dependent upon his parents. He was beginning to feel like a failure letting his parents support him and living in his childhood home, though, of course, we would have been more than willing for him to do so.

I understood how Gary felt, but still I hated to see him leave. I had loved having Gary back home. He entertained and amused us as no one else could do. And Gary's year at home had been a time for me to get to know him better as an adult, as a gay man, not as the adolescent, whom I had hoped, at least for awhile, might not truly be gay. But I knew now he was truly gay, and his gayness was an essential part of who he was. Though I feared that life would always be more difficult for him than if he were heterosexual, I couldn't even imagine him as heterosexual, couldn't imagine him not being gay. And I didn't want him to be different in any way from just exactly the way he was. He was my wonderful son whom I loved and admired. What more could I ask?

Seeing Gary at work over this past year, observing the intensity with which he pursued his ambitions, sometimes allowed me to forget that he still had to survive in a homophobic society where people like himself have to fight for the rights and privileges that come so easily to others. I could forget that he was a member of a discriminated against minority, that prejudice and bigotry would possibly follow him throughout his life.

And I despaired sometimes about his relationship with Darryl. I knew that Gary was still passionately in love with Darryl and that they seemed irrevocably tied to one another. But my own view of the relationship was ambivalent. Darryl kept Gary in such a state of crisis that it was frightening for me to imagine what Gary's life was going to be like with him if they stayed together. I sometimes longed for him to find another partner who might bring calm and peace to his life. Perhaps, though, it was Darryl's very complexity and refusal to be pinned down, to be captured, which made him so fascinating to Gary. Perhaps Gary's need for challenge and excitement were satisfied by Darryl's quixotic nature. He may not have been able to tolerate a calm, peaceful relationship. But whatever my opinions about Darryl might be, they could hardly be expected to influence my willful, strong minded son, and I kept them to myself. What I did understand was that my son was capable of a deep and lasting love, however irrational and foolish it may have seemed to others. Doesn't passion often sway reason, even in those who are among the most rational?

Gary was now ready to move into a new phase of his young life, and in June 1986, he moved back to New York City. He immediately applied through Columbia's job placement system to try to find a writing job. He was referred to Telecom Library Publishers, a small publishing company looking for a writer for a brand new computer magazine. He was interviewed and hired the same day. I remember so well the day Gary called me in Tucson to tell me about the job interview. He was highly excited and told me that Harry Newton, one of the publishers, had offered him a job as a writer and wanted him to start work that same afternoon. He sounded deliriously happy and I was so happy for him. He could be a writer and still earn a living.

Gary wrote several letters to Andy in Brazil telling him about the new job:

> August 23, 1986
> Dear Andy:
>   I've gotten a job that looks to be fun. I'm a writer on a new computer magazine (*LAN*) dealing with the so-called Local Area Network, a way of linking PCs together. The company

already has several other successful magazines, and this one looks to be very marketable. The first issue comes out in about a month, but our deadline is right now. It's very hectic, late hours, not a moment of rest. But it's fun and exciting, like being back on newspaper (high school), with a little added pressure.

The publisher is a quasi-celebrity in the computer/telecommunications world, and is a complete eccentric. Everything is completely informal, we wear shorts to work. It's really ideal for me. A fellow Columbia classmate and I are the editorial crux of the magazine, though he does more and has the title. He's worked with the company for several years already. Everyone seems to like me. Thank God, I finally have a job I like. Love, Your brother.

October 1, 1986
Dear Andy:
    Did you receive copies of the magazine? I wrote much of it, several articles as well as news. Did you notice the Andy Warhol quote I slipped by in the first issue? I'm sure it completely escaped our readers. I have already received a promotion, from writer to "senior writer." I dreamed up the change myself, to hide the fact that not only am I senior writer, I'm sole writer. The "senior" evokes a crew of drones laboring beneath me.

By Christmas 1986, Gary had been working for *LAN* magazine for about six months and thought he could get time off for a brief vacation. Since Andy was unable to get home from Brazil for Christmas, we concocted a plan for the four of us to meet in Rio de Janeiro, which was only about an hour's distance from the Biological Reserve where Andy was living and doing his research. We made reservations at a hotel in Rio right near the beach, and Andy took time off from his work and met Jack and me and Gary, who had joined us from New York, and even went early to spend a few days with Andy in his jungle setting. I have always been grateful that we took this trip as it was to be the last Christmas the four of us would ever all be together.

It was a happy time, walking on the beach, sightseeing in Rio, eating at wonderful restaurants, and enjoying being together as a family. Andy was able to speak Portuguese quite well by then and guided us expertly about the city. If Gary was a bit distracted, we did not notice then, though later, I was to think back and realize that he was occasionally fatigued and usually went to bed earlier than the rest of us. In a letter written to Andy after this holiday, Gary makes comments about AIDS, but gives no hint that he is fearful for himself.

March 3, 1987
Dear Andy:
. . . The AIDS situation is very bad here. So many dying. Liberace. Several friends from Columbia. Kevin, a friend of James and Tom's, just died two weeks ago.
. . . I still marvel at what you do in the jungle every day. It's very grueling. You must be fond of your tiny auburn charges to pursue them with such dedication. You have everyone's admiration here. I'm sorry if I was unpleasant during our trek in Brazil. Love, Your brother.

During the succeeding months of March and April 1987, Gary continued to work as a writer for *LAN* magazine, and the job was an ideal one for him. His writing talents, his organizational abilities, his need for excitement and independence fit the job perfectly, and he was receiving a lot of recognition for his good work. As far as we knew, Gary's life was happy and fulfilling, and he gave us no indication to the contrary. To see both my sons doing rewarding work about which they seemed excited and enthusiastic was deeply satisfying.

All during this time period, antigay prejudice was still rampant and the AIDS word could not be spoken without evoking images of gay sex and of the opprobrium that accompanied such images. Media coverage was increasing exponentially and I would some-times be seized with terrible dread, but I generally managed to convince myself that Gary would not be touched by this terrible disease. But a day was coming, a day which would shatter our lives, the day Jack and I would learn that our son was fated, like so many other young gay men of his generation, to be among those who would die from AIDS.

Chapter 9

The Verdict

It was May 5, 1987, and it was the day Gary was told he had "full-blown AIDS," the day he was given the verdict that was to seal his fate and break the hearts of his parents and brother. Ironically the day had started happily for Jack and me as Andy had just arrived back in the United States from Brazil. He had telephoned us early that morning from the airport in Florida to say he was on his way to visit Gary in New York and wanted his brother to pick him up at the JFK Airport. He asked me to get the message to Gary as his connecting flight was about to leave and he hadn't been able to get through to him. When I reached Gary he sounded very rushed and said he was about to leave for an important appointment and couldn't meet Andy. Happy that Andy was back in the country and that my two boys would soon be together again, I had no premonition of the tragedy awaiting us.

Gary's appointment, which I had assumed was about business, was instead for a bronchoscopy, a procedure used in the diagnosis of AIDS-related pneumonia (pneumocystis carinii, also known as PCP). I can only begin to imagine the terror Gary must have felt as, all alone, he waited for the results, waited to learn if he was going to receive a death sentence. And by noon of that day the sentence came; the bronchoscopy confirmed what Gary had feared. He did have PCP; he did have full-blown AIDS. Gary's uncertainty had ended.

His uncertainty over, Gary did not hesitate. He immediately got on the phone to his father in Tucson to tell him he had AIDS and was being admitted to the hospital. All unknowing, I was in my office seeing patients and Jack was afraid to call me, afraid of what my reaction would be. He decided to wait until the end of the day, to wait until I got back home.

I got home around six o'clock that evening, and Jack suggested we sit down in the family room and have a glass of wine together. Immediately I sensed something out of the ordinary. I don't know exactly why, perhaps an uncertainty in my husband's voice or an unusual expression on his face. We sat down and this is what he said: "Jean, there's something I have to tell you. In all the years we've been together, it's the hardest thing I have ever had to say to you." I heard my husband's terrorizing words, I saw the look on his face, and I knew he was going to tell me something I couldn't bear to hear. He stared at me, his face pale and strange. For just a moment he hesitated, he couldn't seem to open his mouth, but then, his voice trembling slightly, he told me, "Gary is in the hospital. He has AIDS."

Now almost nine years later I still feel the brutal onslaught of the words Jack spoke; I still hear them endlessly repeated in my mind and I still hear also those other words . . . the words I screamed that night, over and over to my husband, "No, no, no. It isn't true. Please, please, tell me it isn't true. It must be a mistake; it's a terrible mistake." Senselessly, hopelessly, pleading with Jack, repeating myself again and again, "Please tell me it's not true. Not Gary, please, please, not my baby. No, it isn't true. I know it's not true." Irrational and inconsolable, I couldn't make myself stop screaming. Jack grabbed me and tried to stop me, tried to make me sit down. But I couldn't stop. I kept crying and screaming the same meaningless words over and over and over.

I cried until finally I could cry no more and my throat had become too raw to scream. Then Jack put his arms around me and for a little while we silently held on to each other. But there was nothing either of us could say to comfort the other. What can comfort a mother and father who have realized their child is going to die? What you want is impossible, you want someone to tell you everything will be all right, but no one can, and all we could do was sit there, locked in a dreadful, imprisoning silence, knowing that our lives had changed forever.

When we thought we could handle it, we made the call to Gary's hospital room and Andy answered the phone. He attempted to reassure us, saying that Gary was doing well and that he was getting the best treatment available. He had been started on intravenous Bactrim, a drug which had been found to be quite effective in controlling PCP. Andy sounded calm and controlled, but he had never before had to confront tragedy, and now he faced the death of his only sibling, his little brother, his best friend. I was sick with fear for him and for all of us.

Then Gary came on the phone. His dear familiar voice sounded soft and weak, but he kept assuring me he was OK. I told him we loved him so much, that there was nothing we wouldn't do to help him, and that we would be with him as soon as we could make travel arrangements. Several times Gary said, "I'm so sorry to cause you all this pain." His simple, selfless statement was to portend the manner in which he would deal with his fatal illness, and it tore my heart. I almost began crying again, but I somehow managed not to. What I tried to tell him then, perhaps awkwardly, was that he need never apologize to his family for his illness. I think he understood.

After our phone call I went to bed, but tormented and frightened, I did not sleep the entire night. Chaotic thoughts of all the things I knew about AIDS were going on in my mind, and everything I knew was terrifying. I knew that once the disease had progressed to the point of an AIDS-related illness such as pneumocystis, it was uniformly fatal. I knew that the entire immune system was gradually destroyed, leading to random and bizarre infections. I knew about gradual mental and physical deterioration, dementia, blindness, and eventual slow and painful death.

But what I had heard or known about AIDS was suddenly not just abstract knowledge. Now it was my own beloved son who had this dreaded disease, a disease meaning that a horrifying death awaited him. The protection and care I had given him throughout his life had not been enough. I had failed him. And all through the night the same pleading, desperate words repeated themselves endlessly in my mind, "No, not my baby. Please don't let him die. Please let this be just a horrible dream"—a hopeless, despairing plea directed I knew not where.

The next morning, dazed, exhausted, and unable to think coherently, I couldn't decide what to do. First I thought I should go to my office, but then I wondered how I could possibly do that, go through the day as though things were normal when nothing would ever be normal again. But I didn't know what else to do.

I only had one appointment that morning, but it would occupy almost the whole morning because it involved an entire family— two divorced parents and their three children. They were from out of town, so I couldn't cancel, but I did ask our secretary to cancel my afternoon appointments. But it was a mistake trying to work with this disturbed family when I was so distracted. Though I struggled to focus my attention, horrifying images and thoughts insistently intruded, images of my son's strong body wasting away, his brilliant mind slowly destroyed, thoughts of my dear child frightened and facing death at the young age of twenty-five, his future, his hopes, his dreams, all ended. My beautiful son with all his promise and all his passion who was not going to get to live out his life.

AIDS, early death, stigma, the words are inevitably linked together and make this illness one unlike any other. The thought of Gary afflicted by this cruel disease was abominable. However, even as I knew the inevitable I also began to deny it. Gary couldn't die. I loved him too much to let him die. And I kept thinking, children shouldn't die before their parents. It's an aberration, it's the ultimate tragedy.

Mind and heart in total turmoil, I somehow got through that morning and remembered that, by a strange coincidence, the psychologists in my office were having their first meeting of a support group that we had been planning for some time. The plan was to meet together over lunch on a monthly basis to talk about coping with the stress of our work and our daily lives. Coping with tragedy had not been part of the plan. But here they were, on that day of my own desperate need, a captive group of colleagues, people I knew well, whom I could talk to, whom I thought would understand.

I was already in the conference room as the others started arriving. They needed only a glance to know something was terribly wrong. Barely able to speak through the tears, I was able to tell them, without preliminaries, just as Jack had told me only a few hours earlier, "Gary is in the hospital. He has AIDS." A profound silence filled the room, but somehow I felt that in that silence my grief was being shared. It was, of course, my first experience of saying aloud, "My son has AIDS," and from this small group came an outpouring of compassion. This experience gave me the courage in the days ahead to always be honest about Gary's illness and how he acquired it. I believed then, and I believe even more so today, that choosing to be secretive about this illness, as many families do, only intensifies the tragedy and makes it more difficult to bear. Secretiveness is also a very clear message that the family is ashamed, and I was determined from the beginning that Gary must never be allowed to think, for even a moment, that we were ashamed of him or of his illness.

Jack and I wanted to be with Gary as soon as possible and began making the necessary arrangements for the trip. We got plane reservations for five days hence. I cancelled my appointments with the exception of a few of the most critical, and the succeeding days went by in a blur. I couldn't sleep or eat. I only went through the motions of living, postponing everything until I could see my son.

Andy was maintaining a vigil in Gary's room and whenever we called, usually several times a day, he always answered. Then Gary himself would try to comfort us by saying he was feeling fine and making progress. But on the evening of May 9, we called and Andy wasn't in the room. Gary answered in a faint, almost inaudible voice. He spoke with us for only a few minutes and then told us he didn't feel like talking and abruptly hung up. Jack and I both started crying, overwhelmed with fear, in anguish because we couldn't help our son and didn't know what was happening.

A few minutes later, Andy called back to tell us that Gary couldn't talk because late that evening he had developed a severe allergic reaction to the Bactrim. His physician was changing his medication to Pentamidine. Now we were even more frightened knowing that pneumocystis was the leading cause of AIDS-related deaths and wondering what would happen if he couldn't tolerate the new medication. I started crying, tears of panic, thinking about Gary dying, feeling the absolute terror and then the total disbelief, "Gary can't die. We can't let him die."

On the same day as this telephone conversation with Andy, although apparently earlier before the development of the allergic reaction, Gary had written the following entry in his journal:

I've been in the hospital four days being treated for Pneumocystis carinii . . . I've always liked the resonance of its
name. It's the disease I was always destined to be greeted into
the world of AIDS by. It's been unpleasant . . . fevers and
nausea, due to the poisonous ministrations of the antibiotics.
Now, though, I feel fine. They tell me that my chest X ray is
normal . . . meaning I'm already over the pneumonia? I'm not
sure. They still must do the whole circuit of treatment anyway.
One thing that frightens me is my intolerance of pain. When
I'm deeply feverish . . . 104 degrees . . . has been the worst. I
actually think about dying as a better alternative. Sickness
eradicates all memories of the feeling of health. You simply
cannot imagine what it is like to feel well again.

The next day, May 10, Jack and I left, late at night, from the
Tucson Airport for New York. We arrived in the early morning of
the eleventh to a cold, gray, and melancholy city, going directly by
cab to the St. Moritz Hotel on Central Park South, a hotel we had
stayed in frequently while visiting Gary in the past—a happier past.

After checking in, we left immediately for the hospital. Gary was
in the Lenox Hill Hospital on 77th between Park and Lexington,
Room 7608. We arrived at the door of his room, scared and desperate to see our son. The door was closed and there was an ominous
sign on it instructing visitors to put on one of the masks enclosed in
a container on the wall. The sign seemed to me to symbolize the
stigma of AIDS. We couldn't bring ourselves to greet our son with
masks on our faces and we ignored the instructions, rushing into his
room. And there he was, our dear child, lying in his hospital bed,
thin and pale, smiling at us. I held him and kissed him and he could
see from my face how devastated I was. I guess he wanted to say
something to help me, and looking at me pleadingly, he said,
"Mother, I still have two more years." I thought this was one of the
saddest things I had ever heard. In the midst of his own suffering, he
was able to think of consoling his parents, and he went on once
again to apologize for causing us pain. All I could manage to say,
also once again, was that he had nothing to apologize for, that we all
loved him, and that we were ready to do anything in this world to
help him.

I kissed Andy and I think I thanked him for being there to take care of his brother, but I don't remember for sure if I did that. I was attempting to conceal from Gary just how terrified I was and trying to maintain a degree of composure. He said he was comfortable and not in pain, that his doctor thought he was responding to the new medication, Pentamidine, which was being given, as had the Bactrim, intravenously. I felt such a great sense of relief just to see my son, to be with him, to hold him. I tried not to think about what might be coming next.

During the first few days we were in New York, we were encouraged by how well Gary seemed to be feeling. On the second day we were there, he asked Jack and me to make an appointment to speak with his physician, Dr. Kevin Cahill, a well-known, highly respected AIDS specialist in Manhattan. We had no trouble getting an appointment with him for a couple of days hence. His office was in a prestigious neighborhood on Fifth Avenue across from Central Park. We arrived early for the appointment, both of us extremely tense. After only a short wait, we were escorted into the inner sanctum of the doctor's personal office. It was a calm, restful, elegant room with period furniture and interesting collectibles and art objects. Dr. Cahill, a rather remote individual, probably a necessary ingredient to do the kind of work he was doing, was extremely kind to us and obviously highly skilled and knowledgeable. The only thing I can actually remember him saying, probably because of the high level of my anxiety, was, "You know the statistics." The hopeless words brought me to tears; I didn't want to believe that the statistics would apply to my son. Gary couldn't die. Denial of the fate awaiting him was already growing in me.

Gary also wanted Jack and me to meet with Dr. Louis Baker. Dr. Baker, an AIDS researcher, was the director of a longitudinal study of gay men in which he assessed their overall physical condition and monitored their T-cell counts, one index of immune status. Gary, unknown to us, had been a participant in this research for a short period of time. We easily obtained an appointment with Dr. Baker, who was affiliated with the Blood Center at Memorial Sloan-Kettering Hospital on East 67th Street. Wandering nervously through the hospital's subterranean halls and tunnels, we arrived at Dr. Baker's laboratory in the basement—a modest, utilitarian space.

Although Dr. Baker had agreed to meet with us, I'm sure he didn't know exactly what we expected. Nor did we know—we were just following Gary's lead. Perhaps what Gary hoped was that these introductions to his doctors would help prepare his parents for dealing with the reality of his illness, would introduce us to his world of AIDS. Dr. Baker was a quiet, kindly man. He said very little, but reached over and held my hand. He did, in some subtle way, manage to convey a depth of understanding of our anguish. In this sad, depressing meeting, Dr. Baker offered us no hope, no reassurance, but nevertheless, we appreciated his kindness. Several years later, we heard that he had retired early, perhaps finding the many deaths of the young men who had participated in his research too much to bear.

Those first few days in New York, Gary was doing so well that Jack and I had foolishly thought that perhaps we could take him out of the hospital for a few hours to dinner; but Dr. Cahill frowned at the suggestion and said no, it was impossible. Since we couldn't take Gary out to dinner, we resolved instead that we would have a dinner party in his room. We were anxious to create some small festivity, some pleasure for Gary, and there were so few ways to do this. We invited Darryl, of course, and other of his friends including Andre, "the Hungarian aesthete" as Gary always called him; Joe, a video editor and close friend; Lou, who was now a ballet dancer, choreographer, and waiter in New York; Winnie, Lou and Gus's sister, also a childhood friend who currently worked in a New York advertising agency; Renee, Gus's girlfriend, who now worked in publishing in New York, and a few others. Nobody acted at all surprised at being invited to a party in a hospital room and they all accepted.

On the afternoon of this party, Jack went shopping for disposable plates, glasses, and utensils, while I walked over to Grace's Market on Third Avenue, between 71st and 72nd, one of the elegant gourmet food stores that abound in Manhattan. I became quite obsessed with selecting exotic foods and wines, hoping to create for our son some brief moments of happiness and perhaps attempting to ward off our own panic over the future. By the hour of the party, Gary had become extremely feverish and nauseated and, although he struggled bravely to enjoy the occasion, he was too sick to do so.

But we proceeded to spread out the food and wine in the confines of his small hospital room, gather together in the midst of tragedy, eat, drink, and even laugh and joke. The hospital staff never intervened to interrupt our strange festivities, although they may have been somewhat puzzled by our daring.

During the following few days, Gary's fevers escalated. He could eat almost nothing and he had become so weak he needed assistance to go to the bathroom. The doctors thought that his symptoms were now due, as previously, not to the pneumocystis, which was responding well to the medication, but to side effects of the medication. Gary's only hope, as we understood it, of recovering from the PCP was a full course of treatment, and according to medical belief at the time, the medication needed to be continued for at least twenty-one days in order to be certain that the pneumocystis was completely eradicated. There was ongoing discussion of taking Gary off the medication. Knowing how deadly the pneumocystis could be, we were terrified by the prospect of discontinuing his medication.

This began the first of the balancing acts that Gary would face as he battled his illness, that is, to decide between taking highly toxic medications with potentially dangerous side effects or leaving potentially lethal infections untreated. This is the constant dilemma of all those with AIDS. If Gary was unable to tolerate the Pentamidine and it had to be discontinued, we were told there was only one other possible medication, an experimental drug that had not yet received FDA approval. To obtain permission to use the drug would require special dispensation from the FDA, something that might be impossible to do within the remaining window of time. However, Gary's fevers were becoming out of control, and Dr. Cahill decided to discontinue the Pentamidine and apply to the FDA for approval to use the experimental drug. We were frantic with worry.

Then Dr. Cahill had to leave town, and the FDA approval had still not been received. Gary was now feeling better since the medication had been discontinued, but the doctor covering for Dr. Cahill, concerned that approval for the experimental drug would not arrive on time, recommended that Gary "just tough out the side effects" and start again on the Pentamadine. Gary agreed. The following days went on like a prolonged nightmare. Gary's temper-

ature raged. He couldn't eat or sleep and was at times almost deliri-
ous. The nurses, in a desire to try to bring down his temperature,
had suggested an electric cooling blanket for Gary's bed. We tried
this briefly, but the ice cold blanket on his poor thin body was
intolerable. He pleaded tearfully for us to take it away, and we
couldn't bring ourselves to refuse him. Instead we all took turns
cooling him with wet cloths, applying them almost continuously.
This seemed to help keep his fever from becoming totally out of
control, though for several days his temperature hovered between
103 and 104 degrees.

Gary almost never complained and he repeatedly told us all how
grateful he was for all we were doing. I tried to help him understand
that he didn't have to thank us, that we did what we did out of love,
not obligation. As I watched my son, so young, pale, thin, and
helpless lying in his hospital bed day after day, I was filled with love
and was in anguish over what he was enduring. There was so frighteningly little any of us could do to alleviate his suffering or to slow
the force of his ominous disease. We felt helpless most of the time.

During these days, Jack, Andy, and I were with Gary in his
hospital room most of the time, trying to comfort him in whatever
limited way we could, trying to capture a little time from doctors
and nurses to ask about his condition, and talking to his friends and
co-workers who came to visit. Andy was totally dedicated to the
care of his little brother, tending to his every need and spending
each night in Gary's room while Jack and I went back to the hotel
for a few hours of sleep. Andy would only leave to sleep after Jack
and I arrived in the morning. No one could have cared more ten-
derly or lovingly for a brother than Andy did for Gary.

Gary tried always to do as much for himself as he possibly could,
but it came to the point where one of us usually needed to help him
out of bed to go to the bathroom. One day I was the only one in the
room and had helped him into the bathroom, always an awkward
task because he was connected to his intravenous lines. I left him
alone in the bathroom, but after a few minutes I heard him calling
me. I found him lying on the floor having fallen because he was too
weak to stand. I helped him to his feet and hugged him, but the sight
of my dear son emaciated, sick, and lying on the bathroom floor
looking pathetically up at me broke my heart.

Gradually Gary began to tolerate the medication better and his X rays and blood gas tests showed that he was recovering from the pneumocystis. His fever was subsiding and he was regaining some of his strength. He began to talk more about his illness. One day, when he and I were alone, he told me that he had almost been relieved when he was diagnosed with AIDS because living with uncertainty and fear for so long had been worse than knowing. He said that he had been having symptoms that made him fearful that he had AIDS for some time, but didn't want to tell us if he wasn't sure. He said that he hadn't been tested to see if he was infected, because during most of that time period there were no treatments available anyway. An entry from his journal illustrates his anxiety during the time before he was diagnosed:

> October 24, 1985—There is something about the discrete entity of the look of paper that is necessary to keeping a journal. I thought of writing on the computer, but it didn't seem right. Until now, my journal has been in the form of letters on a computer disk. My indolence, my fears, my confused thoughts . . . all encourage me to go back to writing a real journal. To be able to ramble with relative impunity. I never escape the feeling of having a reader peering over my shoulder.
>
> I am in a strange position . . . I've concluded again, is this the third time? . . . that I am terminally ill. AIDS has me in its thrall . . . certainly psychologically if not physically. As of yet, I have no signs other than lymphadenopathy, but I am of a morbid turn of mind and am somewhat convinced. I truly don't want to die (at times in the past I could not have said that); I feel a new era in my life coming . . . a new fulfillment and spirituality, if not necessarily happiness. But really, my main feeling is of confusion.

Through all this time of fear about AIDS, Gary had not turned to his family for comfort seemingly because he did not want us to suffer if there was no need. But at least Gary trusted us enough to tell us immediately when he knew for certain. I have always been grateful that Gary never felt, as so many young gay men with AIDS do, that he had to keep his illness a secret from his family. But now Gary knew what he faced and he was very open with us. He told us that he wanted to live his life as normally and fully as possible during whatever time he had left. Adamant that he wouldn't live as a victim, as just a person with AIDS, Gary didn't complain and he never seemed to feel sorry for himself. I had always admired Gary for his wonderful qualities, his brilliance, his wit, his sense of adventure and drama, his intensity of purpose, his bizarre sense of humor. However, I now saw in my son a strength and resolve far beyond his chronological years. I was in wonder over his courage and will. My child was now truly a man.

Gary's major goal, as he started to improve, was to return to his job as a writer for *LAN* magazine. Gary was so fortunate to be working for a company, Telecom Library Publishers, Inc., whose owners were remarkably unprejudiced and compassionate. Right after Gary had gone into the hospital, his immediate supervisor, Aaron Brenner, and the two owners of the company, Harry Newton and Gerry Friesen, wrote a letter about Gary's illness and hospitalization, a letter they distributed to all of the employees of the company. A model of compassion and enlightened thinking about AIDS, especially for the time at which it was written, here is what the letter said:

May 7, 1987
Dear Telecom Library Employees:
As you all know, Gary is in the hospital. He has pneumocystis. It is pneumonia. It is not contagious. He is on intravenous medicine which means that he has a needle in his arm for an hour or so, three or four times a day. His doctors say the medicine will cure the pneumonia in about two weeks, at which time he will leave the hospital and return to work and real life.

At the same time, however, having this type of pneumonia is a sure sign that Gary has Acquired Immune Deficiency Syndrome, or AIDS. This is a fact, a fact that Gary accepts. It is also something that his family and friends accept. They have all helped in any way necessary and will continue. Gary is in good hands. He is receiving the best medicine and the best care possible.

We here at Telecom Library are part of Gary's family. We must also support him in any way we can. For the time being we can do that by calling him, visiting him or writing to him. In a few weeks Gary will return to work. When he does, we can support him in the same ways we always have . . . by being his friends.

We can also help Gary by learning about AIDS. Brochures are available and will be passed around the office. If you want more information, talk to Aaron. Or you can talk to Gary. He is very willing to talk about it. He is not ashamed, nor should he be.

AIDS is a contagious disease. But it can only be transmitted through the exchange of bodily fluids, usually semen and blood. It cannot be spread through casual workplace contact. According to a pamphlet entitled AIDS Hotline: "You can't get AIDS from the air like you get flu. You can't get AIDS from doorknobs, dishes, drinking glasses, plates, silverware, telephones, toilet seats, sharing cigarettes or joints, swimming pools, kissing or handshakes. You can hug someone with AIDS. Adults and children with AIDS need love and care. Don't be afraid to give it to them."

We are not afraid. And neither should you be. We will support Gary in absolutely every possible way we can . . . emotionally, financially, friendshipwise.

Aaron, Gerry, Harry

I saw a copy of this letter almost immediately when I first walked into Gary's hospital room after arriving in New York. He had posted it on the wall right beside his bed. I was overwhelmed with gratitude and relief when I read this marvelous letter. With no uncertainty, this letter affirmed that Gary's employers would not allow Gary to be discriminated against and would protect him from the humiliation and prejudice that often confronts people with AIDS in their workplaces. I have been forever grateful to these three compassionate and generous men—Harry, Gerry, and Aaron—both for their immediate reaction to Gary's illness and for their amazing support during the entire course of his illness and up until his death.

As Gary's symptoms subsided, Jack and I began to make plans for his leaving the hospital. Prior to his diagnosis, Gary had been sharing a very tiny, cramped apartment with a casual friend. Jack and I had not been in this apartment, but Andy told us it was not suitable and he didn't think Gary should go back there. Andy was fearful and we were too that Gary might have to spend more time at home and would need a more comfortable living environment. Housing was incredibly expensive in New York, and even though Gary was earning a very reasonable salary, it wasn't sufficient for him to afford a pleasant, roomy apartment.

Gary's needs mobilized Jack and me. We didn't know how to make our son well, but we could help him have a good quality of life for as long as possible. We embarked upon an apartment search and located one on Mulberry near Broadway and Bleeker. Gary knew the building because his friend Joe lived there. We took a year's lease on a one bedroom on the third floor, 304 Mulberry Street, #3F, and Jack and I told Gary we would subsidize the rent to whatever extent he needed. We would also help him buy any furniture or household items he needed. We had found something concrete we could do for our son.

Gary was now recovering from the PCP and was regaining his appetite and strength. He would very soon be ready to leave the hospital. Andy had decided not to go back to Brazil where he would be so far away until he was certain that Gary's health was stable. Jack and I felt Gary would be in safe hands and we could return to Tucson. On the flight back, I thought of times when our lives were happier, when my little boys were growing up. I could see their beautiful little faces as I held each one in my arms right after birth; I saw them both with their binoculars glued to their eyes trying to identify birds; I saw them poised on the edge of the Indian Ridge swimming pool ready to dive in and compete in a swim meet; I saw them in their purple and gold robes at their high school graduations, and saw them receiving their diplomas and Phi Beta Kappa awards at their college graduations. But the future, what was to come, intruded on the past, and I thought about losing my son, thought of him dying from this terrible disease. A hollow, sinking sensation was in the pit of my stomach, a feeling that would remain with me for years to come. Jack was there in the plane beside me, but somehow I could not communicate even with him. I wanted consolation, but there was no consolation, no relief, just the terrifying prospect of what awaited my son.

As it turned out, Gary's condition, once the PCP was eradicated, quickly improved, and he was back at work soon after we left New York. At his work, the extraordinary attitude of his employers meant that Gary was received with total acceptance and support. I learned more about how the people at Telecom Publishers and *LAN* felt about Gary when I spoke to Harry Newton, one of the owners, after Gary died. Harry told me the following:

> The magazine could not have happened without Gary. His illness affected the company in very interesting ways. I was concerned because we had some uneducated people who could have reacted negatively. This was long before the greater awareness of AIDS that developed. People believed all kinds of things. I was concerned that we would have mass panic, but I took a very aggressive approach. We educated everybody in the office. We acquired enough literature about AIDS for a packet for everybody in the place. We had some meetings. I laid down very strict rules. "If you violate my ground rules in terms of protecting Gary, you get fired on the spot." We brought in a bed so that Gary could rest during the day. We had a series of meetings to organize things around Gary. I think he was slightly embarrassed. We made sure he had a lap top computer and a modem so he could work more easily wherever he was.

Aaron Brenner, who was the editor of *LAN* magazine when Gary went to work for the company, also spoke to me after Gary's death, telling me how Gary's illness was dealt with and how it affected the organization.

> My own feeling was that I loved Gary and that the organization should accommodate to him. If we had been a different kind of organization, it could have been more difficult. The impact was to make people much more aware. It was a group of people who did not know much about homosexuality and AIDS. The way he handled it, his dignity and openness. It shattered a lot of myths. People learned they could live with it and it wouldn't be a problem for him, because Gary had already proven to people what he was. A couple of people had

trouble with it. Some may have been unsympathetic to people in general. Some might have felt uncomfortable with homosexuality. But the *LAN* staff rose to the occasion. We said to Gary, "What do you want?" It was never a question for most of us.

Gary combined, in an unusual way, two interests, a love of literature and a fascination and love for computers. I never met anyone with such a wide range of literary interests and yet the scientific/computer interests and knowledge. It led to a very interesting way of thinking. His sharp wit was special. He was amazingly observant and he thought about everything.

Andy Moore, a co-worker of Gary's, also talked to me about Gary's contributions to the magazine and the company's way of dealing with his illness:

Gary's job was very demanding, intellectually and creatively. He did a great job and everyone accepted him. I think Aaron's and Harry's letter was great. I think what that letter showed me was that when something like this happens, the person needs a special advocate in the organization, to stand up for him and explain what has happened and educate people. I don't think Gary would have done it himself, not because he was ashamed but because he would have been embarrassed to ask for any special attention.

Gary had the tragic misfortune to acquire HIV/AIDS, but had the great good fortune to have been working with people like those at Telecom Library Publishers. They will be remembered and treasured forever by Gary's family. There is no way we can ever repay them for what they did for Gary.

Chapter 10

After the Verdict

Gary was back at his work; Andy, the devoted big brother was still with him in New York, not quite ready to leave his little brother alone; and I was back in Tucson having to content myself with daily telephone calls to be reassured by the sound of Gary's voice. Gary told Jack and me that he felt better than he had in a long time, and over and over he let us know how much he valued our help and support. We could not have responded to our sick child other than the way we did. But AIDS is no ordinary illness, and adult children cannot always take it for granted that their parents will be good to them when their illness is AIDS. The stigma of homosexuality has been so inextricably tied to this illness that many of those infected die alone, estranged from their families, afraid to ask them for help, or even being rejected when they do so.

When Gary returned to his job so quickly after his hospitalization, I was encouraged to cling ever more fervently and foolishly to the hope that his life could be saved. And every time I heard his voice saying he felt fine, my hope was reinforced. I don't believe I could have survived without some degree of hope because to truly face the certainty of Gary's death was simply unimaginable to me. This may seem like denial and it undoubtedly was, but denial and hope are often not so very different. Maybe the difference is, at least in some cases, just one of language, different words expressing the same thought processes and emotions.

AIDS had certainly not defeated Gary. He was as driven and passionate about his life as he had ever been. But the fate that had befallen him had changed his life dramatically as his grand ambitions of the past became channeled much more narrowly. He had been promoted from senior writer to editor of his magazine and his purpose in living became his job. He stopped writing fiction. I believe this was because he realized the severe limitations to what he could hope to accomplish in the time he had left to live. Instead, the magazine became Gary's lifework, and he seemed to accept with grace that it was to be his last creative endeavor. There was a new maturity that came to Gary as he faced his mortality and as he chose his adult identity, to be the editor of *LAN* magazine, not just a person with AIDS, and not even a famous writer of fiction, an identity that he now had to give up forever.

Gary's friends often advised him that working so hard and for such long hours would hasten the destruction of his immune system and perhaps shorten his life. But Gary would live no other way; he would live only if his life could have meaning and purpose and if he had some sense of personal control, over himself and over his world. He refused to let AIDS define his life and said, "If AIDS treatment is going to take over my life or interfere with the freedom to live my life meaningfully, then I don't want treatment. I won't live just to live." To me, my son was truly heroic. He confronted his illness and the inevitability of his death, but while he lived he refused to submit to the fear which I am sure he felt. I hear and read of many such young men, who live their lives creatively and bravely while coping with their impending death. Perhaps it is this facing of mortality while in one's youth that, at least in some, ennobles their lives and brings out the very best that is within them.

After Gary died, Lou spoke similarly telling me how he thought Gary had reacted to his illness and how it had affected his life. In one of our many conversations, Lou said the following:

> I was angry at Gary when he died. I thought he had killed himself because he worked himself to death. However, I now know how important it is to be vital, to accomplish, not just live a pastoral life. (Lou had, by the time he and I spoke, been, himself, diagnosed with AIDS.) It would be like already being dead. Gary defined himself by his work, by his writing. He loved being the editor of a magazine, making decisions, working with a deadline. He was a writer, an editor. Take those away and he would be nothing. How you deal with your illness has to do with how you define yourself. Gary had such a fertile

mind; he would have gone crazy if he couldn't use it. Gary was a driven person.

As the disease progressed in Gary, he preserved all of his energy for his work. He quit doing a lot of other things. He was considered an expert in his field and he was very gratified by his work. Seeing that magazine come out every month, enjoying the travel, the pressure, the deadlines, being in charge.

Darryl made similar comments about Gary's response to his diagnosis, how it affected his life and how it affected their relationship:

> I think when Gary first found out he had AIDS he was terrified. He wasn't afraid to say he was scared. He said, "You're afraid, Darryl, and you just won't admit it." I think I failed him. I just took a strong hand with myself and I shut myself down. I wish that Gary had demanded something from me, but he never did. I was timid in my offers. I wish I had just quit work and nursed Gary. It's remorse I guess or maybe it was just a fantasy. Gary decided *LAN* magazine was it. He just wanted to live a normal life, not a life of someone with AIDS. I do think that Gary dealt with his illness in outstanding and creative ways. He gave up his bohemian life. We both wondered if AIDS was really a blessing and an opportunity.

What seemed to be happening to Gary was that, with the knowledge that he was dying and having decided to commit his life to his work, he withdrew from Darryl and no longer asked or expected anything from him. Perhaps Gary was afraid to expend his more limited emotional and physical energy on a relationship that had brought him so much pain. And Gary was such a proud person that I don't believe he would have asked Darryl for anything after he became sick. Anything coming from Darryl would have to be offered, not asked for, and Darryl apparently did not offer.

From Darryl's viewpoint, though he had no symptoms at the time, he too, was infected with HIV, and perhaps Gary's illness aroused too much anxiety about being forced to confront his own death before he was ready to do so. And in the relationship between the two, Gary had always been the giving one, and I suspect that Darryl couldn't deal with what would have been such a drastic change in their roles; that is, to change from being the one who depends to being the one who is depended upon. Sadly, Gary never formed another romantic relationship and he lived his life after his diagnosis without a loving partner or even casual romances.

Only after Gary died did I develop a closer relationship with Darryl, and only then did I begin to better understand why Gary was fascinated with him and why the relationship, though so conflicted and unhappy, was paramount in Gary's life. Gary was wise in many ways, but he was a "fool for love," and Darryl was his one true love. Darryl talked to me at length about his and Gary's feelings for one another and about his views of how Gary lived his life, both before his diagnosis and after it. Darryl described their love affair in beautiful but very sad words, words which make me grieve to this day, and which tell how tragic and doomed was Gary's only love affair.

I used the word "unique" to describe our relationship and our sexual attraction for each other, but I also saw his uniqueness whenever I just watched him. He was so single minded and he had vision. He had this ability to throw himself into something and just go with it for as far as he could go. I liked the way he became obsessed with things. He was almost manic, sort of unstoppable. Also, he was incredibly forgiving.

Gary was a person totally on the edge. He wanted to try everything which was different. He thought our relationship was like *Who's Afraid of Virginia Woolf?*. I was an Elizabeth Taylor character. Beauty gone bad. He became the overrated intellectual with pretensions. We played these games with each other. He never believed in himself as much as I believed in him. I thought he was a harbinger, a new person. He had incredible courage.

I think he saw me like he was the artist and I was his unhewn piece of stone. If I had been an innocent little boy from the South who knew nothing . . . that's what he thought he was getting into. I pretended to be that way.

And I was enthralled with all the men falling at my feet and I casting them aside. But it was only because I couldn't have what I wanted from Gary. It was a way of getting back at him. At our last fight I told him I felt incredibly guilty that all of this was a way of getting back at his not giving me what I never asked for. Also, it fed my ego and it was safe because Gary was always there. His being betrayed fit into his story. My being self-destructive fit into my story. I couldn't bear to look at what was really happening or I would have had to run away and not look back.

What I felt for Gary I can't express any more. What Gary and I had was beyond words. The details make me quite sad.

Lou also had insights about Gary and Darryl's relationship and told me,

Gary was endlessly fascinated with Darryl's life, his abandonment by his mother, his father's suicide, his retarded sister, his escape from the small town in South Carolina. To Gary, Darryl was a fascinating character. Like Truman Capote, he liked to write about neurotics and Darryl's ups and downs fascinated Gary. It was a romantic story. Two young, good-looking boys arriving in New York, students at Columbia, in love, the city. All the time he was getting hurt by Darryl, he would say, "I let myself keep getting hurt because I love him."

Gary's relationship with Darryl had obviously changed when he became ill, but I was so preoccupied and frightened about Gary's illness that I never tried to find out how he was feeling about Darryl. I wonder if he interpreted this as lack of interest in his love life, or as avoidance of the topic, and perhaps it was the latter. Maybe I didn't want Gary and Darryl together. But all I could seem to think about was Gary's health. Every slight change he reported in his condition or in his medication, any hesitancies or uncertainties in his voice, a cough, a phone call he did not immediately return sent me into a panic.

Sometimes people told me that I must prepare for the fact that Gary was going to die. These attempts to help I rejected totally because I had to convince myself that although others who had

AIDS would die, somehow my own son was different. At some level I knew I was living in a fantasy, but continuing to hope allowed me to survive the years of Gary's illness.

In August 1987, I made a trip to New York to attend a conference of the American Psychological Association, but I went primarily because it would enable me to visit Gary. It was the first I had seen him since he was hospitalized and I guess I must have expected a healthy looking, vigorous young man, but instead he still looked thin and pale, and I was immediately in despair. He kept reassuring me that he was fine and he was excited about my being in New York. We could go to restaurants, the theatre and museums, and see his friends. We did all these things, and Gary seemed to have a wonderful time, but Darryl was seldom with us. I saw him only once or twice, and Gary never talked about him.

While I was with Gary in New York I could see how literally obsessed he was with his magazine, with being its editor. His magazine would be his mark on the world, the mark he would leave behind, not perhaps the one he had wanted to leave, but the one that was possible. I thought my son was courageous and noble. I was immensely proud of him and immensely sad for him.

During this visit, I learned in more detail about Gary's treatment. He had frequent appointments at Memorial Sloan-Kettering Hospital for tests and procedures as part of his participation in clinical trials for AZT. This was an antiviral drug meant to slow the development of the disease. Gary was on the highest dosage level of AZT being used in the experimental trials. AZT often caused nausea and loss of appetite and it had to be taken in the middle of the night as well as throughout the day on a six-hour schedule. Gary was willing to tolerate the side effects and inconvenience because AZT was considered to be the only hopeful treatment for AIDS at the time.

And Gary introduced me to the people who were taking care of him: his primary physician at Sloan Kettering, Dr. Sheldon Brown, a very skilled and compassionate physician; the research director, Dr. Gold; and an outstanding social worker, Jill, who ran the support group. I even attended one of the support group meetings. I was tremendously grateful for the outstanding care Gary was receiving and in awe at the dedication of these talented health professionals devoting their lives to AIDS patients.

During this time period I was becoming more aware of the many AIDS patients who didn't have health insurance or jobs and how different Gary's life was from theirs, how the attitude of his family, his employers, and his friends, as well as his financial situation had protected Gary from the humiliation, loneliness, and inadequate care that many have to endure. I was also reading books such as *And the Band Played On* by Randy Shilts (1987) and being awakened to the reality that both governmental neglect and societal prejudice had kept this disease in the closet and contributed to its spread.

I was constantly reminded also that my dear, dying son was regarded by some as degenerate and perverted because he was a homosexual and because he had AIDS, and had to hear pious proclamations that homosexuals deserved to die. The baby I had brought into the world, loved and cherished throughout his life, was being derided by people who could say he deserved to have AIDS. As a mother, I was devastated to know that my son and other gay men were being reviled by people who had only narrow, stereotyped views of who they were. The pervasive antihomosexual spirit at loose in this country is similar to the extreme anti-Semitism and racism of earlier eras, but it is a prejudice that is still tolerated and that has not become, as the others have, "politically incorrect."

Jack and I were now in contact with Gary mainly by phone. Hearing Gary's voice reduced my anxiety to a tolerable level. He wrote seldom since we talked almost every day. However, he did write occasionally and more frequently to Andy, who had gone back to his research project in Brazil. Excerpts from his letters tell of how he was trying to live a normal life, of his gratitude to his family for their support, and of the indignities of his illness.

Dear Mother:

Do you like my new stationery? I just designed it on the laser printer at my office. I'm feeling very well and eating healthily (if that's a word). I bought *The Joy of Cooking* and cook dinner most nights. I'm getting back my lapsed cooking skills. I'm really enjoying my new apartment.

Thank you for everything you've done, and for the support you've given me in the face of something very difficult to deal with. You've been wonderful and you've made my adjustment to my new situation much easier. Perhaps this isn't very articulate, but you know how much I love you. Gary

In the following excerpts from letters to Andy, Gary is much more open than he ever was with Jack and me about what it was like to live with AIDS. In some of his letters to Andy I can see now how Gary used black humor and his sense of irony to help him cope with what was happening to him and his friends.

September 22, 1987
Dear Andy:
    . . . My various treatments proceed. Our wretched group of 18 in the "002" protocol at Sloan Kettering is like the characters in *The Magic Mountain*. There is Jerry, the actor; Joe, the motorcycle type with tattoo and hideous mother; Ernie, the absurd queen who surely suffers a brain infection; Fred, the babbling Fire Island queen who bristled at my claim that a broncoscopy was painless; Chang, the Chinese with wife and a range of facial expressions from pained to very pained; Juan, the Puerto Rican, who disappears with a syringe periodically; and Irene, the hideous woman who complains that her husband thinks her face is distorted.
    They're not really all that terrible. Jerry, the actor, is really quite pleasant. And the study continues . . . of 16 members, one is dead, five are "off study" which means unable to tolerate the AZT, four with recurrences of PCP. We beg for Aerosol Pentamidine (a preventive drug for PCP), but we are denied until our second bout of PCP.
    Much has happened in the moons since your departure. A variety of minor ailments has kept me laid up for long periods. An anal attack was my introduction to the humiliation of herpes. The pain upon excretion was tremendous. It has cleared up, however, due to my careful ministration with the wondrous Zovirax brand of Acyclovir. "You've done a fine job," Dr. Cahill told me, with uncharacteristic warmth, as he peered through a scope at the reduced lesions in my colon. On yet another front, I am off AZT temporarily due to anemia. I may get a transfusion tomorrow. Then I'll be back on AZT, at

a lower dose. I feel weak but my complexion is a lovely alabaster hue.

My anger is coming out more freely now. I feel a need to vent it. Your turn will come, perhaps in my next letter. I became angry at Darryl the other day and he spoke as if he had enrolled in the upper East Side of Buddhism . . . "You must learn to be more forgiving, Gary. Perhaps if you ate more kale and sea vegetables."

Well, I need to go to bed. Dealing with the hemophiliacs in the festive transfusion room tomorrow will be a bash. A wretched crew, and 90 percent of them infected with HIV. Terrible. Write soon. Your brother.

September 25, 1987
Dear Andy:
 . . . I've just returned from dinner and slide show with B.T. (You remember, he is J.R.'s old lover). He revealed to me an entire subculture of "Radical Faeries," sixties type gay men who live in communes, raise goats, and observe the harmonic convergence with grave seriousness. This is not a small group. They have their own journal and they have regular nationwide meetings. Photos in B.T.'s album revealed nude volleyball leagues, "naturists," and a variety of other bizarre and incomprehensible activities.

My health has been excellent. I was feeling great, going to the gym, and eating enthusiastically. I still feel alright, but my appetite has failed somewhat. Still, I have gotten my weight up to 160. I'm back in shape as well. The lower dose of AZT is certainly more merciful.

Oh, yes, I had forgotten to tell you earlier. I was promoted to Editor of the magazine. My duties are keeping me very busy, to the extent that I busily edit articles even as I am transfused.

Later . . . I have returned from Dallas and from Las Vegas where I went for trade shows for the magazine. I also attended the huge . . . they say 700,000 people came . . . Gay/Lesbian/AIDS March on Washington. I went down with B.T., but he expected me to lodge with legions of the "Radical Faeries" which, as I told you, is a group dedicated to nudity, rustic living, and other activities I didn't wait around to discover. The March was quite amazing, the quantity of people was startling. The papers claimed only 200,000 were there, but there were vastly more. Imagine, for starters, the entire mall filled, from Capitol Hill all the way to the Lincoln Memorial. Love, your brother.

October, 1987
Dear Andy:
   . . . Today I bought a damned pillbox. I expressed an interest in the one wielded by Richard, the Italian AIDS victim. He looked at me as if I were not truly among the fraternity of the terminally ill. "Don't you have one?" he said. "Everyone has one." I felt compelled to purchase one. It cheeps like a sparrow every four hours, without resetting.

Occasionally in Gary's letters he would include strange little poems and anecdotes. He could be deliberately perverse in these writings which often showed his fascination with life's oddities and eccentricities, as in the following little story he included in one of his letters to Andy:

   Leg
   Without a leg, I find it hard to move about.
   Without a leg? Without? Without one leg? You still have
      one leg!
   It's true. I won't deny I've a leg.
   Won't deny? You better not! It's clear as day! No pros-
      thesis could simulate
   the fleshy repulsiveness of your remaining leg!
   Perhaps you're right.
   Right? Of course I am. That leg is thin! Who would
      design such a spindly prosthesis?
   That leg is hairy! Who would manufacture such a hirsute
      limb!
   That leg is liver spotted! Who would dream up such a
      repellant decoration?
   That leg is varicosed! Who would incorporate such a
      feature in a commercially available prosthesis?

No, you've the wrong leg.
Wrong leg?
This is the false one!
This?
This one.
This leg is pristine. White. Hairless. Shapely.
It's my real leg.
And this . . . this is the false?
This is false.
Who designed this false leg?
J & J Limb Co.
Of course!
Of course what?
Of course it would be J & J.
You know J & J?
(Thinks, his eyes roving. He is clearly muddled.) No.

While Gary lived with AIDS and impending debilitation and death, he was trying, through humor and reassurance, to deal with the needs of his grieving family. That he could, in the midst of his own troubles, try to respond to each of us in the way he thought we needed is a testament to his courage.

And all the while he was reassuring me, he was on a roller coaster of recurring symptoms. Fatigue, loss of appetite, anemia, bouts of diarrhea, fevers, night sweats, herpes infections, weight loss, tongue sores, thrush, and difficulties with swallowing were only some of the disturbing effects of his illness. Occasionally he would mention some of these to me, but he was trying so hard to keep me from worrying that generally he glossed over the negatives in favor of positives. I wanted so desperately to believe him that I lived in my own created world of unreality. But the truth was he never stood a chance.

Jean, Andy (age 8), and Gary (age 4) in 1965.

Portrait of Andy and Gary, 1964.

Jack, Andy (age 10), and Gary (age 6) in 1967.

Jean and Gary at his graduation from Columbia in 1984.

Andy and Gary on the family patio in Tucson in 1985.

Gary, age 25, before diagnosis.

Jean and Gary in Gary's New York apartment.

Andy, reading names at the AIDS Quilt display in Washington, DC, 1989.

Andy at a party celebrating the completion of his PhD in 1991.

Jean and Andy on Andy's patio, 1995.

Chapter 11

Another Verdict

Early in February, Jack had an appointment for his regular medical checkup and, instead of the usual good news, was told that his chest X ray looked suspicious. He was referred to an oncologist specialist for another opinion. Jack and I huddled together in the oncologist's office, tense as we held hands and awaited the doctor's interpretation, but still hopeful, until he began bluntly outlining the cruel facts. Jack had lung cancer and it was too advanced and widespread for either surgery or radiation. Chemotherapy was the only possible treatment, and the likelihood of a remission was extremely small, perhaps 5 percent, even with treatment. Stunned, we sat silent, unresponsive, unable to fully comprehend or react. All our thoughts, all our feelings had been focused on Gary for so many months that we couldn't quite make a transition. But within moments the reality started to sink in along with the unbearable thought that both my husband and my son were going to die. And Jack quickly realized that he had to make a decision. Even though the prognosis was so terrible, he told the doctor he wanted to try chemotherapy, giving me a bit of the hope I needed.

It was Jack's nearly forty years of heavy smoking which had insidiously taken their toll, but even after beginning his treatment he continued to smoke as heavily as he always had. His doctor didn't advise him to stop even when I specifically sought his opinion. I think now that this was his acknowledgement of the hopelessness of Jack's condition.

Immersed in Jack's illness and treatment, I was not so totally possessed by worries about Gary. However, I was soon to be reminded. It was sometime in late March 1988 that Andy, having completed his research in Brazil and doing an internship at the

Washington Zoo while also working on his PhD dissertation, decided to visit Gary in New York. He arrived to find that his little brother was desperately ill. Gary had not told any of us he was sick, probably because he knew how worried we were about his father. But immediately upon arriving at Gary's apartment, Andy telephoned Jack and me to tell us that Gary was so sick he couldn't get out of bed without help. His sudden deterioration was apparently unexplainable by his doctors except as just another of the many complication of AIDS.

I spoke to Gary on the phone, and as always, he tried to reassure me, but his weak, tremulous voice told me more than his words. Scared, confused by his symptoms, dependent upon his brother, Gary's will seemed to have faltered. I couldn't stop crying and was telephoning the apartment every few hours. All I wanted to hear was that Gary was getting better, that his fever was going down, but nothing was changing, and my frantic phone calls only made me more frightened.

Andy couldn't remain in New York indefinitely and Gary couldn't possibly be alone. We tried to decide what to do. I wondered if I should go to New York and take care of Gary or go and bring him home. Then I wondered if Andy could fly out with Gary to Tucson. But Gary was too sick to travel. Frantic and indecisive, we talked back and forth like this for several days, trying to form a plan. Andy finally decided that Gary was slightly better and that the two of them could fly home together.

In advance of their arrival time, I drove, almost trance-like, to the airport, oblivious to the beauty of the surrounding desert and mountains, terrified of what I might see when my sons got off the plane. As I waited I thought of the wonderful years before the terror and anxiety of AIDS. I thought of my once strong, healthy son now incapable of even making a simple plane trip without someone to assist him and I tried to prepare myself for what I might see when Gary got off the plane. Andy and Gary were almost the last passengers to emerge, but Gary walked off. He wasn't in a wheelchair, he wasn't being helped or carried, and I could see his shy little smile, endearing just as it always had been. He looked like a very sick young man, thin and pale, but he was walking, slow and wobbly, but walking by himself. I remember feeling so happy, so relieved and realizing how little it took now to give me small moments of joy . . . seeing Gary walk, that was enough that day.

Back at home, Jack was waiting anxiously for us, and as sick as he was, he jumped to his feet and hugged and kissed his sons. It was not the handshakes that many young men and their fathers adopt. Jack had always been physically affectionate toward his sons and, even in adulthood this had not changed. Perhaps it was the enthusiasm of the greeting bestowed by his father, but it seemed only hours before Gary started to feel better, and with each passing day, he was stronger, more energetic. Seeing friends, calling his office, working on some assignments for the magazine, he very rapidly began to recover his strength. Another crisis had come and gone, another reprieve, another renewal of our hope.

Very predictably Gary quickly abandoned his sick role and made arrangements to return to New York and to his job. In the days after he was back at work, he phoned frequently and assured us that he was working productively and doing very well. I wanted to believe that he was well and happy, and it was easy to convince myself that his life would go on.

In May of that same year I began to think that we should have a family vacation. It must have been somewhere in my consciousness that this could be our last vacation as a family, but I immediately tried to stifle such a thought. Andy and Gary were both excited about the plan and each thought he would be able to get away from his work. I made reservations for an apartment in Newport Beach, in Southern California, for the first two weeks of September.

But over that summer, Jack's health started deteriorating quite dramatically. He had been gradually losing weight and strength, but he had continued to play golf, albeit with a golf cart. However, in July, Jack suddenly stopped playing golf. Golf was Jack's passion and when he couldn't play I should have understood that his condition was much worse than I had been admitting to myself.

Other changes were occurring that also should have been warnings. Jack seemed to be withdrawing into his own private world, distancing himself from everyone, drifting away into his world of illness. I tried to get him to talk about his illness, about his feelings, but his pain and exhaustion seemed to be all he was able to cope with. I asked Jack's physician if we should cancel the trip, but he said he thought it might be good for Jack. So, even though Jack was getting sicker every day and was now dependent upon oxygen twenty-four hours a day, we persisted in our ill-begotten plan.

On September 1, Andy arrived in Tucson, as the plan was for the three of us to drive to Newport Beach and meet Gary there. When Andy arrived home he was obviously shocked to see his father so extremely sick and unresponsive. Jack was sitting at the table in our family room and he didn't even stand up when Andy walked in. He barely forced a smile. Jack idolized his children and his failure to respond to his son was totally unlike him. Andy immediately started to wonder if we shouldn't cancel this vacation, but I was so desperate for us to be together as a family, to have this, perhaps final, vacation together, that I was unable to hear Andy's reservations. I had lost all sense of logic and reason.

So we proceeded to leave Tucson on the evening of September 2, and with only a few mishaps arrived at Newport Beach. We picked up the key to the house from our rental agent, Ms. Dola Benish-Miller, whose name, we all thought, was impressive. As we moved into the house, Jack's exhaustion became total, and Andy and I had to practically carry him in. To see my husband like this, debilitated and exhausted, made me realize how selfish and inconsiderate I had been. I had dragged my pathetic, sick husband five hundred miles for a vacation that he was totally unable to enjoy, for what now seemed to be incredibly selfish reasons.

We only had Gary's anticipated arrival to keep our spirits up, and when the expected time came and went, we started to become frightened. Hours went by and still no Gary. There was no way for him to contact us since there was no phone in the beach house, and I began to imagine all kinds of horrors. He had collapsed in an airport or on a plane; he was in a hospital; maybe he was even dead. Andy went out to call the airline and found the flight had arrived many hours ago, almost on time. But at last we heard footsteps on the path and I felt a surge of joy and relief. Gary stumbled into the house lugging a huge suitcase and directing us to, "Please go out and speak to Dola Benish-Miller." After we had gone out and thanked her, Gary revealed the story of his harrowing experiences. He had taken a van from the airport, but had been let off, mistakenly, at the opposite end of Newport Beach from where our beach house was located. The night was dark and he could find no phones or cabs. He didn't know where he was and walked for what seemed to him like hours. He finally found a public phone and, fortunately, he had Ms. Benish-Miller's home number. He literally begged her to come find him.

A young healthy man would, of course, have had no or little difficulty in dealing with such circumstances, but for a young man suffering from AIDS, it was quite a different experience. I struggled to stifle my tears as my son stumbled into the house, thin, exhausted, and yet still not complaining. He even described with great humor how he had to implore and beg Ms. Benish-Miller to come and get him. He loved her name, Dola Benish-Miller, and he always referred to her with her full title.

Gary, as Andy had been, was extremely shocked and sad to see the condition of his father. Jack had already gone to bed, and when Gary came out of the bedroom, after going in to greet his father, he had tears in his eyes. And my tears were inside, as I thought about what was happening to our family. Gary, my dear son, so ill himself, and now, having to worry about his very sick father. My husband, ill and probably near death, and yet worrying about his son. Andy, coping with the impending loss of both his father and his younger brother. Myself, devastated by my husband's and son's illnesses, yet irrationally eager for a family holiday.

Here we were, this family, which until recently had not known real tragedy, faced with the imminent death of two of the four of us, gathered together in Newport Beach, in a rented house on the beautiful Pacific Ocean, desperate in our efforts to have a family vacation despite the tragedies that had befallen us. Efforts doomed from their very inception.

The first two days of the "vacation" proceeded with relative calm. But on the third night of our stay, everything changed. I was awakened during the night hearing Jack struggling and gasping for breath. I reached over to touch him and ask what was wrong, but he couldn't respond. His face was distorted and he was gasping for air. I screamed for Andy and Gary and at the same time figured out that what had happened was that his oxygen supply had run out. I tried to steady myself sufficiently to connect another tank of oxygen, but I was afraid it was hopeless, afraid he was dying. Andy ran to the nearest public phone and called for an ambulance, which arrived promptly. Andy, Gary and I followed the ambulance in the car and then, in the emergency room, the three of us waited, silent and scared, terrified that Jack might be dying. But then, a nurse emerged and told us we could come in and see him. He was alert and conscious, but he had been placed on a respirator and couldn't talk. He looked into my eyes and held my hand. I knew he was completely aware. He made gestures to show us that he wanted a paper and pencil and he started writing down questions asking us to explain to him what had happened. I had a sense of total happiness. My husband was alive. He was here with us. I couldn't think beyond the moment.

We were told to wait in the Emergency Room treatment area until a hospital room was available, and finally we met with a doctor. Dr. S., a physician of East Indian background, was the doctor with whom we first spoke. He was extremely blunt, but, at the same time, sympathetic. He said that Jack was dying. He told us we were deluded, although I don't think he used that exact word, to think that there was anything medicine could do to prevent his death. He spoke philosophically and said that we should accept the inevitable, urging us to think of death not as an ending, but as a transition to another stage of life. I couldn't speak. I was sick with fear and disbelief.

Jack was placed in the intensive care unit of the hospital, and I spent the night on a couch in the waiting room. During succeeding days, my children and I tried to live a life, but it totally revolved around Jack and the hospital. We were in a vacuum, separated from our ordinary lives. Each morning we went to the hospital and remained in Jack's intensive care room as many hours as permitted, huddling about in the intensive care waiting room when not allowed to be with Jack in his room. We obtained a pager so that we could be called during the night, if there were to be an emergency, since there was still no phone in the beach cottage.

Each day brought new medical emergencies, tests, procedures, and numerous consultants. A chest surgeon performed a surgical procedure on several occasions to drain fluid from Jack's lungs, and each time this seemed to produce a temporary improvement in his condition. Still on the respirator, Jack was able to communicate only by writing or body language. The doctors thought he could be weaned off the respirator and begin to breathe on his own. Training by a respirator therapist was begun and gradually Jack's breathing capacity improved and he was taken off the respirator. He could now talk to us and was relieved of the terrible discomfort of the respirator.

During all this time, Gary was coping with his AIDS-related problems. He was on a large array of oral medications that had to be taken throughout the day. He was also on GMCSF, Granulicite Macrophage Colony Stimulating Factor, which had to be injected. Each morning, in that little house on the beach, I watched Gary get up and faithfully prepare and inject this medication into his thigh. He was stoic and uncomplaining as he carried out his daily ritual, and watching him was a painful reminder to me of how sick he was. GMCSF was an experimental treatment, and Gary was among the first in the country to participate in the clinical trials assessing whether the drug could be used safely and effectively to increase white blood cell counts in AIDS patients. It was only later that GMCSF was found to be ineffective and perhaps even dangerous as a treatment for AIDS-related problems.

Even as we despaired about Jack, we also couldn't forget how sick Gary was, and it soon became obvious that he was becoming so fatigued he could barely function. He phoned his doctor in New York, who recommended that he have a blood transfusion. This was not an uncommon thing for Gary, because of the AZT-related depletion of red blood cells. We spoke to Jack's doctor who recommended an AIDS specialist in his own office. After a difficult process of getting this doctor in touch with Gary's doctor in New York, the arrangements were made for Gary's transfusion. I try to remember this period of time and the memories are vague. I know I was beginning to grieve for the inevitability of my husband's death, and yet, at the same time, trying to maintain hope that he would not die. I was also momentarily concentrating on Jack and putting fears about Gary in abeyance.

But Gary himself was simultaneously facing both his own death and the death of his father. One of his usual coping mechanisms was his sense of humor, and he helped himself and helped Andy and me deal with what was happening to our family by reminding us that we could still laugh despite our despair. Each day he would imitate the various persons who regularly visited patients in the intensive care unit and with whom we had daily contact in the waiting room. Leaving the hospital in the evenings, the three of us would usually be laughing hysterically over Gary's imitations and stories and hoping that no one would notice and wonder what manner of persons these were, who could laugh while their father and husband was so deathly ill.

We had fallen into a daily routine, varied only by which doctors we had contact with, or which particular test or procedure was being done, or what Jack's response to that test or procedure was. We couldn't imagine what the outcome was going to be, how it would all end. But Andy and Gary both had commitments that they needed to return to, and I did also. One doctor suggested that I might want to return to Arizona and commute on weekends, but I couldn't imagine leaving Jack.

By chance, one of the intensive care nurses mentioned to us that we might want to consider using medical air transportation to take Jack home. So, after Jack had been in the hospital for over two weeks, we began to make the necessary arrangements to use this service to fly him back to Tucson. Gary needed to return to his job and he departed several days before we were able to complete the arrangements for the flight. Andy's schedule was more flexible and he arranged to stay on and help me with the move. I flew back with Jack in the tiny medical transport plane and Andy drove the car back. Both a nurse and a respiratory therapist accompanied us on the plane as Jack's condition was still so critical. Just the flight itself was terrorizing. The tiny plane rocked back and forth and up and down; it was totally unlike flying in a large commercial plane. And I watched my husband strapped into the stretcher, white and motionless and thought that, at any moment, he was just going to stop breathing. He was totally uncommunicative probably because of the morphine he had been given. I began to believe I had used terribly bad judgment in taking Jack from the hospital and subjecting him to the trauma of this harrowing trip. His stillness and the seeming nervousness of the nurse and the respiratory therapist only intensified my doubts and my own anxiety.

However, we arrived safely back in Tucson and were met by an ambulance, which transported us to Tucson Medical Center where Jack was immediately placed in intensive care. It was now September 19, seventeen days after the beginning of our ill-founded vacation. The next day, Jack seemed to be slightly improved and was moved to a regular medical unit. I was told that he would be able to go home at some point, but that was not to be. He began again to experience difficulty breathing and the cardiac surgeon's procedures for draining fluid from his lungs were ineffective. He was getting sicker almost moment by moment. He communicated very little except to occasionally tell Andy and me that he loved us, or to ask for a drink of water. When my sister June and her husband, Leonard, heard how sick Jack was, they cut short a vacation in the East and flew back to Arizona to be with us. Andy and I were so grateful, but Jack was barely able to acknowledge their presence.

Late on the evening of September 22, the resident on duty suggested that we might want to have Jack again placed on a respirator. I remembered what Dr. S. had told us in California, that there was no hope of recovery for Jack and that respirators or other extreme medical procedures would only prolong his dying. I knew also that legal and medical issues become complex once a patient is placed on a respirator. There is reluctance to turn it off, even when hope is gone. To live on, bedridden and tied to a machine to breathe for him, with no hope of a meaningful life was what Jack would have to look forward to.

Andy was with me, and we agonized over the decision. Should we continue trying to keep Jack alive or should we make the decision to let him die, which he would surely do without assistance in breathing? We decided to telephone Jack's primary doctor, but he was unwilling to advise us as to what we should do. We went back to Jack's room and he happened to be quite alert at the moment. We told him that the doctors had suggested the possibility of being placed on a respirator again to help him breathe. We asked him what he wanted. He shook his head and conveyed clearly to us that he didn't want help to stay alive. He closed his eyes and said no more.

I thought that Jack might be making this decision for our benefit, because he thought it was what Andy and I wanted. Fearful also that Jack might suffer from being unable to breathe if we decided against the machines, I was in a panic and couldn't think clearly. He was so sick and withdrawn that a real discussion with him was impossible. Andy and I sat in the room silently by Jack's bed, holding his hands, looking at him, looking at each other, not knowing what we should do. Then the cardiac surgeon who had performed the chest procedure, and the partner of Jack's regular physician, both happened to come by the room and I was able to ask them if Jack would suffer if we didn't use a respirator. Both told us that he could be given enough morphine to alleviate both distress and pain, although in a sense, the morphine would also hasten death.

By now Jack wasn't talking at all, so the doctors couldn't ask him directly themselves. And all I could think of was that I didn't want my husband to die, I wanted him back the way he once was. But at the same time I knew he was never going to be the way he once was. I was in torment about making a decision, especially because I couldn't be certain if Jack had refused the respirator because he was truly ready to die or if he had refused for his family's sake. And I wondered why I hadn't I been able to discuss all this with him before it became too late. The words "euthanasia," "assisted suicide," "passive suicide," and "mercy killings" revolved through my mind. Was it morally right to deny Jack the right to continue living even at such a price? It was finally Dr. S.'s brutal honesty in Newport Beach that helped me make the ultimate decision to let Jack die. His words have always remained with me. He had told me that my husband was dying, that he wasn't ever going to get better, that the family should quit trying to prolong his life, and that all we were doing was prolonging his death. Few physicians think like this or give this kind of direct advice to patients or their families. I guess I believe that I did the right thing and I think I did what Jack wanted. I will never be absolutely certain.

From the moment I made the ultimate decision, I had to finally acknowledge that my husband, whom I had loved from the time I met him when I was twenty-one years old, was going to die. He could barely communicate by then, except by holding my hand and looking into my eyes. He said a few words, that he loved me and that he was not afraid to die. My illusion, that my husband would get better and come home to me again, was finally gone.

The last night of Jack's life, September 23, 1988, I slept in his hospital room. He was not talking at all, unconscious, I guess due to the morphine. He did not appear at all distressed or in pain. I tried to sleep, but every few minutes I would look over to see if his chest was moving so that I could be certain he was still breathing. I must have dozed off for a few moments, for the next time I looked he was perfectly still; his chest was not moving at all. I got up and touched him and I knew he was dead. He was extremely white and his skin felt cool. He was completely motionless. I held my husband's once beautiful, muscular body, now so frail and emaciated. I kissed him and caressed his face, his body, his hands. I told him that I loved him and always would. I said goodbye, that I would never forget him. And I never have.

Chapter 12

Forewarnings

My husband of thirty-nine years, the father of my two children was dead. I mourned Jack's death, I mourned that my children had no father, and I mourned that my dear, sick son had been robbed of his carefree youth and now had been robbed of his father's love and support. I wanted my husband with me to help me cope with what was coming, to be there as the one other person who knew so well how I felt about Gary and who felt the same as I did. And as I grieved, I still clung desperately to the futile hope that Gary would not die. Sometimes I dreamed that I could keep him alive if only my hope and my will were strong enough.

Then, on October 28, 1988, a little more than a month after my husband died, my eighty-six-year-old father died suddenly, found on the floor of the bathroom by my eighty-two-year-old mother who was suffering from the beginnings of Alzheimer's disease. The call came from my younger brother. Mourning my husband's death and preoccupied by what Gary was facing every day of his life, I barely reacted to my father's death. Numbly, I went through the funeral and then the aftermath. Everything except grief over Jack and fear for my son was excluded from my consciousness. Grieving for my father was to be delayed a very long time.

The days and weeks after the deaths followed inexorably one by one, and Thanksgiving approached. I wanted to see my children and dreaded spending the holiday alone, so I planned a trip to New York where I would stay with Gary and Andy could join us from Washington, DC. I hoped to make the holiday as normal as possible, an absurd wish, I suppose, under the circumstances of our lives. But immediately this wish was denied me. Gary met me at the airport and my image of him as handsome, strong, and healthy, as he used to be, was blotted out. Instead, walking toward me was this very thin, pale young man, looking so sick and tired. I realized, of course, that he actually looked not much different than he had during our summer trip or than he had when he came for Jack's memorial service. However, when were apart for a little while and my only contact with him was through his reassuring voice on the phone, I managed to convert my image of him back to what he was during the days before AIDS invaded our lives. Seeing Gary face to face forced me to admit the harsh reality of his life.

But seeing my sons together and hearing them talk enthusiastically of their work was still deeply pleasurable. Andy was completing his PhD dissertation and working at the Washington Zoo, involved in a career that fulfilled all his childhood ambitions and dreams. Gary was devoting his life to his magazine, excited about his work despite his illness. He and Darryl still maintained contact, but the old fascination and obsession seemed absent. I don't believe Gary had stopped loving Darryl, but I do believe that coping with the complications of their relationship just became more and more impossible as his illness progressed.

Gary was still a participant in the clinical trials of GMCSF (Granulicite Macrophage Colony Stimulating Factor), so each morning, as in Newport Beach, I watched him faithfully prepare and inject the medication into his thigh. And each morning I was on the verge of tears as I watched the resolute manner in which he carried out his morning ritual, a stark reminder that he was staving off the ravages of a terrible disease.

For Thanksgiving Day we had reservations at a nearby restaurant and had invited Winnie and Lou Porcelli to join us for dinner there. But on Thanksgiving morning, Gary awoke feverish and weak. He began taking Tylenol, but as the day wore on his temperature kept rising. Andy and I were desperate to do something to help and persuaded Gary to let us put him in a tub of cool water. He was so weak, Andy and I had to undress him and help him into the tub. I could barely conceal my tears when I saw his poor, emaciated body. There was my child, once so vigorous and energetic, lying in the bathtub, weak, shivering, helpless, yet still so strong in his capacity to keep on coping with the brutalities that AIDS was inflicting upon his weakened body, and trying so hard not to show his brother or me how much he was suffering.

Gary didn't want us to call his current doctor because it was a holiday weekend and he didn't want to inconvenience her. When he finally agreed, we reached the doctor covering for his doctor, who, after hearing us describe Gary's symptoms, thought they were a reaction to the GMCSF. He told us to take Gary to the hospital immediately. It was too late to cancel the dinner, so Andy decided to remain behind to meet our friends, and I would get a taxi and take Gary to Sloan Kettering. Gary didn't object. Slowly and quietly he gathered up his down comforter and wrapped it tightly around himself in preparation for going to the hospital.

Gary was weak and feverish and still clutching his down comforter when we reached the Sloan Kettering Emergency Room. I helped him in and we were greeted casually by a nurse who put us in a waiting room. The nurse took Gary's temperature, which was a frightening 103 degrees, and we waited for what seemed an endless period of time for a doctor. Gary was shivering and very quiet and the sadness in his eyes broke my heart. How cruel, I thought, was the tragic fate that had brought me and my dear son to this hospital emergency room on Thanksgiving night of 1988.

The very young doctor on call in the ER arrived, uncertain and hesitant in manner. An intensely serious, but awkward, interview ensued, and all the while Gary seemed to be trying to humor the doctor and help him relax. Gary was by now so familiar with doctors, hospitals, medical procedures, and hospital protocol, that he often seemed to be more knowledgeable and in control than did the medical personnel. This doctor decided to take a blood sample, but after several bungled attempts, he was still unable to get the needle in Gary's vein. I sensed that this young physician was perhaps unfamiliar with AIDS patients and maybe even afraid of them.

Gary had been extremely patient and polite during the doctor's unsuccessful attempts, but after he had left the room, Gary told me that he found nurses were usually much more skilled with injections and drawing blood than physicians. Indeed, the nurse came in a few minutes later and quickly completed the procedure. Gary complimented her and told her he appreciated her skill and care. I was in awe watching Gary making the effort to be thoughtful and polite when he was so desperately ill.

Throughout this harrowing evening Gary never complained nor did he speak of suffering. In a strange way, Gary's very matter-of-fact manner of dealing with whatever new indignity or crisis came his way seemed to only make him a more tragic figure. He never asked for the slightest sympathy. I knew that night that I admired my son more than anyone I had ever known.

Gary finally got settled into a room and seemed a little more comfortable. Even though I would be more than two hours late, I went to join the others for our failed celebration. We talked about Gary for the rest of the evening. Lou and Winnie thought Gary was working too hard, not eating enough, not getting enough rest. They were frightened about the status of Gary's health and told me that Gary had struggled to protect me from knowing how sick he was. Winnie and Lou loved Gary almost as much as Andy and I, and I knew they would do anything to help him, but this was a dilemma we did not know how to solve. We were all terribly frightened and we resolved nothing that evening.

Back in Gary's apartment on Mulberry Street, Andy and I tried to sleep. We left early the next morning by taxi for Sloan-Kettering. Gary was obviously still sick and feverish. He had had a very humiliating experience during the night. He had diarrhea and was unable to get to the bathroom in time. He had to call a nurse to come help him and clean him up. I felt Gary's humiliation with him, just one more indignity to suffer. I was angry at myself and feeling guilty for having left him and gone out to dinner. I remained in the hospital all that day and then spent the night in his room. By evening his fever had gone down considerably and he slept comfortably through the night. Life immediately seemed better because Gary was better.

My plane reservations were for the next day and I had to decide whether to keep them or stay over. Bill Anselmo, a very dedicated nurse at Sloan Kettering who had been involved with Gary's treatment and his participation in clinical trials, was there and he assured me that Gary was OK and that I could safely leave him. Gary also urged me to return. Looking back, though, I have sometimes regretted that I left Gary then, and also that I didn't abandon everything else in my life and take care of Gary from the time he was first diagnosed. Even now, so many years later, I often wonder if I did enough, if I did the right things, if I couldn't have done more, if I couldn't somehow have loved Gary more, loved him enough to keep him alive. Futile, even absurd, thoughts, but still they plague me.

As it turned out, Gary's symptoms were the result of a severe reaction to the GMCSF and he improved rapidly once it had been discontinued. He was released from the hospital just a few days after I left New York. However, it was soon after this hospitalization that Gary finally admitted to himself and to me that he could no longer handle his demanding work schedule. He called and told me that he had spoken to Harry, his boss, about temporarily working from home and coming to stay in Tucson for awhile. He would have to relinquish the editorship, he hoped only temporarily, but there was a lot of writing and editing that he could do from home with his computer and his modem. Harry, ever compassionate and generous, agreed with Gary's request and Gary arrived back in Tucson in late December 1988.

Grateful that Gary was back home, still I knew how ominous was the meaning of his return. He would never have come back to live at home unless he felt he had no choice. I was faced once again with the frightening reality of his disease. But at least now there was something I could do. I could see him every day. I could help take care of him. When Gary arrived he looked sick, he was thin, he had no energy and for the first time I could tell that he was depressed. He told his friend Lou, "Sometimes I feel like I've come back home to die. I'm in my childhood room. It's too frightening." Gary never said these things to me, and it was only after Gary died that Lou told me what Gary had said. How unbearably sad are these simple words.

Soon after Gary got back to Tucson, however, he had a kind of semirecovery and he began to get back into his highly disciplined work routine. He was working on a national survey of Local Area Networks installers, which his magazine was conducting for the third year in a row. Gary was gathering and compiling the data to prepare a report to be published in the magazine. He spent hours every day hunched over his Macintosh, making phone calls, writing, compiling, and analyzing his data. As he completed each section of his report, he would ask me to read it and make comments. I was deeply pleased that Gary wanted me to be involved with his work.

Gary was still trying to keep me from worrying and so seldom talked about his health. But as I watched him almost endlessly taking medications, using his Pentamadine inhaler to ward off getting PCP again, taking naps in the middle of the day, and struggling to make himself eat when he had little appetite, my heart ached for him. I wanted to be the mother who could take care of her sick child and make him well, but this was no simple childhood illness and my wishes were only fantasies.

After Gary returned to Tucson he started going to support groups at the Tucson AIDS Project and the People with AIDS Coalition. He had never gone to support groups before. Then he found out about a support group sponsored by the Tucson AIDS Project for families and caretakers of people with AIDS. He suggested that the two of us go together to one of the meetings. I had known that these groups existed, but I hadn't wanted to join them. It seemed as though it would be admitting how hopeless Gary's condition was and how desperate I was. I wanted to believe that my son was strong and would never die, so why would I need a support group?

I will never forget that first support group meeting that Gary and I attended together. The leader was a woman I had known previously through my profession and she was extremely kind, gentle, and empathic. Another person in the group that first day was Miles Thompson, whose lover was sick, and who was to become a good friend over the years. There were other parents in the group who were also to become my friends. When we went around the circle introducing ourselves and telling a bit about why we were there, I was stunned when Gary said, "I'm afraid my mother will let my death destroy her life and I don't want her to do that." I was still in such denial that hearing Gary talk about his death in this very direct way brought me to tears. I so desperately didn't want Gary to admit that he was dying. But it became clear to me at that moment that the reason Gary had brought me to this group was to begin preparing me for his death. He had been afraid to make me confront his dying until he had found me a source of support. I then realized also that he was now going to support groups for himself to prepare for his own death. My son was so brave and I was such a coward.

Sometime in February 1989, Gary began to plan a trip back to New York, and I got little hints that he was thinking of trying to resume his work again. Andy had come to Tucson for a short visit from Washington, DC, and he and Gary began planning on returning to New York together. Gary was scheduled to go in for his regular checkup at the University Hospital Infectious Disease Clinic before he left for New York, and he and Andy left early in the morning for the appointment. By noon, they still weren't back, and I began to become anxious. About then Andy called to tell me they were having to wait for some test results, but that they would be home shortly. I sensed something was terribly wrong and began to feel those familiar symptoms of panic—a pounding heart, trembling hands, and frightening thoughts about what new crisis might be coming.

A little later I heard the car in the driveway and ran out to meet my sons. Gary was getting out of the car and as he did so, he fell against a redwood trellis that Jack had built next to the carport when we first moved into our home. One of the redwood slats was broken by Gary's fall. That slat is still broken. For some strange reason, I have never had it fixed. Each time I see it I am reminded of the image of Gary's face looking up at me as I ran to help him up. Gary looked up at me and with a faint little apologetic smile on his face said, "Mother, I think I have PCP again."

PCP, the dread disease that all AIDS patients and the people who love them are so terrified of. I wanted to scream at the unfairness. Gary could see how frightened I was and immediately started explaining, trying to reassure me. He said that the doctors weren't totally sure, but that they thought he should be hospitalized. He, himself, however, was fairly certain it was PCP because he had been having symptoms frighteningly similar to those he had with his first bout of the disease and so he had been suspicious even before he saw his doctors. Gary didn't want to go into the hospital in Tucson, he wanted to go ahead with his plans to return to New York and be hospitalized there if his doctors so advised. I tried desperately to persuade him to stay in Tucson, but Gary, sick or well, was not ever to be deterred by his pleading mother from something he was determined to do.

As it turned out, once Gary got back to New York and saw his doctors, they confirmed the diagnosis and did hospitalize him. Andy, the ever-devoted brother, stayed on for several days, but as soon as Gary started to recover, he returned to his work. Everyone persuaded me that I didn't need to come because Gary was responding well to the medications, which were not producing the severe reactions they had during Gary's first episode of PCP. His friends were visiting him regularly and Darryl was being especially attentive. All, according to the many telephone calls I received, was well.

A two-week stay in the hospital was predicted and it was obvious that Gary could not immediately go back to work but would need a period of time to recuperate. As it turned out, Darryl and Adam, another good friend, had been wanting to come for a visit in Tucson and they said they could coordinate their travel plans to coincide with Gary getting out of the hospital and could accompany him back on the plane.

Darryl and Adam picked Gary up at the hospital and went directly from there to the airport. As I drove to the Tucson airport to pick them up, I could no longer bring forth those visual images of my son as strong and healthy. Now, instead, I remembered his pale face, his thin body, his sad expression. I was almost certain that this time Gary would not walk off the plane by himself. I was prepared, as much as I could be, and when Gary was wheeled into the airport by Darryl, I was crying inside, but I didn't break down. Seeing Gary sitting in that wheelchair and his friends walking, I could only imagine what his thoughts and feelings were. I suffered for him and with him. But he smiled and hugged me in the same old familiar way as always.

Adam and Darryl stayed with us for about ten days, and Gary had determined that they have a good time and see the Tucson sights. He began feeling somewhat better and only used the wheelchair on a couple of occasions. He took them to the Arizona Sonora Desert Museum, to the San Xavier Mission, to Mt. Lemon, and to Sabino Canyon. He planned a backyard barbecue, thinking it would be a real Arizona experience. Darryl seemed very attentive and loving, but I didn't totally trust him and I didn't think Gary did either.

I struggled to make everything normal, to enjoy Gary's being home and to help him provide a good time for his friend and his erstwhile lover. I tried to do alone what Jack and I had determined we would do together when we first learned our son had AIDS: to do what we could do as his parents to make the time he had left in his life as memorable and meaningful as possible. Inside, I was stricken with terror as I recognized how Gary's health was deteriorating and how his father was no longer there for us.

After Darryl and Adam had gone back to New York, Gary stayed on in Tucson for a short while. However, as so many times in the past, once he felt a little better, he wanted to go back to New York and try to work again. It was toward the end of April 1989 that Gary left Tucson and returned to his apartment in New York. I couldn't quite believe his determination, his unfailing will. What a magnificent son I had. And what a magnificent older son who had become an unending support and solace for his younger brother.

Chapter 13

Strange Interlude

Gary had returned to New York and I was alone, grieving over Jack and imagining my son, so far away, facing the never-ending onslaughts of his disease. Although occupied with my work, there were still so many hours when, alone and frightened, sorrow for what my son was having to endure became nearly unbearable. At the edge of my consciousness was the endless refrain, always there in the background, no matter what else I might be doing: "I don't want Gary to die. Please don't let my baby die." The words became a talisman, a desperate, compulsive ritual, my hopeless and futile attempt to ward off the terror of knowing my son had AIDS, of knowing how inevitably the virus was multiplying in his body, of knowing that day by day he was becoming less able to fight off the infections that were eventually going to kill him.

I attended a weekly grief group for widows and also the AIDS support group Gary had introduced me to. I watched, listened, searched for news related to AIDS, and hearing about some new drug or treatment brought about brief surges of hope, but always my heart ached for my son.

Then it was Mother's Day, May 14, 1989. I had been in San Carlos, Mexico, visiting my friend Diana Hosley. She and her husband, Richard, owned a time-share condominium and had invited me to spend a week. It was on Mother's Day that I flew back to Tucson, dreading the return to my empty house and the sad symbolism of the day. To my joy and astonishment, who was there to meet me at the airport but Gary. He said he wanted to surprise me for Mother's Day and he had tracked down my arrival time by calling various friends and relatives. His beautiful familiar smile helped me momentarily forget everything except the pleasure of seeing him. It seemed a bit dramatic to me, even excessive, that he had flown across the country just to celebrate Mother's Day, but I didn't want to analyze his motives, I just wanted to enjoy his being there.

When we arrived back at the house, I found a beautiful bouquet of long-stemmed red roses and a Mother's Day card, and Gary announced that we had reservations for dinner at Terra Cotta, one of our favorite restaurants. I was planning on going to the cemetery to take flowers for Jack's birthday, which had been on May 11, during my stay in San Carlos. Gary wanted to take a nap instead of going with me. I was alarmed by this slight reminder of his illness, but convinced myself that he was just tired from his trip.

The evening was memorable. It was one of those beautiful spring evenings in Tucson, and we sat in the outside patio of the restaurant. Gary was in high spirits, extremely optimistic about his future. He talked of a new therapist he was seeing, who did Heller body work, a type of physical manipulation that is supposed to release emotional tension. Gary said that if I would go to one of these therapists in Tucson, he would pay for it. His suggestion seemed a little odd to me at the time, but Gary's happy mood dissolved any uncertainties or questions I might have had.

Throughout the evening Gary told me repeatedly that he felt better than he had in years and he talked excitedly about his plans for the future. Extreme talkativeness was unusual for Gary, but I interpreted it as a sign that he was better, and I was elated. The two-year mark, which Gary had been told was his prognosis for life, at the time of his diagnosis on May 5, 1987, was now past, and Gary seemed healthier and happier than he had in a long time. Only later did I realize that my interpretations of his behavior were all wrong.

After Gary's death, I found a note in his journal, dated May 5, 1989, saying only, "This is my two-year anniversary." This simple little statement still just tears my heart. Gary was to live only two more months after he made his journal entry, and less than two months after our memorable Mother's Day evening.

Over the next several days, Gary was energetic and euphoric. He raced from one activity to another, making appointments with various individuals, doctors, and groups, and going out with old friends and new acquaintances. He talked endlessly of plans for his career as his magazine had just been sold to another company and he was thinking that he might want to transfer to San Francisco where the new company was located. He seemed quite grandiose and described the many demands and stipulations he would make of the company before he would consider taking a job with them.

Several nights after Gary had arrived back home, he said he wanted to have Gus and Gus's mother and sister over for dinner. Since I had appointments with patients all day, I asked Gary to pick up a few things at the grocery store. However, when I arrived at the house that evening Gary wasn't there. He raced in about a half hour later with too many grocery bags to hold the items I had asked for. For everything I had requested, instead of the one item, there were two, three, or four, plus many additional things that I had not asked for. This seemed a little strange, but again, I didn't place any great significance on it. What I saw was what I wanted to see, that Gary was happy and having fun and that he seemed to have more energy than he had had in a long time.

During the evening, Gary talked almost constantly. He was extremely funny and entertaining and he was enthused about a plan, which he described in detail, to produce an off-Broadway, one-man show featuring Lou Porcelli. The idea all revolved around Lou's recent experiences as a waiter at a bar mitzvah party for thirteen-year-old twins in New York. Lou, with his usual flair and dramatic excess, had been regaling Gary with a detailed story of the extravagance and ostentation displayed at this event, and Gary seemed to have hit upon the notion that Lou's interpretation was worthy of a money-making, off-Broadway production. Several times he said, "We're all going to be rich. We won't ever need to worry about money ever again." I thought Gary was just joking and didn't take any of this seriously. Looking back later, the oddities of Gary's behavior that night should have been obvious, but I think I was so desperate for hope that I failed to recognize that something was seriously wrong.

It was a wonderful, unforgettable evening with the Porcellis. As so often during the course of Gary's illness, there were these special times of pure pleasure and joy, when we seemed to be able to totally forget that Gary was dying, or perhaps it was that these occasions took on their special significance just because of our not knowing how much time Gary had left, of not knowing how many happy occasions he might have in his future.

The next day I went to my office, leaving Gary on his own. He had plans that evening to go to a meeting at the People with AIDS Coalition and I had a date to go out to dinner with two of my friends, Rachel Burkholder and Jan Pearson. I spoke to my friends about Gary at length during dinner and about how hopeful I was because he seemed so well and so strong. I remember feeling incredibly elated that night, thinking maybe Gary had had some miraculous recovery.

Gary hadn't returned home by the time I arrived, and so I went to bed. I didn't hear him come in, but during the night, I heard the TV going in his room and I thought I heard him talking. It was very late and I was worried, so I went to his door and asked him if he was OK. He said he was fine, not to worry, to go back to bed, which I did, although after that I couldn't get back to sleep. I could still hear him talking, and then I heard a loud crash as though something had fallen. I raced back to his room and knocked on the door. He told me to come in and there he was in bed with books and papers spread everywhere. The TV was on the floor, having somehow fallen off the table. Gary brushed this all aside, saying I shouldn't worry, that there was no problem. He appeared to be writing something and told me he was preparing a speech that he planned to give the next night at a People with AIDS Coalition meeting. He again assured me he was fine, but I had a sense of foreboding.

The next morning, I left the house to go to my office, assuming Gary was asleep as I heard no more strange noises or talking from his room. When I arrived home that evening, I had expected Gary would have gone to his meeting, but he didn't mention it, and he and Gus were both there. I fixed dinner for them, but Gary seemed restless and ate only a few bites. Gary was again talking rapidly, at times almost nonstop, and now his thoughts seemed rambling and disconnected. He said he needed a good night's sleep, that he hadn't slept at all the previous night, and that he might need to go into a hospital so he could sleep. Gus pulled me aside and said he was worried about Gary and thought we should take him to a hospital.

Then I began to sense that Gary was becoming suspicious of me. He had purchased a new briefcase and he was holding it close to his body and telling me not to touch it. I knew we must do something drastic and I tried to reach doctors whom Gary had seen, but I couldn't reach anyone. I couldn't understand the significance of the briefcase, although I was later to discover that he had purchased a very tiny cassette tape recorder, which he was keeping either in the briefcase or hidden in his pocket. He had been taping all of his conversations as well as his private thoughts and feelings. I transcribed these tapes after Gary's death and learned more of what was happening in his mind during that time. Through the tapes, I learned that Gary had come to believe he was a reincarnation of Christ, and that he believed he was meant to be an AIDS messiah. The previous night, when he could not sleep, he had been searching through the Bible trying to find out what age Christ was when he began his ministry, trying to confirm that Christ was the same age then as he, Gary, was now. He wanted to find out also how old Christ was when he died, believing that he would then know how long he himself still had to live. Here is a brief excerpt from the tapes where Gary is talking to himself:

> At least I'll live to age 35. I told Gus I'll have to die of some AIDS-related thing. It's a little bit frightening. I'm not upset. Probably I'll be ready to die after 7 or 8 years of this treatment. No wonder Jesus . . . I totally understand everything now. Reading the Bible you know, I've never read the Bible except briefly. I mean I haven't even read portions. I was never brought up with the Bible and yet, I know it all on a subconscious level and, of course, you know about the Bible when you live in America.
>
> And I thought it was when Jesus was between age 27 and 35, which is what got me started looking. But this Bible is ridiculous. It took me all night. Maybe they hid that part. If it was to make someone read the Bible more, it certainly worked. And Joseph Campbell's book doesn't have any mention of Jesus's age when he died. Really, I'm not manic anymore, I just want to literally get out of the house tonight and relax.

I didn't know that night, as I tried to figure out what was happening with my son, that Gary believed he was a reincarnation of Jesus Christ, and I didn't know that he had told Gus he was afraid to be in the house with me. But I knew something was terribly wrong and the hospital seemed the only course open to us. Gary wanted to go to University Hospital where he received his primary care through the Infectious Disease Clinic. Gary drove with Gus in his car and I went alone. Gary didn't want to ride with me.

At the Emergency Room the three of us roamed aimless and confused. Everything seemed slightly unreal. If I had been thinking like a psychologist, I would have thought Gary's symptoms, the grandiosity, the rapid and rambling speech, the paranoia and suspiciousness, the inability to sleep, the excess energy, were exactly like those of someone in a manic episode of a bipolar (manic-depressive) disorder. But, instead I thought that his strange behavior must be AIDS related. AIDS dementia was the word on the fringe of my consciousness, but I wasn't really thinking clearly because I was so afraid.

Gary was eventually interviewed by an admitting nurse who decided he should see the psychiatrist on call. An hour or so went by as we waited, and Gary was becoming agitated. Gus decided he must leave because he had to get up early the next morning to go to his office where he was now an attorney in a law firm. Gary didn't want Gus to leave and kept insisting that I should leave and Gus should remain. But, despite Gary's pleading, Gus left and Gary and I were left alone.

Soon, the nurse came back and took Gary to an examining room to wait for the psychiatrist. He was vehement that he didn't want me in the room with him, so I hugged him, even as he stiffly resisted, and went to wait in the hall. I was in total turmoil, panic-stricken, confused. Here we were in a hospital emergency room, Gary sick with this stigmatized and fatal disease, and now, afraid of me, hostile toward me. AIDS had turned our lives into a horrible nightmare, just as I had been regaining hope.

My knowledge of what went on between Gary and the psychiatrist came from a transcription of his tape recording. Gary's paranoid and delusional thoughts are evident but he still has his sense of humor and his wit:

Psychiatrist: (After introductions) Are we on tape?
Gary: Yeah. I'm not trying to sue anyone, even in my paranoia, so just don't think about it.

Psychiatrist: OK Why are we on tape? It just makes you feel better?

Gary: My attorney wants me to do it. I always do this when I go in the hospital.

Psychiatrist: Have you had problems with doctors and stuff that you have an attorney and have to tape things?

Gary: Never. It's never been a problem at any hospital. It's just that he's very cautious.

Psychiatrist: How come you have an attorney?

Gary: Well, he's like my best friend too. He's just starting out.

Psychiatrist: Is he representing you for a certain reason now?

Gary: Yeah, it all started out because the company I work for is being sold and so there are a lot of issues. Now I just need to be insulated. I think I'm out of any manic phase, but I have stayed up for 36 hours. I definitely don't need Haldol, but it would be interesting to try the experience. The night before, the Bible. I don't know the Bible at all because I wasn't raised a Christian. I wasn't raised anything. And suddenly I was looking in the Bible and also in Joseph Campbell's book. I was hoping it had something. So I stayed up all night. . . . I was looking for this stupid fact. I mean you would think, how old was Jesus? I guess this is grandiose. How old was Jesus when he was baptized by John the Baptist? I looked for three hours in the Bible and another three hours in Joseph Campbell's book. I mean, I'm definitely having delusions to an extent. They're actually not delusions. I've got to sort of say that to calm everyone down. My mother will freak out if I said I thought I could be like an AIDS messiah. All I say is I could be.

Psychiatrist: Do you have AIDS?

Gary: Oh, yeah. For two years. And I've been much worse off than this. I've been very depressed. I work 70 hours a week and I was so broken down by that. I didn't know how to say no.

Psychiatrist: So why did you come in tonight?

Gary: To get away from everyone. My best friend, Gus. You can tell him anything. You cannot tell anything to my mother because she will react very strangely.

Psychiatrist: How have your thought processes been? Do you feel they have been going kind of fast?

Gary: (He laughs.)

Psychiatrist: Why is that funny?

Gary: I think that's pretty obvious to everyone even to you. You haven't gotten a chance . . . I've been talking about a mile a minute, going like 45 rpm. That's exactly the experience I'm having. This tape really isn't for my attorney.

Psychiatrist: It's not for your attorney? Why did you tell me that?

Gary: Well, it is for my attorney and he's also my best friend as well. I just wanted him to preserve all this.

Psychiatrist: Have you ever felt like this before?

Gary: Oh, definitely. Not that I was a messiah, but just recently I was working through a lot of hostility.

Psychiatrist: Have you been hearing anything?

Gary: It's all verbal. You know, all the ideas.

Psychiatrist: Do you feel like somebody is out to get you?

Gary: Well, no one currently at all.

Psychiatrist: Who was?

Gary: My mother, in her own strange way. I need a highly controlled environment where my mother cannot see me.

Psychiatrist: Let me ask you some other questions. Are you suicidal? Are you thinking about hurting yourself or hurting anyone else?

Gary: No. Am I truly delusional in any large sense?

Psychiatrist: Not in a large sense, but maybe in a small sense.

Gary: I mean, are the things I'm saying. I mean I have a lot of plans for helping in the fight against AIDS.

Psychiatrist: It sounds like this is a time you need to get some insulation.

Gary: Yeah, I just have to get . . .

After the interview, the psychiatrist came out and told us both that she thought Gary should be admitted, but that he would have to go to another hospital because University Hospital didn't have a psychiatric unit at the time. I suggested Tucson Psychiatric Institute because it was a hospital where I had staff privileges. It was around 1:00 a.m. by now. As Gary and I went out to the parking lot, he stayed at a distance from me and was reluctant to get into the car.

During the drive to the hospital and the long admissions process, Gary became more and more distant and strange. He kept clutching his briefcase to his side and while we waited for him to be interviewed and admitted, he kept telling me to leave the room. When I tried to kiss him goodbye, he pulled away. My loving son had turned against me and even seemed to think I was his enemy.

After I finally got home, around 2:30 a.m., I couldn't sleep, haunted by what was happening to Gary. My own thoughts were now racing as Gary's had been. What is in Gary's future? How will he endure what is to come? Is he about to die? How can I ever accept that he is really going to die? How can it be that he is afraid of me? Beneath the obsessiveness, I was just so scared. I wanted not to believe what was happening. I wanted the past back, those happy days when I didn't know my son had AIDS, when I thought he had a glorious life ahead of him. Why Gary? Why did all this happen to him? I tried to make sense out of the tragedy that had befallen my son, but there was no sense, no meaning, just the inexorable blows of fate and other blows to come.

The next morning, I went immediately to the hospital. But Gary was obviously reluctant to speak to me and said that he was much too busy to talk, that I would have to come back later. I was able to talk to Dr. Robert Winsky, whom I had asked to be Gary's attending psychiatrist. Dr. Winsky had seen Gary that morning and agreed with me that we should have a neurological evaluation to find out if Gary's symptoms were the result of AIDS affecting his brain. Dr. Winsky ordered an MRI, and late that night he called to tell me that Gary's MRI showed brain lesions.

I think I had been afraid all along that Gary's bizarre symptoms might be AIDS related, which would have to mean that his brain had been affected by the disease. My heart sank. The brutality of those words, "brain lesions," just struck me like a physical assault. How much more could my dear son bear? I wanted so desperately to protect Gary, to keep him safe, to stop his suffering, but I was afraid more was coming and that nothing I could do would stop it.

The next morning, I telephoned one of Gary's doctors in New York, Dr. Sheldon Brown, at Sloan-Kettering. I told him about Gary's diagnosis with brain lesions and asked him to explain what that might mean. Dr. Brown said that there were several possibilities; one was progressive multifocal leukalencephalopathy (PML). If this were the diagnosis, there was no treatment and Gary would only have two to six months to live. Another possibility was toxoplasmosis, for which there was treatment, but treatment which was quite toxic. Another was lymphoma, again for which there was treatment—both radiation and (I think he said) chemotherapy. I'm not certain, but I believe the fourth possibility Dr. Brown mentioned was that the AIDS virus itself had invaded Gary's brain. I was sick at heart, and Dr. Brown could not offer me even a little reassurance. But I was a mother, and a mother loving her sick child can be totally unrealistic. I still clung to the tattered shreds of my hope, even as they relentlessly slipped from my grasp.

After the MRI results were known, making it clear that Gary's symptoms were AIDS related and not just psychiatric, Dr. Winsky contacted Dr. Petersen, Gary's AIDS doctor, who recommended that Gary be immediately transferred back to University Hospital. Gary was moved by ambulance that day. By now, his attachment to his briefcase had apparently abated because he left it behind along with all his other belongings. I was told later by the Tucson Psychiatric Institute (TPI) staff that Gary had refused to take anything with him when he left, blithely announcing that his belongings were unimportant, that he had no further need of them. I had to go to the hospital later and collect them.

After Gary's death, Dr. Winsky described to me his impressions of Gary during the hospital stay:

> My first meeting with Gary was on May 18, during his two-day stay at TPI. Gary's presentation was dramatic and colorful. He was manic, very verbal, very intelligent. One of his symptoms was paranoia about you (his mother). He was very fearful of you. He took his affection and turned it around. If he had been in New York, he may have selected his best friend for this treatment. His fear wasn't super-intense. He was also very grandiose and there was a strong religious component. He thought he was another Jesus. He had lots of high energy; he was very talkative. It was clear that his efficiency and his organizational skills were just excellent. He was very impressive. Despite the terrible prognosis, it was difficult to feel

sorry for Gary or to feel sad. He was just so positive and so energetic; I thought if anybody could have a miracle cure it would have been him.

The first day and night after Gary was moved to University Hospital, he refused to see me, instructing me vehemently that he did not want me to visit him in the hospital. However, the second morning he phoned very early demanding to know why I wasn't there. Of course, I rushed to the hospital immediately and once there I knew that our relationship had returned completely to normal. Gary seemed totally happy to see me and obviously not suspicious. Never again, to the very end of his life, did I see any sign of his being afraid of me.

He was, however, still extremely excitable and manic, still talking a mile a minute. His conversation was quite brilliant, focusing on broad philosophical and literary issues, and tying together insights from various books, plays, and current events. He appeared to have some type of obsession with Donald and Ivana Trump, the New York "power couple," much in the headlines in those days. He talked about them frequently in a ridiculing yet, at the same time, admiring manner.

Gary also talked at length about his experiences at TPI. In a quite grandiose way he spoke of the significant impact he had had on many of the patients at the hospital. There was a patient who never spoke and was in a wheelchair. Gary said he had told her that she was being neglected and he urged her to constantly ring the bell that had been placed on her wheelchair. He thought he was empowering her. Another patient was hospitalized for alcoholism and he urged this patient to immediately check out of the hospital and go to AA, telling him that psychiatrists knew nothing about alcoholism. Another young woman was, in Gary's opinion, just having marital conflicts, and he told her she should not be in a psychiatric hospital and should not be on psychotropic medications.

Gary also told me how he had attempted to teach all of the patients at TPI a new way of playing Monopoly. Instead of trying to win money, he instructed each player to lose as much as possible, and the person who lost the most was actually the winner. Gary laughed when he reported that the patients didn't seem to quite grasp that this was a significant improvement over the original form of the game.

Gary was so happy and excited that it was hard to think of him as desperately ill. However, there were other signs of his illness and signs also of the effects on his brain. He was having problems with coordination and with walking. When walking, he tended to veer off a bit to the right and to seem a little unsteady on his feet. When he picked things up he would place them back on the extreme edge of a table or tray, where they could easily topple off.

During the hectic days, I kept in constant contact with Andy in Washington, DC. He was trying to organize his schedule, get airline reservations, and come to Tucson as soon as possible. He arrived the second night after Gary had been transferred to University Hospital. I picked him up at the airport and we went directly to Gary's room. It was around 10:00 in the evening, but Gary was awake and seemingly exhilarated. He immediately started talking and didn't stop for more than a moment at a time for almost an hour. Again, his conversation was philosophical and literary, with a few Donald and Ivana Trump references thrown in.

Gary hadn't seemed surprised to see Andy or even particularly glad. However, when we told him we were going to leave, he silently pulled Andy onto the bed beside him, put his arm around him and then beckoned me to get in on the other side. We just lay there, our arms around each other, not saying anything. The picture is still engraved in my memory, the three of us, just lying there, arms around one another, together in that hospital bed, not talking, not crying, just lying there silently.

I had spoken to Dr. Petersen right after Gary's admission to ask him if he would order a psychiatric consult because of the manic and paranoid symptoms. We were incredibly fortunate that the psychiatrist turned out to be the very gifted and compassionate Dr. Alene Levine. She had also had previous experience working with AIDS patients, which was just luck, since the majority of psychiatrists at that time knew little about AIDS-related psychiatric disorders.

Gary immediately liked Dr. Levine, and affectionately began to call her Lorraine Lorazepam (lorazepam being the generic name for the tranquilizer Ativan, which she prescribed for Gary). This name was soon spread throughout the hospital creating considerable amusement among Dr. Levine's colleagues and the hospital staff.

Dr. Levine soon decided to prescribe Haldol, a major tranquilizer and antipsychotic medication, to control Gary's manic symptoms, the grandiosity, paranoia, and agitation, all of which persisted, though in a slightly less intense form, since the Ativan had been started. Dr. Levine knew that Haldol could increase seizure potential because of Gary's brain lesions, so she sat by his bedside through the entire first intravenous administration of the drug, which took about an hour and a half. Gary tolerated the Haldol well and within a few days his grandiosity, hypertalkativeness, and paranoia began to subside.

Dr. Levine was worried about the possible side effects of Haldol, even though it had so quickly reduced most of Gary's psychotic symptoms. She did a great deal of research and learned that Valproate, a medication often used in seizure conditions, had been recently reported to be successful with manic states, and had been used on occasion with AIDS patients with psychiatric symptoms. She decided to gradually discontinue the Haldol and replace it with Valproate, which seemed to work just as well as the Haldol had and was less likely to cause seizures or other dangerous side effects.

After Gary had died, Dr. Levine described to me her impressions of Gary and of our family at the time she first met us:

> I have to go back to the original time sequence. I got a call from the hospital on Sunday asking me to do a consult for Gary. I was told he was an AIDS patient and that he had had an MRI showing brain lesions. He was described as manic. They did not feel he was imminently suicidal or homicidal, but help was needed in controlling his symptoms. I was told the consult could wait until Monday, but I did not want to wait. I felt I should see him that day.
>
> I remember walking down the hall, seeing the chart, going into the room, seeing his smile. His smile just stopped me. He was rambling in his speech, jumping from one thought to the other. He didn't seem distressed. He was very enthusiastic telling you and Andy all these things and ideas he had put together. I knew it would take a lot of research to understand neurologi-

cally what was happening. But I was also very concerned
about you and Andy, your faces. I didn't know then if Andy
was Gary's lover or brother, but it didn't matter. You were both
looking for hope. That initial contact between the patient and
his family was memorable. The family dynamics. I was
impressed with your ability to disagree in the presence of one
another and not hide it. I haven't seen many families like that.

It seemed that Gary's belief that he was a messiah, of sorts,
remained strong, even after the medications had taken effect, and he
spoke of it to Dr. Levine and sometimes to Andy and to Gus. However, he didn't talk to me about it, and when I asked him, he just
laughed and minimized it as nothing.

I gained more insight into this messiah complex from another
tape recording he had made just prior to his hospitalization. He
made this tape during a lunch he had with Charlie, one of the
volunteers at the People with AIDS Coalition and at the Tucson
AIDS Project. Gary had just met Charlie and had established an
immediate rapport with him. They spent a lot of time together
during the first few days Gary was back in Tucson. Here are some
excerpts from that tape:

> **Gary:** I hope you don't mind if I tape our conversation. You may
> think I'm utterly mad. If this is madness, I'm euphoric, but I
> know what the doctor will say, "I'm crazed with dementia." But
> since I got this little machine my anxiety level has dropped
> remarkably. All AIDS patients should have these machines
> because they forget everything. You don't have to worry about
> forgetting or about losing everything. I don't know why I didn't
> get one of these before. I see why attorneys invented them. I was
> up all last night driving everyone crazy, keeping them awake too.
> **Charlie:** Insomnia?
> **Gary:** No, not at all. I was like visionary in terms of . . . I never
> have any real visual visions, more like verbal visions. But the
> way I have visions is just to talk. That's why I want this tape
> recorder because then I can remember all these visions. This is
> totally grandiose, but people are all following me now and listen-
> ing to me. I have had all the experiences Jesus must have had.
> Have you read Gore Vidal's *Messiah*? Anyone can be a messiah,

you know, if they can talk; and I can talk, let me tell you, like no one I know. I also read Joseph Campbell (*The Power of Myth*) last night.

Charlie: You had a busy night.

Gary: Yeah, I said to the group [AIDS support group], " AIDS is the best thing that ever happened to me." People in the group just looked at me and they thought, "Oh, no, really, this one's totally lost it; dementia has set in." These were all people who have been newly diagnosed. You know, a lot of newly diagnosed people have found solace from my knowledge.

From Gary's words it is evident that he now viewed himself as having a special mission in life. He believed he had insights and knowledge about AIDS that he was meant to reveal to the world. This was certainly grandiose, and, I guess, one would have to say, delusional. But on the other hand, Gary's belief was consistent in some ways with his lifelong patterns, the level of consciousness he possessed, the way he was always searching, always passionate, always focused intensely on a goal.

In retrospect, I think that Gary's belief that he was an AIDS messiah was a masterpiece of invention. His so-called delusion could be viewed as his strategy for coping with his impending death and with the changes taking place in his brain and body. He had a grand purpose to engage his mind and emotions during his last days on earth. Dr. Oliver Sacks, the famed neurologist and author, who has written at length about his patients with neurological syndromes and how they cope with their diseases, has written something very pertinent to Gary's way of coping with the assault of AIDS on his brain. "The study of disease," says Sacks (1995), "demands the study of identity, the inner worlds that patients, under the spur of illness, create." Gary did create his own inner world, a world that gave him both comfort and purpose. Gary's belief that he was an AIDS messiah also reminded me of Prior Walter, a character in *Angels in America*, Tony Kushner's award-winning Broadway play, which I saw long after Gary's death. Prior, who had AIDS, said, "Maybe I am a prophet. Not just me, all of us who are dying now. Maybe we've caught the virus of prophecy."

Several other people who were around Gary during this time period also spoke to me of their impressions of him when he was at the peak of his manic period. Dr. Petersen said the following:

> Some AIDS patients cope by depending upon religion. Although Gary seemed to suddenly acquire some spiritual beliefs, they seemed not to be a retraction or retreat from the world as some are, but more an active way of mastering the experience, that is, becoming a reincarnation of Christ rather than a belief that God was helping him or would save him.

And here is what Gary's dear friend Gus said:

> It was such a weird experience being with Gary. It stands out because it was so extraordinary. It was like if there is a God, it was his last gift to Gary. He was just so florid and uninhibited. It wasn't that it wasn't Gary, it was all Gary, but at a fantastic level, almost surrealistic. We should have written down the things he was saying and studied them; the associations he made with literature and the kind of fusion or synthesis he was making with ideas was amazing. I think if Gary had lived he would have made some significant contribution. Some part of that is always luck, of course. I think I'm a pretty intelligent person as people go and there are very few people I think are smarter than I am. I used to say when I was a kid that Gary was a genius. But now I can tell you I have formulated a very considered opinion and I can say Gary was a genius.

My friend Genevieve Ginsburg knew Gary as my son, but also knew him during the writing of her book on widowhood, *To Live Again*, when he helped her with editing and with using her Macintosh computer. She told me about the conversations she had with him during this period and said the following:

> It all kind of reminds me of Mozart on his deathbed. He just kept working and creating. Most of us just kind of give up when we are dying. With Mozart and, I think, with Gary, there was energy-projecting life still going on. Was it brain pathology or genius? Maybe people like Gary try to rapidly live the lives they are not going to have.

Gary remained in the hospital for approximately ten days. It was recommended that, after discharge, he have nursing care at home and continue on the psychotropic medications as well as the AZT and aerosol Pentamadine, which he had been taking prior to his hospitalization.

As it happened, a good friend of Gary's from childhood, Judy Epstein, was a nurse and on the register of the home health agency that had been recommended by the hospital. Judy asked her agency to place her on the case and she was with us on the day Gary got out of the hospital. He had been pleading to leave the hospital and was elated about going home. The moment we got back to the house, Gary told Judy he was going to call the Gadabout, a salon where he sometimes had his hair cut, and see if he could get an appointment. He was able to get one right away, and he and Judy jumped into the car and raced off to the salon. He got a new style of haircut and looked wonderful, if a bit disheveled. By now Gary was paying very little attention to his clothing and he had put on a very strange combination of baggy plaid shorts and a ragged old shirt from his high school days.

After Judy and Gary returned from the hair salon, Gary wanted to go to a movie; so the four of us, Judy, Gary, Andy, and I, trouped off to the theatre. It is amazing to me even now how we could still have those times when we were able to be so happy and almost oblivious to our tragedy.

By now I was starting to wonder if we really needed a nurse, though Gary certainly enjoyed Judy's company on his various outings. After two similar days, we decided that he didn't need home nursing care. Over the next few days, Gary continued to be quite active, although he was upset that he couldn't drive because of his ongoing neurological symptoms, his unsteadiness and poor coordination. I would drive him to his gym almost every day, although I didn't know exactly what he was able to do there. He usually went off unshaven, in one of his strange garbs, and I worried that people might ridicule him. Often when we were out together I would see people staring, but Gary seemed oblivious to the opinions of others by this point. I'm sure that what other people thought about him was not important now. But still I couldn't stand the idea that anyone would make fun of my son or humiliate him in any way.

Somehow, the thought of Gary, as thin and sick looking as he was, there at the gym with all of those body builders and muscle men was just heartbreaking. I was, as always, impressed by my son's will and his unyielding spirit.

Gary's neurological symptoms were still very noticeable. His walking was unsteady and he still had this strange habit of placing objects teetering on the edge of tables or counters. I was constantly grabbing things that I thought were about to fall. He was also still having difficulty writing and was using his tape recorder to substitute for his lifelong writing habits.

For psychiatric follow-up, Gary had been referred back to Dr. Winsky, since Dr. Levine was on hospital staff and did not have a private practice. Gary's first appointment with Dr. Winsky was about a week after his discharge from the hospital. Andy and I asked Gary if we could go with him to the appointment because we weren't sure Gary would be truthful about his symptoms. Gary didn't object at all. He began the interview by telling Dr. Winsky that he planned to go back to New York within the next few days. Andy and I had been discouraging Gary from returning to New York because we didn't think he was well enough to travel alone or take care of himself once he got there. Dr. Winsky also discouraged him and suggested that he make another appointment about ten days hence and postpone his departure at least until then. Gary seemed to acquiesce.

During the session, Dr. Winsky asked him about the messiah issue. Gary just laughed and said, "Oh, it's only a metaphor." As it turned out, Gary had been secretly taping this session with his little microcassette recorder. His detailed answer to Dr. Winsky's question about his "delusions" was,

> You've got to understand. I think I could, due to my verbal ability, change a lot of people's attitudes toward AIDS. Make it HIV infection instead of AIDS, which, in a way, is a spiritual affliction. It's not really a disease. HIV infection is the disease. If I can be a messiah of sorts. I got a little grandiose. It's nothing.

After Gary had died, Dr. Winsky made the following comments about this visit:

On the May 30 visit in my office, Gary was still very high energy, but he was calm and relaxed with you. There was no point in trying to talk him out of his delusional material. He was wanting to exercise control. That was obvious from his presentation. Of course, that would only be natural for a young, energetic man, but some people with such an illness would not be that way.

When Dr. Winsky later learned about Gary having taped the session without any of us knowing, he said the following:

It was very gutsy. Gary was a fighter and this was another way of compensating, of coping. Gary was always engaged, always thinking. Also, Gary had a particular type of objectivity, an ability to be objective about oneself; he could look at himself. There is a name for this type of objectivity, but I can't remember it. Shakespeare had it; other great writers have had it.

Dr. Winsky later wrote me that he remembered where his reference to objectivity came from. It was from Keat's philosophy of "negative capability," which refers to the capacity of an individual to tolerate uncertainties, mysteries, and doubts, to allow the mind to entertain all possibilities. Gary did have these capacities, revealed in his adventuresome spirit and his magnificent passion for all that life had to offer.

Chapter 14

Final Days

I thought Gary had seemed to agree with Dr. Winsky's recommendation to postpone his return to New York, but he had no intention of doing so. Immediately after his appointment he began phoning airlines to make travel arrangements. The mere thought of Gary making this trip alone and being in New York by himself terrified me. His unsteadiness and poor coordination were more and more obvious, and I could picture him weaving precariously through the thronging crowds in New York, could imagine him stumbling off the sidewalk into the congested traffic. But, at the same time, I understood that my son was struggling to maintain, in whatever way he could, some control over his fate, over his life. I stopped trying to dissuade him.

Gary made his reservation for the morning of June 7, and I drove him to the airport; Andy had returned to Washington, DC, the previous day. I watched my dear sick son walk unsteadily onto that plane and I tried to believe that a normal life in New York would be possible for him. It was not to be. The very next day, while in my office, I received a frightening phone call. It was Gary, telling me he was having trouble dialing the phone, that he couldn't write, and although he didn't say so, I knew he was scared and confused. He hung up very abruptly and then a few minutes later called again, and then again and again. On about the fifth call, he told me he wanted his doctor to admit him to the hospital, but she had refused and had told him she would just see him at his next appointment, which wasn't until three days hence. He was obviously distraught and I tried to calm and reassure him as best I could. His calls suddenly stopped, and the absence of the calls was even more frightening than the calls themselves. I then called his apartment and a strange male voice, authoritative and identifying himself as a police officer answered. I was by now totally distraught myself, but the policeman assured me that Gary was OK, and said he was there because Gary's doctor had called the police, saying that her patient was threatening suicide and needed emergency hospitalization. The policeman told me that he was only allowed to take Gary to the nearest hospital, not to Sloan Kettering. I didn't want Gary to go to a strange hospital where he was unknown, so I asked the officer if he could help Gary get a taxi instead, and he agreed. I felt so helpless, thousands of miles away, unable to do anything for my son, terror-stricken that he might be suicidal. My only thought was to reach Andy who was so much closer than I; I phoned him at the Washington Zoo. I was greatly relieved to find that Andy was already aware of what was happening as Gary had been telephoning him also, and he was in the process of making arrangements to go to his brother.

After enough time had elapsed for Gary to reach the hospital, I telephoned and spoke with a nurse who said he had been admitted and that I could speak to him. Gary's voice was tired and strained. He insisted that he hadn't really been suicidal, but that he was frightened because his hands weren't working and he was having difficulty walking. He told me he felt his only recourse was to threaten suicide because his doctor would not see him or arrange for him to be hospitalized. I didn't know whether to believe his explanation or not. If he weren't really suicidal, how desperate he must have been to threaten that he was. Panic was such a familiar feeling now, but no less frightening just because I knew it so well.

Several hours later, Andy had arrived in New York, located Gary at the hospital, and called me to say Gary was safe and would probably be released from the hospital the next day. I immediately decided to fly to New York the next morning and either bring Gary home with me if he were willing, or stay there with him if he weren't. I got an early flight the next day and arrived at Gary's apartment around 6:00 p.m. Andy was there with him, and Gary was lying on the couch, so quiet, so sad looking. We talked and he agreed that he would go back to Tucson with me the next day. I was relieved, but his passivity seemed ominous and so unlike my son. I wondered if his passivity was a sign that he was at last giving up.

Our flight home was uneventful on the surface, but inside I was in turmoil. Gary was even more unsteady on his feet than he had been before his return, so I was trying to stay very close to him during the trip, and found myself constantly grabbing at his elbow to steady him. He didn't resist. I grieved for my dear son seeing the resigned, sad look on his face and watching his once swift and graceful movements, now slow, clumsy, cumbersome. How demeaning for Gary, that his mother had to come take him home after his confident departure only a few days earlier.

We arrived back home and Gary immediately went to his room. I went in a little later to kiss him goodnight and he said, "Mother, I'm so humiliated." I told him he had no reason to be humiliated, but how feeble my words sounded in the presence of his obvious sorrow and his sweet sad face. It was almost unbearable to see Gary so defeated and disheartened and to realize that AIDS seemed to have, at long last, robbed him of his spirit and his will.

Early one morning, only three days after our return, I was in my room getting ready to go to my office when I heard Gary calling. I found him struggling to get out of bed. He couldn't stand up and he was disoriented and confused. He kept saying he had to go to the bathroom, and I finally got him there, practically carrying him. Once in the bathroom, he didn't seem to know why he was there. He was staggering and falling. In a complete panic, I thought I should call an ambulance, but suddenly he seemed to regain a bit of equilibrium and to be somewhat less disoriented. I decided I would try to get him dressed and into the car and take him to the hospital myself. Once there, he was seen very shortly by Dr. Mandel, one of his regular doctors, who made immediate arrangements to admit him.

A hospital neurologist, who had been asked to consult, soon appeared in Gary's room along with his team of residents and students, this being a teaching hospital. The neurologist did a mental status exam and asked Gary basic questions such as the date and year and the name of the president. Gary couldn't answer any of the questions. He didn't seem to even understand what he was being asked. He was slumped over in his bed, his head bowed. I couldn't believe what had happened to my son. It seemed as if his mind had been destroyed. I could hardly begin to grasp the horror of this scene . . . the medical team standing around and solemnly nodding as their leader interviewed Gary. Their complacency angered me. I wanted to make them all understand what my son was really like and what it would be like to have lived with AIDS for over two years.

The neurology team left the room, and Gary looked up at me and said in a soft, child-like voice, "Mommy (he hadn't called me Mommy since he was about six years old), I'm so scared." This was the first time during his entire illness that he had ever admitted to me that he was scared. I lay down beside him on the hospital bed, put my arms around him, and just held him for awhile; and what I remember saying was, "I'm here, honey. I'll help you."

I remember also that, while all of this was happening, there were a lot of other people who had come to the hospital and were there in the room. I must have called my office to say I wasn't coming in that day and somehow conveyed my anxiety, because two of my partners, Joan Rosenblatt and Cheryl Karp, were there; and Sonia, Gary's nurse from from the Tucson AIDS Project was there; and Gus and his mother. I can't really remember how it happened that so many people were around.

Later more extensive tests were ordered. An MRI was done that afternoon and an EEG was ordered for the next day. Finally, Gary was settled down for the night. He seemed to have calmed down, and at about 10:00, after he was asleep, I went home and tried to sleep myself. Before going to bed, I called my sister June in Phoenix. She must have sensed how frightened I was because she said that she and Leonard would be in Tucson the next day.

When I got to Gary's room the next morning, he was like a totally different person. He was completely alert, articulate, and happy to see me. Such a joy it was to find him like this after the horrifying experience of the previous day. Right away, he began talking of getting out of the hospital and going home.

Within minutes after I had arrived, the neurological team appeared with a few new members attached, no doubt to let the neophytes see firsthand the terrible effects of brain damage and AIDS dementia or whatever it was they anticipated as a result of the previous day's examination. I couldn't help feeling triumphant and gratified when my son greeted them from his hospital bed with great charm and vivacity, inviting them all in and inquiring after their well-being. The expert doctors looked a bit nonplussed and no one asked Gary the year, the date, or the name of the president.

The MRI results came back later in the day, and Gary's original tentative diagnosis of progressive multifocal leukoencephalopathy (PML) was changed to toxoplasmosis, one of the opportunistic infections which AIDS patients are susceptible to and which persons with healthy immune systems seldom get. This diagnosis meant that there was medication that might be helpful, and it was started intravenously that same night. I knew that the medication could be toxic and have serious side effects, but the change in diagnosis brought some hope, because at least now there was treatment available, unlike the PML, for which there was no known treatment.

By that evening, June and Leonard had arrived. I was so grateful and appreciative knowing the many demands in their own lives that they were ignoring to help Gary and me. There were other people also helping us during this time: the Porcellis; Sonia, a nurse from the Tucson Aids Project (TAP); Rosa Cotayo, a psychologist friend of mine whose brother had died from AIDS; my friend Rachel Burkholder; Don and Gene, a couple who were volunteers from TAP; Marcia, another TAP volunteer; Charlie, Gary's new friend from PACT and TAP; Miles Thompson, my friend from the AIDS support group; and, I think, several others.

June, Leonard, and I spent the days in Gary's room, leaving just to eat or to do absolutely necessary errands. All the while my thoughts were focused on my hope that Gary would recover from this setback as he had from all the others. But Gary seemed to be getting weaker and weaker and needed assistance even to get out of bed. He didn't speak to me about being the reincarnation of Christ, but he still spoke about it to Gus. There were no signs of other delusional or irrational thinking as might be expected from someone who believed he was Jesus Christ.

Gary was still telephoning his friends in New York, including Darryl on occasion. However, he was telling everyone he spoke to that he had broken up with Darryl and that their relationship was over. Their breakups were so far from uncommon that I didn't quite know how to interpret this particular one. When Gary spoke with

Darryl on the phone, he was usually quite brief and superficial. As far as I know, he never asked Darryl to come to Tucson, maybe because his feelings were truly changed, or maybe because he was afraid of a refusal. Gary was primarily preoccupied with getting out of the hospital, each day begging me and the doctors to let him leave.

Dr. Levine was back as Gary's psychiatrist, and Dr. Mandel and Dr. Petersen were his AIDS doctors. At one point, Dr. Levine and the clinical director of the psychiatry department asked to meet with me and, in a very tactful way, suggested that when Gary left the hospital he should go into a nursing home. The thought of my son in a nursing home was monstrous. I told the doctors how reluctant I would be to do such a thing to my son, but I did agree to go and look at the one they recommended. June, Leonard, and I went that afternoon to Posada del Sol, one of the few nursing homes that, at that time, would even take AIDS patients. The place was bright and clean, but most of the patients were either elderly and demented or were young, accident victims, severely brain damaged, and in wheelchairs. I was in tears by the time we left and told June I couldn't let Gary live in a nursing home. I knew he would never tolerate such a placement.

I conferred again with the doctors and with home health services and it was finally agreed that Gary could go home with skilled nurses coming in every eight hours to administer his intravenous medication. So, on June 19, we took Gary home once again. He so much wanted to be out of the hospital and back in his home, and for the first day or so he seemed even happy. But he was terribly weak and could only walk a very short distance at a time. I remember June and I walking with him each day, holding his arms as he wobbled up and down the hall and through the house. He could barely stand without assistance. And now his little tape recorder was useless because his coordination had become so poor he couldn't operate it.

I think it was at this point that Gary realized he was not going to get better, he was never going to write again, and the whole meaning of his life was gone. He was depressed and very quiet, but he was clinging to his friendship with Gus who was trying hard to see him every day. One day, Gary was expecting Gus to come to the house to have lunch with him. He had gotten himself out of bed and with great effort, taken a shower and shaved. Then Gus called and said he couldn't come because something had come up at the office. This visit with Gus was absolutely all Gary had to look forward to that day—he, whose life had always been filled with exciting projects, purposes, and goals. His disappointment was heartbreaking. But he was still so brave, so gallant. He didn't complain, he tried not to reveal how disappointed he was.

I was overcome with the sense of absolute helplessness. There was nothing I could do to give my son back his health, to alleviate his anguish, to heal his pain, to give him hope. What was happening to him was just beyond endurance and yet he and I both had to keep enduring. Over and over the words repeated themselves in my mind, "I don't want Gary to die. I don't want him to die." At night I would cry myself to sleep and during the day I would try to pretend to be normal.

At one point I became convinced that if I could figure out a way to help Gary write again, I could keep him from dying. I ran all over town buying things, a new desk, a new lamp for the desk. I rearranged his room and his books to give him more space. I was doing things that made no sense, even to me. I was irrational; I knew it, but I couldn't stop myself.

During this period, June stayed in Tucson while Leonard went back and forth to Phoenix for a day or two at a time to catch up on his work. Andy was planning to come from DC but we didn't know exactly when he would arrive. We just lived from day to day trying to do anything we could think of to make Gary comfortable or to allay our own anxiety. I believe I was hoping for a miracle.

On the morning of June 22, the nurse arrived around 7:00 a.m. to administer the intravenous medication and, despite repeated attempts, was unable to get the needle in either of Gary's arms. His veins by now were almost totally collapsed from the hundreds of times needles had been put into his arms. June and I decided to take him to the hospital where there were nurses with specialized skill in doing intravenous procedures.

Frightened and nervous, June and I managed to get Gary to the hospital. He was too weak to walk very far, so we put him into a wheelchair and wheeled him through those now-so-familiar hospital doors to the outpatient clinic. A nurse appeared almost immediately, and Gary obediently and, in his now highly practiced fashion, thrust out his thin little stick of an arm. Even this highly skilled nurse had difficulty getting the needle into Gary's collapsed veins. I couldn't bear to watch and I was crying inside for my dear, valiant boy.

When the nurse finished, Gary said he needed to go to the bathroom, but he was unable to get out of his wheelchair. June and I had to take him into the bathroom ourselves and even help him take down his pants. Each day now was bringing new humiliations as Gary's poor exhausted body continued its relentless decline.

Now that the home nurses were unable to administer his intravenous medications, I was afraid to take Gary home, so June and I took him in his wheelchair upstairs to the Infectious Disease Clinic to see if Dr. Mandel or Dr. Petersen would admit him to the hospital again. Gary just seemed to be allowing us to do whatever we wanted. It was so unlike him, but he seemed too exhausted and depressed to even care.

Dr. Mandel finally examined Gary after we had waited in one of his offices for almost two hours, with Gary lying quietly on an examining table, and June and I restlessly pacing the corridors or trying to comfort Gary in whatever way we could. Dr. Mandel did decide to admit Gary, but we had another long wait until a bed was available. We finally got him settled into a room, all three of us by now exhausted and unnerved. It was getting late, and Gary fell asleep, so June and I went out to dinner at a nearby restaurant and then returned to his room. We went in. Gary was asleep. June and I were silent. There was nothing for us to say, our feelings too overpowering for words.

June and I arrived early the next morning at the hospital, and Gary seemed slightly better and more relaxed. More tests were being done, and it seemed the doctors were now wondering if he also had CMV (cytomegalovirus), another of the opportunistic infections common only in individuals whose immune systems are seriously impaired. We took Gary in his wheelchair up to the ophthamology clinic for an examination by an ophthalmologist, as loss of vision is one of the damaging effects of this particular infection. I can still picture Gary sitting there in his wheelchair waiting patiently to be examined to find out if he is going to be told that he has been given one more horrible diagnosis. I was under the impression that the results of this examination had been negative. I think Gary told me this because he didn't think I could handle one more thing, and was, even then, still protective of me. Only after Gary's death did I learn that he did, indeed, have CMV in addition to everything else.

I believe it was on about the third or fourth day of this hospitalization that there seemed to be a dramatic change in Gary. He no longer seemed depressed; he even seemed euphoric again. The reason quickly became evident. He had made the decision that it was time for him to die. He told me he was thinking about dying and asked me to contact the Hemlock Society; he began speaking to numerous other people about assisting him with suicide. He also told me he was going to ask Gus to draw up a living will and bring it to the hospital for him to sign.

In the midst of all this flurry of activity, Gary wanted something special from me. We were alone in his room, and he told me that he was hoping I would given him permission to ask his doctor to stop all treatment. That moment, his words, and the pleading look on Gary's face will live in my memory forever. To give him permission to die, that is what Gary was asking of his mother. It was the only gift I had left to give my son, to allow him to keep some control even at the very end of his life. There was no alternative for me but to say yes, though it grieved me beyond belief. My son was truly going to die. I was able finally to acknowledge it to him and to myself, and I was able at last to ask him how he felt about dying. He gave me an incredible, radiant smile, and looking directly into my eyes, he said very quietly, "I think it will be beautiful." Gary was ready to meet his fate, and was facing death with all the power of his being, even as his mother could not.

Later in the evening, Gus came with the living will and we gathered around Gary's bed—June, Leonard, Rachel, and I—while Gus read the will aloud and asked Gary if he understood what he was signing, that is, a wish to have no extreme measures, including respirators, used to keep him alive. We were all crying now, but were also just in awe of Gary, of his spirit and his courage. My sister June said later, "He just looked so trusting, like such a little boy. He was not at all afraid. I saw no fear, no indecision. He seemed very confident that this was what he wanted."

The next morning when I arrived at the hospital, Gary was tense, anxiously waiting for Dr. Mandel's morning visit. The moment the doctor walked into the room, Gary told him that he wanted all his treatments stopped. He spoke with absolute certainty. Dr. Mandel looked over at me and asked, "Do you believe Gary is capable of making this decision?" and I answered with equal certainty, "Yes, he is." It was done. I now accepted the sad, bitter truth: My son would soon be dead and I was helping him hasten his death.

I went into the hall with Dr. Mandel. I wasn't crying. I looked totally calm. I tried not to let myself feel the fear because if I did I could not help my son do what he needed to do. I did want to make sure that Gary would not suffer undue pain or distress and I asked Dr. Mandel about that. He said he would prescribe morphine, which would prevent pain. I knew from what we had learned with Jack that morphine would probably also hasten death. I asked when we could take Gary home, and he said probably not until Monday because it was difficult to discharge patients on the weekend. This was Saturday. I knew I had a lot to do before then. Arranging for nurses, hospital beds, transportation home by ambulance, on and on. This busywork would keep my terror under control.

Gary had fallen asleep by the time I got back to his room. Soon after, his lunch arrived and I woke him up. He looked at his meal and with a slightly puzzled look on his face he said, "Hamburger. That doesn't seem too appropriate." It took me a moment to realize that Gary thought this was to be his last meal. He believed that Dr. Mandel knew what he really wanted and would give him something to help him die. I looked at my son and said, "Honey, the doctor isn't going to help you die. You're just going to have to let death come naturally." A few tears came into Gary's eyes and rolled slowly down his pale cheeks. Then he spoke with a sad resignation, "Oh, well, I guess that's the way it will have to be."

June 27, 1989. I brought Gary home in an ambulance—home to die. Back to the home of his childhood. I had prepared the dining room for Gary's last days. It was a more accessible room than his bedroom, and it would be easier for me to be close to him. The furniture was moved aside and his hospital bed installed. Gary was taken from the ambulance on a stretcher to the hospital bed in the dining room. He was never to get out of that bed, the bed he died in.

The one thing Gary had asked of us all was that we would help him die quickly, and no one was able or willing to do that. Gary's oft-repeated wish from the time he was first diagnosed with AIDS was that he would be able to die with dignity. In my own view, Gary died with unsurpassed dignity. But what he wanted did not happen. Once Gary had decided that meaningful life was over for him, he did not want to linger on in a hospital bed, unable to even turn over by himself, helpless as a baby, totally cared for by others. Yet this is what happened. He lived one week like this . . . in a bed in the dining room of his childhood home.

One week was to ensue before Gary died on July 3, 1989, four days before his twenty-eighth birthday. The week went by in a blur of confusion, anxiety, and hectic activity. We had nurses around the clock, but there was still just so much to do. June and I were preparing and buying special foods and trying to get Gary to take a few bites. We helped bathe him and change the diapers he now had to wear. We tried to talk to him whenever he was awake. We watched over him. We loved him. We wanted Gary to know he was loved, protected, and cared for; that he would not die alone in a hospital with strangers. These things kept us busy, occupied us, and so we lived as though in another world, separate from everything that was happening away from that room, that house. Sometimes June and I would put our arms around each other, crying, without words.

Gary was semicomatose much of the time and would be alert and awake only a few minutes out of each day. When he would awaken and recognize me, or when he would say a word or two, my heart would leap and it was as though the most wonderful thing in the world had happened. It took so little to give me these brief moments of happiness. One day Gary awoke and said with a surprised, lilting expression, "Mother?" I really believe that, at that moment, Gary thought he was already dead and was totally amazed that I was there, wherever he was.

The nurses who came in were constantly trying to get him to try various things to drink or eat. His reaction usually was to say, "I'll try." I think they all loved him, his sweetness, his gentleness, his brave acceptance of his fate. I could tell. Not one seemed disturbed or reluctant to be treating a patient with AIDS.

Andy arrived on June 30. I brought him home from the airport directly to "Gary's room" in the dining room. Gary was surprisingly alert and said, "So, you did get here." He held out his thin, pale hand to his brother who grasped it, hugged him, and said, "Didn't you know I would?" His greeting to his brother was among the last words Gary was ever to say. From then on, as though he had been staying alive and alert for Andy's arrival, he went into an almost comatose state. We could barely get him to eat or drink anything and he slept almost all the time.

I went to see a counselor at the Hospice, who advised me that I should prepare for Gary's death by a formal ceremony of letting him go. That night, Andy, June, Leonard, Gus, and I gathered together around Gary's bed, and although he seemed totally unaware, we each told him what he had meant to us during his life and we told him good-bye. We were all crying and holding hands. I knew none of us would ever forget this moment. I thought my heart would break once again. How could a heart keep breaking over and over? I was overwhelmed with the love I felt for this child of mine who had suffered so and yet who had never become bitter or angry, who had faced his death with sublime honor and dignity. These last days and weeks of Gary's life had revealed ever more clearly to all of us who loved him the ultimate strength of his character and personality. He had not allowed the social stigma of his disease or his homosexuality to stigmatize him as a person. He had lived a productive, creative life. He had lived and was now dying with dignity. I thought Gary was triumphant in the way he had coped with the tragedy that had befallen him. I was proud to be his mother.

Lou and Winnie Porcelli arrived from New York on Sunday, July 2. They came into the dining room and were in shock to see Gary so obviously close to death. Lou kept saying, "He looks so beautiful," and then he ran out of the room and disappeared into the neighborhood. I still don't know what he did or where he went. That night, the Porcellis wanted Andy and me and June and Leonard to come to their house for dinner. I was afraid to go because I didn't like being away from Gary for any length of time, but Don and Gene, from the Tucson AIDS Project, who had dedicated themselves to helping care for Gary during his last days, had come by and said they would stay with Gary along with the nurse; they urged us to go. The Porcellis only lived a few streets away from us, and we could get home immediately if necessary, so I finally agreed. We were actually able to enjoy the evening, sharing memories from the past and talking mostly about Gary.

When we got back home, I sat by Gary's bed holding his hands and telling him how much I loved him. He did not answer. I finally went to bed. Strangely enough, I was able to sleep. The next morning I awoke early and immediately went into the dining room. The nurse was sitting there saying nothing. But I looked at Gary and knew something was terribly wrong. He started gasping. I held him and looked into his eyes. I could see he was dying. I ran to the phone to try to call the doctor, although I had been told there was no reason to do this and I knew what Gary wanted. I was supposed to let him die. How can a mother let her son die? I couldn't reach the doctor. I was distraught, frantic. I ran back to Andy's room screaming. He came racing out, and June and Leonard heard what was happening and came running out of their room. We were all hysterical. I can't remember exactly what happened. My son was dying. My baby. Gary gasped his last breaths and died in my arms. I held him close and kissed him, caressed his thin, dear body. His valiant battle was over. I did not know how I could live without him.

Chapter 15

Grief, Loss, and AIDS

As parents we forever try to repress our troubling fears that something tragic might happen to one of our children. Imagining our child dying is a thought so horrifying that we instinctively build powerful psychological defenses to protect ourselves from truly believing such a tragedy could ever happen to us personally. When my sons were young children, the eighteen-year-old daughter of a friend of mine died, and I remember how I struggled to convince myself that neither of my children could possibly die. I believed with certainty that if one of my children were to die, I could not go on living. But it happened; my own child acquired a fatal illness and two years later, my child died.

I did, of course, go on living, but after Gary died there were times I was alone, with no one to see or hear, times I would lie on the floor screaming aloud as I had when I first learned he had AIDS, "No, I don't believe it. It's not true." My plaintive cries contained the deep and hopeless longing that my son still lived, the longing to believe I had been captured in a horrifying nightmare. But the nightmare was real, my son had died, and all the longing in the world would never turn his death into a dream. Each day, I awoke with the same hollow feeling inside my body, awoke to a barren world, a world Gary would never inhabit again. I would never see my son again, never touch him, never hear his voice. And the inescapable words repeated themselves endlessly in the deepest recesses of my consciousness, "Gary is dead; my little boy is dead."

Now that my son had died, how strangely insignificant seemed the fact of his gayness. How difficult to believe I had ever thought his being gay was a tragedy. Being gay is not the tragedy; what is tragic is that any parent can reject a child simply because the child is gay. And, of course, the death of one's child is the ultimate tragedy.

Gary's death brought me to the realization that if I did not acknowledge in a very public way his sexual orientation and the cause of his death, I would be denying his identity and his worth and, even more shameful, I would become a collaborator in the stigmatization of AIDS. I knew that Gary's death obliged me to become even more actively involved in the fight to tear away the veil of secrecy and shame that hovered over AIDS and homosexuality. One of the first decisions to be made in an AIDS death is what to say in the obituary. Will the survivors use subterfuge and euphemisms or will they be honest? Gary's obituary was prepared to clearly indicate that his death had been from AIDS and the inclusion of Darryl as a survivor made obvious his homosexuality. I also wrote a tribute to Gary, which I read at his memorial service, a tribute symbolizing a mother's love and pride in her gay son. It was something I could still do for him when there was nothing else left to do. This is what I said:

> Being a part of Gary's life, being his mother, has been a special privilege for me. His father, Jack, felt the same as I, as does his brother Andy. Gary brought his unique perceptions and abilities into our lives and we are forever changed.
>
> I am deeply grateful for what I have learned about courage from my son during his struggle against AIDS. He lived his life fully, and he never felt sorry for himself. Gary made his own decision, as he did concerning everything else in his life, about when to die. When he became aware that he could no longer be a fully functioning human being, he requested that all treatments be withdrawn. This occurred a little more than a week before his death. His doctors and his family accepted his decision and admired him for his bravery.
>
> As for Gary being gay, his family not only accepted it, we loved that part of him as we loved everything else about him. Being gay was as essential a part of his nature as were his other characteristics . . . his creativity, his boundless energy and enthusiasm, his bizarre sense of humor, his logical mind, his iconoclasm, and his strong will.
>
> If you were fortunate enough to really know my son during his life, you could not help but admire and appreciate him. If

you had any prejudices or negative feelings about homosexuality, these should have been eliminated by knowing and understanding Gary. I am forever proud of him.

After Gary's memorial service the agonizing prospect of closing up his apartment and taking care of his possessions awaited me. My sister and brother-in-law, ever generous and kind, volunteered to accompany me to New York to help. It was during this trip that I discovered that Andy, my older son, was also gay.

This is how it happened. The day was July 16, 1989. June and Leonard were away from the apartment on an errand, and I was alone, crying and sorting through Gary's belongings: his papers, his clothes, his correspondence, his records, his household items, his books, his photographs. Each little object seemed precious and I wondered if I could bear to give away or discard anything that had been meaningful to him. I had the foolish, irrational fantasy that I should preserve his entire apartment just as it was forever. Logic seemed to have escaped me. I read through some of Gary's school papers, and they reminded me of his unique manner of expressing himself, of the way his mind worked. I wandered aimlessly through his apartment, stripped of his presence, soon to be stripped of those things he cherished.

One of my tasks was to sort through Gary's personal papers and it seemed to me that I should return letters to the people who had written them. As I worked on my task, I suddenly came across a long computer printout. It wasn't in an envelope like the other letters, and at first I didn't think it was a letter. As I tried to figure out what it was and who had written it, a sentence about Andy leaped out of the page. The printout was a letter, and it was a letter from Darryl to Gary. The sentence was about Andy keeping a secret from his parents and how Darryl thought Andy's secrecy had affected Gary.

Instantaneously I knew what the secret was, although never before had I even the vaguest suspicion that Andy might also be gay. Shaken, I went to the phone and called Andy in Washington, DC, though he was expected to arrive within days to help us with the apartment. Without preliminaries I asked him, "What secret have you been keeping from me?" He admitted the secret is that he is also gay.

For a moment Andy sounded like a stranger, someone with whom I was dispassionately discussing the abstract topic of sexual orientation. And all the while we were having this discussion I was thinking, Andy isn't gay. How could my thirty-year-old son be gay and I, his mother, never have known? It was incomprehensible. Never had I considered, even remotely, the possibility that both of my sons were gay, that I was the mother, not of one, but of two gay children. But in grieving the death of one son, I quickly realized that the sexual orientation of my other son is of no matter. What mattered was the possibility that Andy might also be infected with HIV. He immediately assured me, even before I asked, that he was not. Andy was alive, he was healthy, he was the same outstanding young man he has always been. I could only be grateful.

However, what disturbed me then, and still does, is not that Andy is gay, but that he had hidden his homosexuality from me for so long. I have tried to understand and he has tried to explain his secrecy over those many years. He knew he would never be rejected by his family, knew that we had never stopped loving or supporting Gary, but still Andy kept his secret. He did tell me that after Gary's diagnosis, though he was almost certain he, himself, was HIV negative, he wanted to prevent any additional stress that his coming out might bring to his parents in the midst of the tragedy of Gary's illness.

But what of all the years before Gary's diagnosis? Andy's explanation was that he didn't want his parents, me in particular, to be hurt or disappointed. He had never forgotten my first reaction to learning that Gary was gay and he was apparently afraid of something similar. My initial response to Gary's coming out was so much more salient in Andy's mind than my transformation over the years. Andy couldn't believe his father and I could possibly be happy to have our only two children both be gay and to know we would never be grandparents, would never have daughters-in-law. Andy's secrecy was, of course, just another sign of how society views homosexuality. Andy grew up in a homophobic society that told him clearly that homosexuals are not quite normal and that no parent would really want his or her child to be one. The minds of young homosexuals, as they grow up, are relentlessly molded by these frightening messages. Thus, the reluctance of young gays to confide in their parents, even in parents whom the child does not expect to be rejecting. The possible disappointment of the parents is enough to deter many from coming out to their families.

After Andy arrived to help with closing up Gary's apartment, he and I had little time to discuss this new revelation. Instead we had to make the many difficult decisions about Gary's belongings and to organize the packing, the moving, the negotiations with the landlord, and on and on. Each of us selected those things most meaningful to us to keep and we gave away things we thought Gary would have wanted Darryl or other specific friends to have. We invited Gary's friends to a small farewell dinner in his apartment so they could come to say good-bye and each select from among his books those they wanted to remember him by. Our mournful task had been accomplished, and we all went home to separately grieve in our own ways.

Back home, Gary's absence haunted me, an absence that was powerful and compelling. I sought out what solace I could and found it most in support groups with other grieving parents. This was a place where I could talk as much and as long as I needed to about my son, about what he was like, about what it was like being his mother, about the way he died, about the anguish, all the while knowing that others in the group would listen and would understand.

Each of us in these groups had a desperate need to keep talking about our own particular child, and rarely could we do this elsewhere. Exposure to intense grief makes many people uncomfortable, and, though there were a few notable exceptions, after the first few months had passed people seldom spoke to me about my dead child, perhaps because of the common and terribly mistaken belief that it is better not to talk to survivors about their loved one who died as it will only remind them of their tragedy. As if one would forget if not reminded. A grief support group is a unique place where the grief-stricken feel free to express over and over the depth of their pain.

Some writers have pointed out that parental loss of a child is unlike any other death, the grief being unusually complicated by the tremendous emotional investment that parents make in their children, in the hopes, dreams, and expectations they have for their children's futures. I had survived other significant deaths, my husband's, my father's, close friends. But with Gary's death I had lost not only my child, but I had lost an essential part of my being, my identity. Being Gary's mother was a basic part of who I was.

Also, when a child dies, survivor guilt is especially overwhelming. Parents should not outlive their children. This is not the natural course of life. I would have gladly suffered for my son and would have gladly died that he might live. This is the unending lament of almost any mother who has outlived her child.

The loss of Gary's special gifts and talents made his death seem even more tragic to me, although Andy has told me that Gary's being special shouldn't make his death any more tragic than the death of any other young person. While this may be true in some sense—certainly my suffering is no greater than that of other mothers who have lost children—still I can't help but dwell on what Gary might have done, might have accomplished in his life had he lived. Perhaps I am just overidealizing my dead child or perhaps not. I cannot know what my child would have accomplished. What I do know is that he will never grow old, but that I will keep track of his age each year until I die, each July 7, another year added to his age, another year measured by his absence.

Indelibly impressed in my memories also are the many joys Gary brought to my life, and, even in the deepest moments of grief, I am grateful that he lived and that I was his mother. All of those many memorable aspects of his character and personality are my legacy from Gary. I treasure also my older son and I will always believe that Jack and I, for no reasons I will ever understand, were granted a rare privilege to have been the parents of our two special children.

In mourning Gary's death, I have read and thought a great deal about grief, and have come to disagree with the common view that grief is a temporary condition from which one should gradually recover. I also began to question the theories about certain recognizable and inevitable stages of grief that must be "worked through" and resolved so that the bonds with the loved one who died can be broken and life can go on. These theories make grief sound like an illness to be cured, or an experience to be gotten over.

There are writers who question these popular assumptions and theories about grief and who believe that some bereaved individuals, especially bereaved parents, are not able and, indeed, do not wish, to forget their loved ones and move on with life. A good source is Therese A. Rando's (1986) edited book titled *Parental Loss of a Child*. In this book, one of the authors movingly describes the loss of a child as a dismemberment, an irretrievable loss, and says that, after such a loss, ". . . the rest of one's life is indelibly defined by a condition for which there is neither a reversal nor an adequate prosthesis" (Fish, 1986, p. 417).

Margaret Stroebe and several co-authors (1992) wrote similarly in a journal article titled "Broken Hearts or Broken Bonds." These authors have suggested that living with a broken heart may be preferable to the more unbearable loss of breaking emotional ties with the beloved and that, at least for some, grief may not be a temporary condition but may last as long as one lives.

Relieved to learn that my feelings about Gary's death had been experienced by other grieving parents, I came to accept that, for me, it was more intolerable and more painful to try to forget my child and get over his death than to keep him as a presence in my life. I ceased trying to recover; I ceased trying to get over Gary's dying. I came to understand that time does not heal all wounds as the old adage would have us believe. I learned to live with resignation rather than with the more hopeless struggle to recover. The truth is that I will never get over Gary's death. I have simply adapted to what cannot be changed.

I personally do not believe in an afterlife; I believe in the total and absolute finality of death. But I also believe that those who have died live on in the memories of those who loved them and in the acts we perform to remember them. Since Gary died, I have found ways to stay close to him, ways to live that will preserve his memory and give some meaning to my own life. I have worked on this book. I have become involved in AIDS and gay rights causes and in programs to inform educators and parents about sexual orientation and about the special needs of gay youth. Gary's brother and I and his friends made a quilt panel in Gary's memory for the AIDS Memorial Quilt. I collect and organize Gary's own writings. And most of all, I think about and remember him every day of my life.

All of this may sound as though I just feel sorry for myself, and I do feel very sorry—not as much for myself, however, as for my son's lost life. In my own life I hope to remember Gary and carry on some of the things he had to leave undone. Gary's impact and his influence can live on in me. The living presence of my older son has had an equal impact, and he is a great joy and comfort in my life. Andy is healthy, successful in his profession as a zoo curator, and happy with his chosen life partner, my dear son-in-law.

Homophobia and AIDS have had a terrible impact upon our family, and we will never get over our loss. The fact that the disease Gary died from was a socially stigmatized disease exacerbated our loss. To know your child died from a disease that has been referred to as the "gay plague," a disease considered by some to be only what homosexuals deserve, has been damaging beyond words, and that attitude continues to damage other families. Homophobia explains the initial disinterest of government leaders, the medical community, and the American public in dealing with this disease. As long as only homosexuals got AIDS, politicians, the public, and even some in the medical profession thought it could be ignored. Two of our presidents, Ronald Reagan and George Bush, could barely bring themselves to say the word AIDS. Gradually, however, it was learned that the virus causing AIDS was transmitted through blood and semen, and that it was not only homosexuals and IV drug users who were at risk, but also hemophiliacs, persons who had received blood transfusions during surgery, and even ordinary heterosexuals and infants of mothers who carried the virus during their pregnancy. The concept of "innocent victims" came into vogue.

There seemed to be a pervasive societal indifference to those persons with AIDS who, by exclusion, were not "innocent victims," who were only getting what they deserved when they became infected, and who were undeserving of sympathy or compassion. As for their families and loved ones, it was as though they didn't exist, as though "noninnocent" people with AIDS were so outside the human community that they did not have families or people who loved them and suffered with them.

A moving history of the neglect of AIDS by the government and the health care system has been reported in Randy Shilts' compelling book, *And the Band Played On: Politics, People and the AIDS*

Epidemic (1987). Shilts' book describes how governmental neglect contributed to the widespread dissemination of the AIDS virus in this country and to some deaths that might have been prevented with earlier and more active intervention by the government and by the medical community.

Both Presidents Reagan and Bush took moralistic positions about AIDS and attempted to ignore its relevance for the general population. Even the respected U.S. Surgeon General C. Everett Koop, who had been so forthcoming on other controversial issues, took his time when it came to AIDS. Shilts (1987) pointed out that Koop had been totally silent about the AIDS epidemic for over five years, and that 27,000 individuals were already dead before he spoke out. But, nevertheless, it was Dr. Koop's report, titled *The Surgeon General's Report on Acquired Immune Deficiency Syndrome* (1986) which stirred the nation to action, and Koop will long be remembered for this historical accomplishment.

The Surgeon General's report, and a resolution passed by the U.S. Senate calling on the president to appoint a national AIDS commission, at last propelled Reagan to action, and in 1987 he appointed a commission to advise him on the epidemic. The presidential commission findings led Congress, in 1989, to establish the National Commission on Acquired Immune Deficiency Syndrome. The commission issued its report, *America Living with AIDS,* in 1991. This report defined AIDS as a frightening epidemic threatening the entire globe and it openly berated the Bush and Reagan administrations and Congress for failing to help prevent the spread of AIDS and for failing to adequately fund medical research. The commission insisted that politics, ideology, and unwillingness to talk frankly about sexual behaviors and drug use were among the reasons that so little had been done to contain the epidemic. But it was prejudice and homophobia which had been the major barriers to action and the commission urged all levels of government to overcome prejudice and work toward their common goal of HIV prevention.

President Bill Clinton has shown a greater awareness of the dangers of the AIDS epidemic than our two previous presidents and has spoken more frankly about the topic. He has not been afraid to speak the word AIDS. He also appointed, for the first time, a high-level position in his administration to coordinate AIDS policies and programs. He and Vice President Gore and their wives attended the 1996 AIDS Memorial Quilt Display in Washington, DC, and even participated in the reading of names of those who have died. The medical and scientific research communities have responded heroically, and professional organizations such as the American Psychological Association and the American Psychiatric Association have directed efforts into research and education about AIDS.

However, the stigmatization of people with AIDS continues as well as do those underlying prejudices fueling it. In my own state, Arizona, we have an AIDS education statute that makes AIDS education voluntary, not mandatory, and the legislation explicitly prevents those schools that choose to voluntarily offer AIDS education from giving students information about homosexual orientation.

In 1994, the United States Senate, led by Senator Jesse Helms, attempted to pass similar legislation that would have denied federal educational funds to any school district with programs which referred to homosexual orientation as an alternative lifestyle or which provided counseling to gay students or referral services to gay programs. Fortunately these restrictions were deleted in committee. And in Arizona again, there was recently a movement in the state legislature to ban gay support groups in all public schools and universities. These antigay legislative efforts at both the state and national levels are often clothed in the rhetoric of "family values," but they reveal clearly how antigay prejudice still obstructs AIDS prevention programs. The fact that adolescents are especially at risk for AIDS seems not to matter to those legislators who are willing to risk the lives of our youth by their unwillingness to allow schools to provide students with clear, unequivocal AIDS prevention information.

The callous ways in which our country and its leaders initially responded to AIDS has affected all those who have suffered and died from the disease and also those who love them. For my son and others like him to. have had to live and die with a fatal illness is tragic enough, but that they also had to live knowing that their illness was considered shameful was an added psychological burden they should not have had to bear.

Governmental indifference and pervasive antigay prejudice have reinforced the shame and stigma associated with AIDS and have contributed significantly to the disheartening phenomenon of families isolating themselves from their sick children and keeping it secret that the children have AIDS. But then, how are parents, themselves usually not knowledgeable about AIDS or about homosexuality, to react when a president of the United States is afraid to mention the word AIDS and when homosexuals are still regarded by many as abnormal?

As a mother, when I discovered my son had AIDS, I was grief-stricken and heartbroken, but I had an additional fear, the fear that he might be discriminated against, scorned, and humiliated. I tried to do everything possible to protect my son from humiliation and hostility and to show him that his family loved and supported him and would never be ashamed of him. Nevertheless, when Gary died I had to face the reality that AIDS was still viewed by many as a shameful disease.

Those of us who have lost loved ones to AIDS are the ones who should be messengers to society—messengers of love, understanding, and compassion for those suffering from the disease. This is our responsibility but also our privilege. Just as it is important for parents of gays and lesbians to come out of the closet, it is important for families of persons with HIV/AIDS to come out of the closet. Secrecy only compounds the sorrow over an AIDS death while openness about the disease and about homosexuality helps dispel the added grief that results from shame and secrecy.

When a mother comes out and says, "My child is gay; my child has AIDS," she is giving a strong message to others that there is no reason to be ashamed, only a reason to grieve, and that a parent whose child is homosexual and who dies from AIDS grieves in the same way as any other parent whose child dies. This is a lesson that can be taught best by those of us who love someone who has died from AIDS—someone not among that group of "innocent victims," a group whom society more easily empathizes with. We must stir the consciousness of a nation and awaken empathy for our children and for all those who have suffered from this disease. In so doing, our grief will not be diminished, but at least it will not be compounded by shame and secrecy.

A personal message from a parent can be a powerful way to help change social attitudes. As I have spoken publicly about both my sons' homosexuality and about my younger son's death from AIDS,

I seldom encounter anyone who has been openly hostile. This may not necessarily mean that those who hear the message are tolerant. Some may simply be embarrassed to express their prejudice openly to a mother whose child has died; but, nevertheless, they hear a parent's unique viewpoint.

Gary was less affected by the stigma of AIDS than many under similar circumstances because he received strong support from his family, his friends, and his employers, and because he had excellent health insurance. But how troubling it is that so many people with AIDS do not have family or employer support and are often subjected to rejection and discrimination. This is particularly true for the poor, the unemployed, the uninsured, and often for those of minority backgrounds.

I am still angry about the rampant prejudice in our country toward homosexuals and toward AIDS, and I am angry that our government and even the medical establishment failed to confront the AIDS epidemic in the very early years. Vast numbers of young gay men, including my son Gary, may have become infected simply because they did not know of the existence of a sexually transmitted virus that could kill them and because they were not given the information, soon enough, that could perhaps have saved their lives. It is hard for me to forget that had our government acted sooner and more aggressively to help stop the spread of HIV, the life of my child and the lives of many other mothers' children might have been saved.

Since Gary's death, Lou and Darryl, two of the people closest to him in his life, and who were very dear to me, have also died from AIDS. Lou died a slow and painful death on July 23, 1992, and Darryl died on November 4, 1993. Both, fortunately, were surrounded by family and loved ones at the time of their deaths, Lou in Tucson and Darryl in New York City. Many other of Gary's friends have died or are HIV positive. Almost the entire network of his friends have died or may die, all in the prime of their lives. It is too sad to bear.

I often picture Gary and his friends, young and strong, striding happily through the bustling streets of Manhattan, laughing, partaking of the city's excitement and promise, thinking their lives are ahead of them, and all the while living, unknowingly, on the edge of disaster.

Chapter 16

Memories and the Right to Die

During the last days of Gary's life he asked several people, directly or indirectly, including his physicians, to assist him in suicide, but none were able or willing to do so. Gary's physicians, though highly enlightened individuals and perhaps philosophically in agreement with a terminal patient's right to die, were constrained by medical ethics, by the law, and in some cases, by their own belief systems, from granting Gary his desire. They all grappled with the complexities resulting from his request.

Both my husband and my son reached that same point in their lives, where choosing to die may be a rational decision, an active decision of taking control rather than just passively waiting for death or hoping for a miracle to reverse the dying process. I watched Jack and Gary go through these final stages of terminal illness and I watched them both decide to stop treatment when they realized they were not going to recover. Their physicians did not demur and were also willing to prescribe morphine for pain, which no doubt hastened their deaths. This might be considered a passive form of assisted suicide, although some would argue that point.

Living through these devastating experiences with my husband and my son persuaded me that medical ethics and laws about physician-assisted suicide should change in order to take into account those individuals who so strongly desire the freedom to choose to die rather than to live with great pain or with greatly diminished capacities. Why should physicians or society as a whole insist that patients prolong their lives in order to satisfy some abstract principle, even when those lives have become so severely limited or filled with such pain that life is no longer worth living? Who, in these circumstances, but the individual himself has the right to choose, to make such a highly personal decision?

AIDS, as a particularly horrifying disease and one that has affected primarily young people, has heightened our attention to the complex issues of voluntary euthanasia and physician-assisted suicide. AIDS has brought into the medical system on a scale never before seen, a group of young patients who have educated themselves about their disease, who are proponents of patients' rights, and who are not so willing to do exactly what the doctor orders. These patients are often unusually knowledgeable about their illness and extremely active in making decisions about their treatment. Because of their intimate knowledge of the terrible onslaughts and assaults of a slow AIDS death, they are often more likely to consider suicide or to ask for help with physician-assisted death. This is particularly the case for those who have tragically lived through multiple losses of their friends and lovers.

Physician-assisted suicide or voluntary euthanasia has long been debated in this country and it has its strong proponents as well as opponents. More open discussion was brought about by the formation of the Hemlock Society in 1980, an organization that has fought for the right of terminally ill persons to choose suicide or assisted death. Derek Humphry, one of the founders of the society, has written several books on the topic, including *Final Exit: The Practicalities of Self-Deliverance and Assisted Suicide for the Dying* (1991).

Perhaps the first physician to address the issue openly in a reputable medical journal under his own name was Dr. Timothy Quill. He wrote a letter to the editors of *The New England Journal of Medicine* (1991) in which he encouraged physicians toward a better understanding of those patients who are unwilling to live through the final stages of a terminal illness. He proposed that doctors should recognize the patient's right to choose the time he or she will die. Dr. Quill admitted in this letter to having helped a leukemia patient to die by giving her sleeping medications and informing her what dosage level was dangerous.

Dr. Quill was brought before his state medical board for an investigation into whether he had been guilty of medical misconduct, and the board determined that he had not. The medical board made a specific distinction between Dr. Quill's actions and those of Dr. Jack Kevorkian, the Michigan physician who has helped numerous persons to die and who has propelled this issue forcefully into the public eye. The distinction made by the board was that Dr. Quill had a long standing professional relationship with his patient, whereas Dr. Kevorkian did not have such a relationship with those individuals whom he had assisted in suicide.

However, despite the distinction made by the Michigan medical board, I believe that philosophically, the same issues are involved in both kinds of cases. First, does an individual have a right to make his own decision about when to die if he is terminally ill, in intolerable pain, or if he has such diminished capacities that, in his own personal view, his life is no longer meaningful? Second, should those most qualified to help him carry out his decision in a humane and caring way—i.e., physicians—have the legal and ethical right to do so? The reason so many people have been forced to seek out Jack Kevorkian, and even Dr. Kevorkian's own rationale for his crusade is that patients' own doctors will not assist them in dying.

Dr. Quill went on, later, to write a book, *Death and Dignity: Making Choices and Taking Charge* (1993), in which he continues his eloquent support for patient rights and argues, "Caring humanely for the dying and trying to help them find a dignified death is a fundamentally vital role for physicians."

Another physician, Dr. Sherwin B. Nuland, has written a moving book, *How We Die: Reflections on Life's Final Chapter* (1994), in which he describes the details of death in six different terminal illnesses, discusses the limitations of medicine in the face of death, and suggests that medicine has lost proper humility. Of most particular interest is Dr. Nuland's chapter on AIDS, in which he refers to the disease as ". . . one of those random crimes that nature now and then perpetrates on its own creatures." In Dr. Nuland's opinion, AIDS is a crime that God has nothing to do with, despite frequent pious arguments to the contrary. He describes AIDS as ". . . a plague of death upon the young" and says that there has never been a disease as devastating as AIDS.

Dr. Nuland discusses physician-assisted suicide, especially in the context of high-tech medicine where the fight against death assumes that medicine rather than nature should win. He believes that medicine attracts people with more than ordinary personal anxiety about death and also with a strong need to be in control. Thus, the physician deems a patient's death as a failure and makes intense efforts to preserve life at any cost and whatever the quality of that life may be. Dr. Nuland believes in physician-assisted suicide, but, like Dr. Quill, under very carefully orchestrated and considered circumstances.

Dr. Nuland, in his book, relates a personal story about the suicide of Dr. Percy Bridgman, a Nobel prizewinner in physics, who worked until the age of seventy-nine laboring on the last of his scientific works, all the while suffering from terminal cancer. Dr. Bridgman, in the throes of a terminal and painful illness, shot himself, and left a suicide note saying, "It is not decent for Society to make a man do this to himself." Dr. Nuland suggests that Dr. Bridgman's poignant words are a plea for the individual's right to ask his doctor to help him end his life.

A most compelling and eloquent book, written by law professor Ronald Dworkin titled *Life's Dominion: An Argument About Abortion, Euthanasia, and Individual Freedom* (1994), offers further insight into the issue of assisted suicide. Dworkin believes there is an unusually close parallel between how an individual feels about euthanasia and how he or she feels about abortion. He writes that although both proponents and opponents of abortion and euthanasia believe in the sanctity and sacredness of human life, these two groups have very different interpretations of what these beliefs mean in an individual life. Dworkin's arguments are complex and cannot be summarized easily, so I will limit myself to attempting to describe his position on euthanasia and leave out his very forceful position on abortion.

Dworkin does not suggest that euthanasia should ever be a common procedure, and he acknowledges that many people do want to be helped to live as long as possible, no matter what their medical condition or quality of life. But he believes that individuals should have the freedom to decide for themselves how and when they wish to die, in the same way that they should have the freedom to decide how to live their lives.

For some people, to end their lives in a comatose state, in prolonged agony, or with extremely diminished capacities, would destroy the overall meaning and dignity of their lives. The way they die is perceived by such persons to be an integral part of how they have chosen to live their entire lives. Dworkin believes that the United States Constitution, properly interpreted, should protect one's right to die, in conformity with one's own intensely personal beliefs and values.

My own feelings as a mother were much more complex than those I easily extol in the abstract. I could never have helped Gary to die myself. I have read numerous books and articles about individuals who have assisted a terminally ill loved one in suicide, but they have usually been written about or by adult children who helped their sick and aging parents to die or about an elderly person helping an elderly spouse. I have not heard of a parent who actively assisted in the suicide of a sick child. There may be such cases, but I think they would be rare. The protective, nurturing love that a normal parent feels for a child makes active participation in the child's death almost a psychological impossibility.

I know that I was truly grateful for each additional hour or day that Gary lived. A little smile or his speaking a word or two to me were sufficient to give me moments of happiness during his final days. I clung to these as to a lifeline. But I recognize that my feelings were totally selfish. I wanted Gary to continue to live as long as possible for me. I think a physician is the person who could best help someone like Gary who knew what he wanted, who was able to articulate it, and whose wish to control the timing of his death conformed to his lifelong value system and his personal philosophy. These are the reasons why, despite my desperate longing to keep my son alive as long as possible, I was able to support his decision to terminate his treatment. I do not know if I would have been able to support his decision had he succeeded in finding a doctor willing to actively help him end his life. However, knowing Gary's persuasive powers, he may have been able to prevail upon me to do so.

Gary was fortunate in being under the care of sensitive, thoughtful physicians and of having many supportive friends and family members who loved him. During his final days he impressed many people with his manner of dying, his openness, and his courage. Here are some of their remarks about their impressions of Gary.

Dr. Eskild Petersen spoke not only of Gary but also of the difficulties that physicians face in treating terminally ill patients and of the irrational attitudes of society toward death and dying:

> Gary was extremely articulate and a major concern of his was whether he could retain the ability to function as a writer. He wasn't afraid of dying. He was willing to confront his mortality. Not all AIDS patients are. Even some who appear to be able to confront their deaths still cling to hope and are willing to try by extraordinary means to prolong their lives. Very few actively make the the decision to stop all treatment. If the people they care for and are close to cannot let go, the patient is unlikely to.
>
> The type of patient Gary was is much easier for the physician to deal with. The physician has difficulty not imposing his own beliefs upon the more passive patient or the one who will accept whatever the doctor suggests. It is easy for the doctor to fall into a manipulative role with these passive patients and the doctor must actively fight against this.
>
> Society's difficulty in confronting death is also a major factor in the way the patient and the family deal with it. Death tends to be an event which we try to protect ourselves from, for example people dying in hospitals rather than at home.

Dr. Richard Mandel, like Dr. Petersen, spoke not just of Gary as an individual but also of the difficulties doctors have with decision making when treating terminally ill patients and of the need to balance individual patient desires and the social good:

> Despite how ill Gary was at the time I was his physician, I was impressed with how clear thinking he was. He had obviously prepared well for the eventuality of his death. Upon hearing the facts regarding the status of his illness, he followed through with his decisions in a very lucid manner. I felt respectful of the clarity of his mind in the face of what was going on. He faced his death very courageously.
>
> Gary took control over his own destiny and he allowed his doctors to help him. A lot of people in his situation force their doctors to make all the decisions, or others have unrealistic

expectations about what the doctors can or should do. Gary was very dignified and very logical.

The doctor's role is to try to help the patient make good decisions about treatment, but ultimately it is the patient's decision. Some people want to give up when they shouldn't and then the physician needs to encourage. Some want to continue when further treatment is futile. As we physicians are getting better at facing the issues related to death and terminal illness, I think it is making things easier and better for the patients. I am more and more attempting to discuss these issues with patients before things become futile.

It is a physician's responsibility to both think of his patient and of society. There are limited resources and it is the physician's responsibility to consider this issue.

Dr. Alene Levine, Gary's psychiatrist at UMC, was the doctor who knew him most intimately, and her sensitivity and compassion helped sustain him during his remaining days on this earth. She had the following to say about Gary:

Gary's initial presentation was more euphoric than sad. He was having spiritual revelations, but he had accepted death. He seemed to make a knowing decision to live while he was dying. He seemed to feel he had become one with the messiah. When he was going through the manic episode, there was not the distress or pain. Part of the later depression was in losing what had helped him define himself.

Gary presented himself well, as a whole person. He talked a lot about his mother. Whatever soul searching he needed to do about dying, it seemed he had already done. He wanted help in how to help his mother. He didn't want to have to spend the little time he had telling his mother he didn't have much time left.

I have been a physician for eleven years and in the health care field for twenty-three years. Except for one other person, I never knew a patient like Gary. He was very exceptional. He seemed to have already made a lot of decisions, but he wanted something more from his mother and his brother. He had to get past your hoping he would have a cure or that something would save him. How do you not destroy your loved ones and yet tell the truth about what is going on? During his last hospitalization, when you (his mother) were able to communicate to him that you understood that it was not going to be long before he died, he seemed so relieved.

I only saw Gary cry once. That was the day they told him he had CMV in his urine. The toxo, the herpes, the PML. He was crying and he said he didn't give a damn if people kept coming to him and telling him he had one more thing. He wanted to go home, to stop treatment. He was not going to stay hooked up to IVs. He started analyzing all the doctors and the medical establishment. One doctor who came in and told him he had one more thing, Gary just wondered what was going through that doctor's mind. He felt that the doctor didn't want to touch him or be close.

Gary just orchestrated everything, but you and Andy both helped. Gary let his doctors know what he wanted. That gift for communication let him do what he did. If you can say anyone died with style, Gary died with style. If someone tried to script dying in a film, it could not be done as well as Gary just did it automatically.

During his third hospitalization he wanted me to assist him in suicide. I remember sitting with him and I told him I wouldn't. He seemed to know I wouldn't do it. I wondered if Gary didn't bring out the best in his doctors. I felt that he was the one doing the teaching. I was amazed at how his brain functioned and his personality prevailed, his goodness and kindness, even with the tremendous neurologic insult which had occurred from the brain lesions. I remember having thoughts that meeting Gary will have a tremendous impact the rest of my life. I thought about what the loss will be to those people who knew him his whole life and about the impact he must have had.

Everyone who knew Gary talked about the additional component to grief over his death, that is, what Gary would have created if he had lived, how Gary would have touched people who didn't know him through his work. Like an artist who may have died prior to creating their best work. There was something very dramatic about Gary's death. I think part of it was these different levels of grief.

I think the most important thing was Gary's being able to talk about dying, to accept that he was dying, and yet to continue to live while he was so close to death.

Dr. Rosa Cotayo, my psychologist friend and Gary's, had also experienced the tragedy of AIDS. Her only sibling, her brother, had died just about the time Gary had been diagnosed. She had lived in New York City prior to moving to Tucson and she visited there frequently, where she would sometimes call Gary and have lunch or dinner with him. Rosa visited Gary frequently while he was in the hospital. Here is what she told me:

> One of the first things I was struck with was his sense of humor, the way he used language to bring out the humorous side of even his own situation. I was also struck by the fact that, at his age, he had the ability to face what was coming realistically, doing what he could with the time he had left, but at the same time acknowledging he was going to die.
>
> Gary had the ability to talk to his family about the disease, the treatment, etc. He was just very open, more so than I have seen with others. I think there is often in families less talking about the disease, the effects, the treatments than I observed in your family. Some people dying from AIDS are so self-concerned, so narcissistic, but Gary was able to transcend his own immediate problems and concerns and be concerned about his family. He was consciously trying to protect you, particularly, from pain.

Sonia, a nurse from the Tucson AIDS Project, knew Gary only during the last months of his illness. She said the following about him:

> Gary had more character and more integrity than any other patient I knew. He used humor and was able to laugh at himself and at his predicament. Even when he became semi-comatose he was affirmative. He was so gentle and beautiful. I think the deepest recesses of one's character come out when one has a fatal illness.

Don and Gene were volunteers from the Tucson AIDS Project who helped Gary so much during the last weeks and days of his life. They were untiring in their attention to him and in their willingness to do anything that might alleviate his suffering or make his last days a little better. This is what they said about him:

> On one occasion in the hospital when we were the only ones with him, he suddenly said, "You know what I want, don't you?" We knew he wanted to die quickly and that he wanted us to help. He had stopped all of his medications at that time. We told him that we knew what he wanted and that ethically we wanted to help him, but legally it was out of the question. He was very philosophical about our response and he accepted it. We thought, "What a brave little son of a bitch."
>
> We have seen this active attempt to die among other AIDS clients we have worked with, but not too often. We usually get mixed statements, people saying they want to die, but then they continue with all of the medical treatments. To know what is happening, the physical and mental decline, and to dread it . . . when you're intelligent and can make the decision, we believe it is the individual's right to commit suicide, but we just couldn't legally help him.

Miles Thompson is my friend from the AIDS support group. He never knew Gary until Gary and I came to the support group only a couple of months before Gary died. Miles started visiting Gary in the hospital and was a good friend during Gary's last weeks. He said the following about Gary's reactions to his illness and to death:

> Gary was the first person of those I knew who died from AIDS for whom I was there throughout the final stages of life. The thing I felt was most singular about Gary was that his attitude was so very resolute, so very realistic. He was saying, "Mother, I'm going to die. I know that and I want you to give me permission to do what I need to do rather than insisting that I live to be just a body, to be hooked up to machines." He really wanted his mother to give him permission and accept the fact that he was going to die. He wanted to retain his dignity. He seemed almost more concerned for his mother than for himself.

One day when I went in he talked to me about the Hemlock Society. I told him I would get the phone number. I did get it for him. After that he seemed to think I had arranged something for him. After you told me about his decision to terminate treatment and how he wanted your support and how you gave it, I went in and told him, "I heard about your decision and I do support you and it's what I would do." He said, "Oh, Miles, I do appreciate that. You don't know what it means to me."

What impressed me most about him was his biting the bullet, facing what was happening. He wanted to do that with dignity. The word stoic comes to mind. He was not coldly stoic, but stoic with acceptance. I don't like it, but. . . . Gary has become my role model for dying, even though he was much younger than I.

I will end these memories of Gary with a poem written for him by his friend Adam O'Connor who has since also died from AIDS. Adam read his poem at the second memorial service for Gary held in New York City at the Gay Men's Health Crisis a few weeks after his death.

For G.B.

I just saw a bird in the road . . .
A sparrow, believe it or not,
and quite a handsome specimen.
How you used to hate these sparrows!

So, you see, when I thought of you
It was with all your fire on . . .
Your fire, and science, and wit.
A young man right out of the West:
How new you appeared, how modern.
"I'll never be as new as him,"
is how I always summed it up.

I only glimpsed you far ahead,
And you kept the distance growing.
But you, better maker, tell me:
What am I to make of this bird,
This dear dead sparrow that I found.

I really saw him, but of course,
He's an old symbol of God's love.

"Not a sparrow falls from the branch
That God doesn't see it tumble . . . "
And see the people pass it by,
And see worse as the day grows warm.
Well . . . you knew the hardy sparrow
So little in need of watching.

When I see the *rara avis*
Which is symbolic of nothing
But is splendid in the instant
I will watch well for the moment
And see a bit of what you saw.
And make a bit of what you made.

Chapter 17

Homosexuality:
Facts, Fallacies, Feelings

As the mother of homosexual sons, I have loved and admired two outstanding individuals who happened to grow up to be gay. I watched them as delightful, vibrant, affectionate children who became productive, responsible adults and contributing members of society. Their sexual orientation did not lessen them or detract from their worth in any way. Sometimes I think that if those in our country who dislike and demean homosexuals could only have had the experience I have had, of rearing and loving gay children, anti-gay prejudice would soon disappear.

However, as a mother of gay children, I also learned of the disdain, ridicule, even hatred directed toward people who when they fall in love, do so with someone of the same sex. Such exaggerated reactions to such a simple, harmless human characteristic. But those who differ from the majority in this one way are truly singled out as the social outcasts of contemporary society.

Although it has become socially unacceptable and politically incorrect to openly express prejudice toward ethnic, racial, or religious minorities or toward women, no such opprobrium attaches itself to antigay prejudice. As a striking example of the social acceptability of prejudice toward homosexuals, General Colin Powell, Chairman of the U.S. Joint Chiefs of Staff, in the early 1990s, appeared perfectly comfortable in stating publicly that to allow openly gay individuals to serve in the armed forces would be demoralizing and would jeopardize the effectiveness of the military. He recommended such people should be discharged.

General Powell seemed to have forgotten that very similar arguments were once used to justify why blacks should not be integrated in the armed services. Had it not been for President Harry Truman's 1948 executive order, which forbid discrimination against blacks in the military, Colin Powell might never have had the opportunity to become General Powell. Today there would be public outrage if a white U.S. general were to make the remark about African Americans that General Powell made about gays.

President Bill Clinton, soon after his election, attempted, as he had promised, to lift the ban on gays in the military, but the generals and the U.S. Congress forced him to capitulate and to adopt instead, a vague, hypocritical policy, popularly called "Don't ask, don't tell." Under this new policy, if you are gay and in the military, you should never mention it, you should stay in the closet. This policy is merely a cover-up for blatant prejudice. A gay, former Air Force staff sergeant, Tom Paniccia, who had been stationed in Tucson, Arizona, testified eloquently before the United States Senate, describing this ruling as ". . . forcing people like me to live a lie."

Denying openly gay or lesbian individuals the right to serve in the military represents just one isolated example of the acceptability of openly expressed contempt toward homosexuals, even by the leaders of our country, while overt prejudice toward other minorities is generally condemned or at least frowned upon. Peter J. Gomes, a professor of divinity at Harvard, has referred to homophobia as the "last respected prejudice of the century."

Prejudice toward gays has gone so far as to result in blatant attempts to deny to homosexuals the ordinary legal protections taken for granted by other citizens. As an example, the state of Colorado, in 1993, passed a constitutional amendment nullifying civil rights protections for homosexuals. Similar ordinances and statutes have, in recent years, been enacted in other states and cities. Fortunately, when the Colorado amendment was appealed, the U.S. Supreme Court, in the 1996 *Romer v. Evans* case, struck it down on the basis that it would specifically deny constitutional protection to a particular group of people. Justice Anthony Kennedy, writing the opinion for the majority, said that no state ". . . can deem a class of persons a stranger to its laws." This landmark decision may herald a new era in the liberation of gays and lesbians in our country.

As the mother of gay children, I became much more sensitive to the destructive effects of homophobia on the lives of young people who are growing up gay or lesbian. I learned how blind and oblivious I had been to homophobia, as are most parents, preventing us from being of any help to our gay children in their struggle to grow up. Parents are not told in all those parenting books and articles we study so assiduously that we may have children who will grow up to be gay. It is as though homosexuals spring up out of nowhere, not out of families, and so families are totally unsuspecting and, thus, incapable of giving their gay children the support they need so badly. Despite avid attempts of certain family values proponents to deny homosexuals entry into their exclusive club, gays also come from families, have families, and believe in the value of families.

My personal experiences as a mother have affected my attitudes toward homosexuality far more than all my professional training as a psychologist. Through experience, I came to understand why many gay youth, including my own dear sons, feel compelled to keep their sexual orientation hidden for fear of being ostracized and humiliated. And I came to realize how ill informed I was as a parent and even as a psychologist about sexual orientation. And most disturbing of all I was to learn how sadly lacking in basic information about homosexuality are most educators and even many mental health professionals.

Whether one approves of homosexuality or not, and whether homosexuals consist of 1, 2, 5, or 10 percent of the population (the statistics are unclear and conflicting), there will always exist a group of young people who will grow up to be gay or lesbian. Those of us who are parents or educators, or who work with young people in any capacity, should be aware of the difficulties experienced by these youth, and should learn how to help them cope with the stresses of growing up so that they can become healthy, responsible adults.

As a civilized society, we must not abandon one entire group of people because of prejudice and ignorance. We must openly address the issues of why antigay prejudice is so rampant, why so many people fear and even hate homosexuals, and how we can best correct the mistreatment that has resulted.

Perhaps one of the most obvious reasons for the pervasiveness of antigay prejudice is the common fear or dislike of the unknown, that which is different; and for a heterosexual, the homosexual is unknown, is different, is even incomprehensible. It is widely recognized that one of the most effective means of reducing prejudice toward a stigmatized group is through having a positive personal experience with an individual member of that group. But since gays and lesbians are so often hidden in their closets, the people around them are unaware that they actually do know someone who is gay or lesbian, that they have a friend, a family member, or a co-worker who is homosexual. The discovery that one's son, daughter, best friend, or co-worker is gay can profoundly and permanently alter one's views about homosexuals. The growing inclination of homosexuals to disclose their orientation will mean many more opportunities for heterosexuals to learn that they do know a gay or lesbian person and that gays and lesbians are, in most ways, not essentially different from themselves.

Another major source of antigay prejudice is the belief that homosexuality is immoral and unnatural. Such prejudice is often based on religious teaching and is difficult to address other than through greater understanding and tolerance within the religious community itself—something that is beginning to develop within certain religious groups. Insofar as homosexuality being unnatural, it only seems unnatural to heterosexuals. To a homosexual, his feelings are perfectly natural and are not perversely chosen, but instead are discovered as they gradually emerge throughout childhood and adolescence, in just the same way as do the sexual feelings of a heterosexual. In regard to immorality, morals have nothing to do with sexual orientation, but with the manner in which one expresses love, concern, and respect for one's sexual partner as well as for other human beings.

Another major source of antigay prejudice is the pervasiveness of certain negative stereotypes about homosexuals—stereotypes that have little basis in fact. These stereotypes and myths about homosexuals have grown up out of ignorance, fear, and the failure to realize that the negative characteristics attributed to homosexuals do not apply to the majority of homosexuals. To address the destructive effects of homophobia, these false beliefs must be brought to public consciousness and challenged at all levels of society.

One of the most common of these myths is that homosexuality is a type of mental illness, a sickness, and that no normal person could possibly be sexually attracted to someone of the same gender. This belief was long perpetuated by mental health professionals whose primary contacts with gay persons had been confined to those seeking mental health treatment. As I have discussed at length in an earlier chapter, psychological research (Hooker, 1957; Gonsiorek, 1977, 1982, 1991; Reiss, 1980) has clearly demonstrated that homosexuals do not differ from heterosexuals in terms of the prevalence of mental illness or serious psychiatric disturbance in each group. Of course, there are mentally ill, seriously psychiatrically disturbed people who are homosexuals, just as there are mentally ill heterosexuals; but homosexual orientation is, in and of itself, not a mental illness and does not create mental illness. There are unique psychological stresses which affect homosexuals as the direct result of the oppression and discrimination they face in their lives and which may interfere, at least temporarily, in their life adjustment. Nevertheless, most emerge as psychologically healthy adults.

Another of the false beliefs about homosexuals is that they are child molesters who prey on innocent children. Scientific research regarding this issue has demonstrated that gay men are no more likely, even less likely, according to available studies, to be child molesters than are heterosexual men (Burgess et al., 1978; Groth and Birnbaum, 1978; Jenny, Roesier, and Poyer, 1992, 1994). These studies all found that homosexual persons are actually less likely to sexually approach children than are heterosexuals. Jenny's study found, for example, that only two homosexuals were involved in 269 cases of sexual molestation of children studied at the Colorado Health Sciences Center and Children's Hospital. Dr. Jenny, in a reference to her study, stated, "A child is 100 times more likely to be molested by a heterosexual partner of a relative than by a homosexual."

One cause for the confusion and misunderstanding is the assumption that males who molest male children are homosexuals. In fact, most of these child molesters are what are known as pedophiles. Pedophiles lack the desire for mature sexual relationships with other adults, and, instead, are sexually fixated on children, whether they be male, female, or both. Many pedophiles have never had an adult sexual relationship, either homosexual or heterosexual. Pedophilia is often equated with homosexuality when the molestation is of a male child by an adult male. This misperception leads people to unreasonably fear homosexuals having any contact with children. The majority of homosexuals, like the majority of heterosexuals, abhor the thought of children being encouraged, coerced, or forced to have sexual contact with adults. And the majority of homosexuals, again like the majority of heterosexuals, do not harm or infringe upon the rights and feelings of others in their sexual practices.

Another of the common myths is that being homosexual is just a personal preference, a sort of perverse choice that is inherently immoral, and that only personal motivation is needed in order to become heterosexual. This myth has been challenged from many fronts. For example, as I have earlier mentioned, there are a number of research studies that suggest biological and/or genetic influences in the establishment of sexual orientation. Among these studies is one conducted by Simon LeVay (1991), that found differences in the hypothalmic area of the brain of homosexual men as compared to heterosexual men. Another study (Allen and Gorski, 1992) found that an area of the brain (the anterior commissure) was 34 percent larger in homosexual males than in heterosexual males.

Studies that suggest a possible genetic, inherited component in sexual orientation include one by Bailey and Pillard (1991). These researchers found that in 52 percent of identical twins, when one is gay the other is also; and, if a nonidentical twin was gay, his cotwin was also gay in 22 percent of the cases. Although these findings suggest a partial genetic component, if only genetics were involved, it would be expected that with identical twins, if one is gay the other would always be gay. Further evidence for a genetic component to sexual orientation was found by researchers at the National Cancer Institute (Hamer et al., 1993; Hamer and Copeland, 1994). Hamer and his colleagues found that homosexual brothers share certain sequences of DNA on the X chromosome. This finding suggests the possibility that a predisposition to male homosexuality may be inherited through the maternal genes.

These studies do not constitute evidence that genes or biological factors alone determine sexual orientation, but rather that they may play a part, may have some degree of influence. The general conclusion of the majority of scientists who have studied the issue is that sexual orientation is an extremely complex human characteristic and, like many other such characteristics, is probably shaped through a very intricate interaction of biological, psychological, and social forces (Money, 1987).

What may be more important, however, than seeking a cause of sexual orientation is that, once it is established, usually very early in life, it is not readily susceptible to change. If you are heterosexual, you have only to imagine how difficult it would be to change your sexual orientation, to become homosexual, in order to understand the near impossibility of changing what is such a basic part of your nature, your very identity. Such a change, if it were possible, would involve much more than merely changing your behavior. It would require changing your emotional, romantic, and sexual feelings and your very concept of self. There are those individuals, however, who have a bisexual orientation and have the capacity and inclination for sexual, romantic relationships with either same- or opposite-sex partners. The statistics in terms of the frequency of bisexuals in the population at large is unclear at this time and may depend in large part on the differing definitions of bisexuality.

Though there are mental health professionals who claim, based on clinical case examples, that they have changed the sexual orientation of their clients, no credible scientific evidence, backed up by valid, empirical studies, exists to support their claims. Haldeman (1991) has reviewed reports of these so-called "conversion" and "reparative" therapies and has concluded that they reinforce the stigma associated with homosexuality and that the practitioners of these therapies offer no credible evidence to support their theory that sexual orientation can be changed. The majority of mental health professionals who have examined the research now believe it is unprofessional, some believe unethical, to attempt to convert people from homosexuality to heterosexuality, and believe also that such attempts stem primarily from social prejudice masquerading as treatment, treatment having the potential to be detrimental and harmful.

Martin Duberman, in his book *Cures: A Gay Man's Odyssey* (1991), describes eloquently the many years he spent with therapists who tried unsuccessfully to change his sexual orientation. His therapists reinforced his sense of deviance about his homosexuality and insisted upon the necessity of his becoming heterosexual. He never became a successful, happy heterosexual, despite his years of therapy, and was only able to repair the psychological damage engendered by the therapy when he finally acknowledged to himself that he was truly homosexual and that there was nothing wrong with being so.

Another myth is that exposure to homosexual role models such as teachers or parents will result in harmful effects on children and will influence their sexual orientation. This belief leads many people, who might otherwise be more tolerant, to believe that homosexual teachers should not be permitted in the classroom and that homosexual parents should not be allowed to have custody of children.

Most of the research that has been done regarding this issue has focused on homosexuals as parents, and since a parent is usually the most significant role model in a child's life, this research is pertinent. There are a number of published research studies examining the effects of being reared by a gay or lesbian parent (Green, 1978; Golombok, Spencer, and Rutter, 1983; Kirkpatrick, Smith, and Roy, 1981; and Patterson, 1992, 1996). These studies found no significant differences between children raised by homosexual parents and those raised by heterosexual parents in terms of social/emotional adjustment, peer relationships, or sexual orientation. The studies demonstrate that gay or lesbian role models are not harmful to children and do not influence their sexual orientation.

Insofar as teachers are concerned, any teacher, whether homosexual or heterosexual, who behaves in a sexually inappropriate manner with children should certainly not be tolerated. And the notion that just being taught by an openly gay or lesbian teacher could lead a child to be gay goes against any reasonable interpretation of the way sexuality develops. The development of a homosexual orientation does not come about as a result of hearing about homosexuality or by being in the vicinity of homosexual people. Homosexuality is not contagious, and homosexuals do not convert young people into being gay.

The many false beliefs and myths about homosexuality perpetuate prejudice and negative feelings toward gays and lesbians and they also have a powerful influence upon the social and emotional development of children who are growing up to be gay. As a child develops and begins to become aware of sexual feelings, the feelings are validated and supported by society when they are directed toward individuals of the opposite sex. Little boys are expected to get crushes on little girls and little girls on little boys. On the contrary, if these feelings are toward members of the same sex, the child or adolescent receives strong messages that his or her feelings are wrong, perverted, or even evil.

It is only necessary to imagine what it would be like to grow up believing that your sexual feelings and attractions are condemned by your parents, your teachers, your peers, and your religion, in order to be able to imagine what many gay/lesbian youth experience as they come to the recognition of their sexual orientation. These youth are confronted with the dawning and frightening realization that they may be members of a despised and stigmatized group. Those who are suspected of being gay by their peers are often subjected to verbal harassment and even physical assault. For example, in studies conducted with young gay and bisexual males, Remafedi (1987) found that the majority reported regular verbal abuse from classmates and one third had been physically assaulted. In another study (D'Augelli, 1996) over 80 percent of gay, lesbian, and bisexual youth who were surveyed reported verbal attacks, 34 percent had been threatened with physical attacks, and 13 percent had been actually physically assaulted. These figures make it clear why so many gay youth do not disclose their sexual orientation while they are still in high school. But even for those who do not disclose, who are not readily identifiable, and who may not have been harassed or assaulted, the clear evidence all around them of the disregard in which people like themselves are held, has to be traumatic.

Gay youth also do not have the positive role models that they need in order to help overcome the stigma. The role models gay and lesbian youth need are openly homosexual individuals who are successful, respected members of society with positive, healthy relationships. This lack of positive role models is not because there are no such individuals, but because so many homosexuals, even now and even as adults, find it necessary to conceal their sexual orientation. This is particularly true for teachers, often the role models for heterosexual youth. Teaching is a profession which makes it more than usually difficult for its members to come out of the closet.

In addition to the lack of positive role models, the victimization experiences resulting from harassment, and the societal messages that homosexuality is abhorrent and perverted, the young homosexual usually has no family support. It is typical that the adolescent is afraid to reveal his or her sexual orientation to the family for fear of disapproval or rejection. A youth from a racial, ethnic, or religious minority who experiences prejudice or discrimination usually has a family to identify with and has emotional support from the family. But the parents of a sexual minority youth are seldom homosexual, are usually not aware of their child's orientation, and were they to become aware would likely not be supportive.

The negative stereotypes and the stigma associated with homosexuality cause many adolescents to struggle against identifying themselves as gay or lesbian. Many totally deny their sexual feelings even to themselves and try to conform to social expectations to be heterosexual, or they may convince themselves that their homosexual attractions are temporary and will disappear when they are older. Others recognize and acknowledge to themselves that they are truly homosexual, but still pretend to others, their friends and families, that they are heterosexual. Another, usually much smaller group is openly gay during adolescence. This may occur by deliberate choice in certain courageous individuals, or, for others, may occur involuntarily because they are more easily identifiable by others as gay or lesbian. The latter often fit some of the more common homosexual stereotypes, for example, extremely feminine boys, who may or may not be gay. The stigma and harassment is just as often directed at boys who do not fit the typical masculine image, but are not gay, as it is for those who are. Gender nonconformity—that is, being unlike the stereotypes for your gender—is often just as stigmatizing as is homosexuality, although this is much truer for males than for females. The tomboyish girl is not usually stigmatized in the same way as the so-called effeminate boy.

The various adaptations that young gays and lesbians have to make as they cope with their feelings may result in enormous pressures during their growing up years and may lead to serious adjustment problems. Gay youth often have difficulty in forming a positive sense of their own identity and may begin to feel worthless and even sinful, internalizing the homophobia all around them. Hating their sexual orientation, they may be led into self-hatred.

As these youth become aware of being so different from their peers, they may also isolate themselves. Questions about their sexual identity go unanswered because they are afraid to confide in anyone, fearing that their hidden secret will be discovered. They may believe that if they were to tell their parents, they would be rejected, sent away for treatment, or even thrown out on the street.

Some gay and lesbian youth become depressed and even suicidal. There are a number of studies (Gibson, 1989; Remafedi, Farrow, and Deisher, 1991; and Roesler and Deisher, 1972) that show gay and lesbian youth are at a much higher risk for suicide or attempted suicide than are heterosexual youth.

The conflict about their sexual orientation may also predispose gay youth to substance abuse and school-related problems. And another very frightening outcome is the higher risk for young gay males of acquiring a sexually transmitted disease, including HIV/AIDS. The self-hatred and low self-esteem that characterize some homosexual and bisexual youth may lead to fatalistic, hopeless attitudes and predispose them to risk taking in the area of sexual behaviors as well as in other areas of their lives.

Ethnic minority gay and lesbian youth may possibly be at even greater risk of suicide, substance abuse, and school failure than are white youth. These youth often experience a dual discrimination based upon their minority status as well as upon their sexual orientation. In some instances, they may also face special problems within their own ethnic group due to cultural and familial attitudes about homosexuality.

The dangers and unique difficulties of growing up gay or lesbian in our society are evident. Are there ways in which the dangers and difficulties can be minimized? I have given a great deal of thought to this question, using my personal experiences with my own children and my professional experiences as a psychologist, talking to gay/lesbian youth and adults, and reviewing the available literature. Although there are no simple, definitive answers, there are a number of reasonable approaches that could be taken, and some of these are beginning to occur already.

The education of parents and of potential and future parents about homosexuality and the possibility of having a gay/lesbian child would be a major step in helping gay youth to avoid at least some of the problems and roadblocks that now occur in their growing-up process. As mentioned previously, there is little such information available in parenting books or classes. Professionals who write parenting books and articles or who teach parenting classes need to become better informed about sexual orientation and should include information about homosexuality in their writings and public presentations.

Parents need to be exposed to the basic facts about sexual orientation and need to learn that the homosexual stereotypes are merely that, just stereotypes. Parents need to learn that most of the myths about homosexuals are not accurate and to realize that much of the prejudice toward homosexuality derives from these destructive myths and misunderstandings.

Parents need to know that once their child's sexual orientation is established, it is not likely to be changed and that attempts to change it may result in serious psychological damage to the child. They need help to realize that if their child turns out to be gay, it is not their fault, first of all because there is nothing wrong with being gay, and second, because there is no evidence that parental influence causes homosexuality (Bell, Weinberg, and Hammersmith, 1981), and there is nothing the parents can do to prevent it. Most important of all, parents need to realize that their support and love for their gay child can enable that child to live a productive, happy life and help him avoid the pain and confusion that come from fear of parental rejection.

As noted earlier, one of the ways parents can become better informed about their child's sexual orientation and can learn how to be supportive to their gay or lesbian child is by becoming involved with Parents, Families and Friends of Lesbians and Gays (PFLAG), which has chapters throughout the country. Many books helpful to parents of gay/lesbian children are also now available and can be found in the references at the end of this book.

However, since parents often do not realize they have a gay or lesbian child or a child who may eventually grow up to be gay, the education of all parents and potential parents should focus on general attitude change and reduction of homophobia. Parents usually convey in daily subtle interactions with their children their attitudes about homosexuality. A message is certainly conveyed when there is absolute silence about the topic. And other messages are conveyed which will either suggest to children that their parents are tolerant and accepting of diversity, including sexual diversity, or will convey instead that they are highly intolerant of those who are different, especially homosexuals.

Parents who express tolerance in general and tolerance specifically toward homosexuals will be giving a powerful message to the child or adolescent who is beginning to be aware of his or her own feelings of homosexual attraction. Just as powerful a message will be conveyed when comments or behavior of the parents suggest to the child that they consider homosexuals to be immoral or perverted. The casual remarks that parents make or the things they don't say will gradually inform their children of how their parents feel about homosexuals.

My older son told me that one of the things that was helpful to him when he was growing up was that he had heard me and his father occasionally make remarks that led him to think we were not judgmental about homosexuality and did not believe that homosexuals were deviant, awful people. I have unending regrets that we did not convey a greater depth of understanding and tolerance than Andy's memories reflect. What would have been much more helpful would have been to very explicitly tell our children that antigay prejudice is wrong and is just like prejudice toward persons of a different color or a different religion.

Educating parents to teach their children tolerance of those who are different and respect for the dignity of all human beings are worthy goals, even for those whose children will not be gay. Parental attitudes can go far in educating future generations that differences among people should be appreciated and respected, not vilified and condemned.

Just as important as the role of parents in helping gay youth is the role of the school. Since most gay/lesbian youth are, in effect, invisible during their elementary and high school years, educators often believe that they are so extremely rare that no attention or help for them is needed. However, even those school administrators who are more aware that there is likely to be a significant number of gay youth in their student body are often fearful of parental reactions if the issue were to even be mentioned. Despite the reluctance of educators to acknowledge the needs of gay youth, the needs exist, and our society is hopefully reaching the point where schools will begin to accept some responsibility for meeting these needs.

Probably one of the most significant contributions schools could make would be to provide information to all students about the range of acceptable sexual behaviors in a nonbiased, nonjudgmental manner. My sons and others have told me that what would have been helpful to them when they were beginning to recognize their homosexual attractions would have been a very simple class presentation of information about sexual orientation, pointing out that homosexuals are not perverted or abnormal, and that being homosexual doesn't mean that one can't grow up to be a normal, healthy adult. To provide emotional support to gay students and reduce prejudice in the nongay students will require schools to teach that homosexuality exists, that homosexuals deserve the same respect as anyone else, and that no one needs to be ashamed of being homosexual.

Schools also need to become much more aware of the dangers, psychological and physical, that sexual minority youth face, and to take responsibility for providing a safe learning environment for these students. In 1996, for the first time in this country, a gay former student in Wisconsin sued the school district he had attended during junior high and high school for failing to protect him from the repeated abuse of other students. The Lambda Legal Defense and Education Fund took on the case and appealed it to the federal Seventh Circuit Court of Appeals after it had been dismissed by the federal district court. The Seventh Circuit Court ruled that the student had valid equal protection claims based on sexual orientation and gender discrimination. The court ruled that discrimination based on sexual orientation was unconstitutional and found the three school administrators liable. In an out-of-court settlement the young man was awarded civil damages of $900,000.

The Wisconsin court decision may have a significant impact upon school administrators in regard to their responsibilities to gay students and should remind them that these youth must be provided with a secure atmosphere free from discrimination, harassment, violence, and abuse. This will require schools to have explicitly stated policies that prohibit discrimination, including discrimination based on sexual orientation, policies that emphasize respect and tolerance for diversity. Once policies are in place, they must be strongly enforced.

School employment practices are equally important, and the school policies should prohibit employment discrimination that would prevent the hiring of openly gay teachers, staff, or administrators. Positive gay and lesbian adult role models in the school setting could be of significant influence toward helping gay youth develop more positive conceptions of themselves.

Sex education courses in school need to include explicit and nondiscriminating information about sexual orientation and sexually transmitted diseases, especially AIDS. Gay male adolescents, in particular, are at risk for AIDS and need clear, unambiguous education about prevention.

To help convey positive images of gays and lesbians, students should be exposed to knowledge about homosexuals who have made significant contributions throughout history. Their homosexuality should not be glossed over or ignored, nor should it be overly emphasized unless it is crucial to the individual's work. Casual reference to sexual orientation in the context of the curriculum can do a great deal to bolster the esteem of the young gay or lesbian and teach the straight students that creativity and significant achievement are not the sole prerogative of heterosexuals.

School counselors, as well as mental health professionals outside the schools, have a vital role in helping reduce the stress of those youth growing up gay. Most of the gay youth seen by school counselors or other therapists will not readily identify themselves as gay or lesbian and will, instead, express many of the same kinds of problems and concerns as other adolescents. Counselors should have overcome any personal prejudices that they may have, and should be open to the possibility that the adolescent they are seeing may have concerns about sexual orientation or sexual identity issues. The obvious presence in the counselor's office of books about sexual orientation and posters that give information about gay youth support groups or other gay-related services will immediately give the young person who has sexual orientation concerns the message that this counselor is someone whom he or she can feel safe talking to. The counselor must also be comfortable enough to ask directly about sexual orientation in the same manner in which he or she obtains other significant information about the youth. The issue should be raised in a very nonjudgmental, matter-of-fact way, and the assumption of heterosexuality should be avoided.

For example, in asking about dating or sexual involvement, a good beginning approach is to ask in a very neutral way whether the young person has any concerns about dating, about sexual feelings, or about relationships, and to convey that some young people are attracted to the opposite sex and some to people of the same sex. This approach tells the gay youth that the counselor is someone who will not be shocked or judgmental, and even if the youth is unwilling to acknowledge homosexual attractions or concerns at the time, he or she will, at least, feel accepted and may be able to confide more later.

There is no need for counselors or therapists to be afraid they will encourage homosexuality by talking about it or that talking about it will put the idea into the young person's head. Indeed, some youth who have concerns about their sexual orientation will, in the course of counseling, be helped to realize that they are not homosexual. It is entirely possible for adolescents to have occasional homosexual fantasies and thoughts and even to have engaged in homosexual behavior, and yet be primarily heterosexual in their orientation. Premature labeling of a youth as homosexual is, of course, very unwise and must be guarded against. But by providing an atmosphere of acceptance and exploration, the counselor can often help relieve the guilt and shame that the sexually questioning youth may be experiencing.

The important task is for the counselor to provide an atmosphere in which the young person can express his or her sexual concerns or sexual identity conflicts and not feel judged or shamed. The most crucial message that can be given is that whatever one's sexual orientation may turn out to be, it is possible to have a meaningful, productive, and happy life.

When a young person has become convinced that he or she is gay, it is not the counselor's role to inform the parents or anyone else about the youth's sexual orientation. However, if the adolescent expresses a wish to disclose to his family, the counselor needs to understand that this may precipitate a family crisis. The counselor needs to explore in depth whether the youth realizes the risk he is taking in disclosing his homosexuality. The discovery that a child in the family is gay is likely to produce intense shock and depression in the family members, and the child faces the possibility of rejection or even abuse. The young person should be helped to anticipate the possibility of such reactions if contemplating telling his family about his orientation and assisted in the process if he decides to disclose.

When parents do learn that they have a gay child, they will need information, education, and support. Referral to support groups such as PFLAG is recommended so that family members can be helped to understand, accept, and support their child, and at the same time deal with what it means in terms of their own identity as a family to have a gay or bisexual child.

Another important role for the counselor is that of being supportive to gay students who wish to form gay/straight student alliances or support groups in the school setting. These groups provide a safe forum for students to discuss sexual orientation issues and hopefully will include both gay and straight students. Such groups are now in existence in a number of schools across the nation, and, despite efforts to ban these groups in states such as Utah and Arizona, the Equal Access Act as passed by the U.S. Congress, requires public secondary schools to allow gay-related student groups if the schools receive federal assistance and allow other noncurricular student groups to meet on campus. Schools, by virtue of this act, cannot deny gay youth groups the same rights as other student groups.

Unfortunately, when young people with concerns about their sexual orientation approach mental health professionals outside the school setting, they do not always find an unprejudiced therapist who is knowledgeable about homosexuality. Although there has been significant progress in educating mental health professionals about homosexuality, there are still therapists who are not sufficiently informed in regard to the critical issues or who are homophobic themselves. Parents will sometimes approach a counselor or therapist with the specific hope or goal that the therapist will be able to change the child's orientation, and some therapists are willing to agree to such a request. In the opinion of the majority of mental health professionals, those who are adequately trained in this area, it would be unprofessional for a therapist to agree to such a request from parents. Instead, the therapist should make clear to the parents that the young person's feelings will be explored in an effort to help him or her clarify any sexual identity concerns, but that no attempt will be made to change or influence sexual orientation. Giving an unrealistic hope of a "cure" to parents or to the youth can result in incredible harm and can exacerbate the young person's feelings of guilt and shame.

I have little to say about religious intolerance of homosexuality, except to point out the strange discrepancy between religious values and human values that must exist when a religion singles out a specific group of human beings as less worthy of respect and human dignity than others. Fortunately, there is an emerging movement among some religious leaders encouraging the promotion of tolerance toward homosexuals, a movement that may have a tremendous influence on social attitudes. Certain churches are far in the lead in this movement while others lag far behind and use the Bible to justify their continuing prejudice.

I hope we will someday openly confront the pervasive homophobia in our society and recognize it for what it is, just another form of prejudice toward those who are different, not justifiable by claims that gays and lesbians are immoral and sick. I hope that gay youth will some day have the same degree of respect and the same rights as other youth so that they do not have to live with secrecy and go through their school years being ashamed of who they are. It often seems, as Gary wrote in his little seventh grade essay, that children in our society, particularly, perhaps, those children who will grow up to be gay or lesbian, have many fewer protected rights than do adults. And so I would like to propose that all children should be entitled to certain rights protecting them from prejudice and discrimination, and helping them to grow up safely while at the same time teaching them the importance of tolerance toward those who are different from themselves.

For example,

1. The right to live in a society that respects all minorities, including sexual minorities, and where all forms of social discrimination, including homophobia, are condemned
2. The right to grow up in a home where tolerance and respect for others is taught and where discrimination toward minorities or women is not tolerated, a home where homophobia is considered a form of prejudice like any other
3. The right to receive accurate, nonjudgmental information about sexuality and sexual orientation, particularly information about the erroneous myths and stereotypes associated with homosexuality
4. The right to receive age-appropriate, accurate sex education, including education about unwanted pregnancy and sexually transmitted diseases, especially AIDS
5. The right to know openly gay adults who are responsible, productive citizens
6. The right to grow up knowing no one in this country will be deprived of his or her civil rights because of sexual orientation or being a member of a minority group, and knowing that hate crimes will be identified as one of the dangerous outcomes of prejudice
7. The right to grow up knowing that no profession or vocation will be closed because of sexual orientation, gender, or membership in any minority group
8. The right to receive religious education in a church that is tolerant of diversity and of sexual minorities
9. The right to have teachers who are unprejudiced and who are knowledgeable about minority cultures, sexual orientation, and child and adolescent development
10. The right to attend schools where discrimination based on sexual orientation, gender, race, ethnicity, or religion is prohibited and where tolerance of diversity is actively promoted

Great strides toward providing safe and accepting school environments for gay youth have been made in Massachusetts, under the leadership of its governor, William Weld. In 1992, Governor Weld, in a visionary move, established the Governor's Commission on Gay and Lesbian Youth because of his concern about gay youth suicides and violence and harassment against gay and lesbian youth. The governor's commission, after a careful study, issued a report (1993) identifying the problems faced by gay youth and made specific recommendations for how schools could remediate these problems and provide an atmosphere of dignity and respect for these young people. The recommendations included training teachers, adopting antidiscrimination policies to protect gay students, providing relevant information in school libraries, establishing support groups for students to discuss gay and lesbian youth issues, and including gay and lesbian issues in school curricula. The recommendations were approved by the State Board of Education in 1993. The governor and the state of Massachusetts are to be commended for their accomplishments and far-reaching vision. Perhaps the model Massachusetts has provided will influence other states and communities to follow a similar path. Evidence of the influence this report has had upon gay youth in Massachusetts can be found in the proliferation of gay/straight student alliances and other gay-related student groups in the high schools in Massachusetts. Whereas most states have no or few such student groups in their schools, Massachusetts has more than seventy schools where these groups have been established (Buckel, 1996).

Until some of these perhaps radical changes in social and family attitudes come about, many young homosexuals will continue to engage in those strategies which may not be psychologically healthy in the long run, but which sometimes help protect them from the negative repercussions of being identified as gay or lesbian during their school years. One of these is to pass as straight. For those young persons who don't fit the stereotypes, this may be relatively easy to do and may allow them to go through their adolescent and high school years without suffering from overt discrimination. This strategy may sometimes be adaptive in the short run, giving the youth time to acquire self-respect and competencies that may make it easier to cope with the social stigma of being gay in a straight world. Another strategy is to convince oneself that the homosexual attractions are just temporary and will dissipate in time. Many young gays truly do believe this, primarily because they don't fit the gay stereotypes they know about and, therefore, believe they must not really be gay. For these youth it isn't so much a matter of pretending to be straight as it is of believing they must be straight because they can't accept that they could truly be members of a group so despised by others.

However, these kinds of individual protective mechanisms are usually based on the young person's internalization of society's homophobia, and can lead to destructive habits of blocking emotions and avoiding intimacy. In a more ideal world, where the practices just discussed have been implemented, one where antigay prejudice would be much less virulent than it now is, these kinds of defenses would be unnecessary and the young gay or lesbian would feel just as good about his or her sexual feelings as does the young heterosexual, and would no longer have to deny and hide.

Despite the innumerable difficulties that gay youth may experience during childhood and adolescence, many not only overcome them but are able to reach extraordinarily high levels of achievement and creativity in adulthood. Some believe there is even a higher frequency of creative accomplishment among gays than among heterosexuals, perhaps due to the adverse circumstances gays have to overcome, but there is no solid evidence of this, just impressions. In general, gays and lesbians possess the same broad range of positive and negative characteristics as heterosexuals do and their sexual orientation, like heterosexual orientation, is only one aspect of their identity. I believe the negative homosexual stereotypes will eventually be overcome as more and more gays and lesbians come out and publicly acknowledge their sexual orientation. And I foresee a time when antigay prejudice will be viewed as identical to prejudice toward those of a different race or religion, when homophobia will no longer be an acceptable prejudice.

I have the hope that gay youth will one day grow up in a society that will accept them as they are, and the hope that all parents of gay children will one day love and appreciate them just as they love and appreciate their heterosexual children. And I have the hope that one day no child will have to grow up thinking he is inferior just because he is homosexual.

References

Allen, L.S. and Gorski, R.A. (1992). Sexual orientation and the size of the anterior commissure in the human brain. *Proceedings of the National Academy of Science U.S.A.*, 89, *(No. 7199)*.

Bailey, J.M and Pillard, R.C. (1991). A genetic study of male sexual orientation. *Archives of General Psychiatry,* 48, 1089-1096.

Bawer, B. (1993). *A place at the table: The gay individual in American society.* New York: Poseidon Press.

Bell, A.P., Weinberg, M.S., and Hammersmith, S.K. (1981). *Sexual preference: Its development in men and women.* Bloomington: Indiana University Press.

Buckel, D. (1996). *The equal access act.* Unpublished memorandum. New York: Lambda Legal Defense and Education Fund, Inc.

Burgess, A.W., Groth, A.N., Holmstrom, L.L., and Sgroi, S.M. (1978). *Sexual assault of children and adolescents.* Lexington, MA: D.C. Health.

Campbell, J. with Moyers, B. (1988). *The power of myth.* New York: Doubleday.

Cass, V. (1979). Homosexual identity formation: A theoretical model. *Journal of Homosexuality,* 4, 219-235.

Cass, V. (1984). Homosexual identity formation: Testing a theoretical model. *The Journal of Sex Research,* 20, 143-167.

Coleman, E. (1982). Developmental stages of the coming out process. In J. Gonsiorek (Ed.), *Homosexuality and psychotherapy: A practitioner's handbook of affirmative models* (pp. 31-44). Binghamton, NY: The Haworth Press, Inc.

D'Augelli, A.R. (1996). *Victimization of lesbian, gay, and bisexual youths in community settings.* Paper presented at the annual meeting of the American Psychological Association, Toronto, Canada.

Dew, R.F. (1994). *The family heart: A memoir of when our son came out.* New York: Addison-Wesley.

Duberman, M. (1991). *Cures: A gay man's odyssey.* New York: Dutton.

Dworkin, R. (1994). *Life's dominion: An argument about abortion, euthanasia, and individual freedom.* New York: Vintage Books, Random House.

Fairchild, B. and Hayward, N. (1989). *Now that you know: What every parent should know about homosexuality.* San Diego, New York, London: Harcourt, Brace, Jovanovich.

Fish, W.C. (1986). Differences of grief intensity in bereaved parents. In T.A. Rando (Ed.), *Parental loss of a child* (pp. 415-428). Champaign, IL: Research Press.

Gibson, P. (1989). Gay male and lesbian youth suicide. In M.R. Feinleib (Ed.), *Report of the secretary's task force on youth suicide, Volume 3: Preventions and interventions in youth suicide* (3-110-3-142). Rockville, MD: U.S. Department of Health and Human Services.

Ginsburg, G.D. (1987). *To live again: Rebuilding your life after you've become a widow.* Los Angeles: Jeremy P. Tarcher, Inc. Distributed by New York: St. Martin's Press.

Golombok, S., Spencer, A., and Rutter, M. (1983). Children in lesbian and single-parent households: Psychosexual and psychiatric appraisal. *Journal of Child Psychology and Psychiatry,* 24, 551-572.

Gonsiorek, J.C. (1977). *Psychological adjustment and homosexuality.* Social and Behavioral Sciences Documents, MS 1478, San Rafael, CA: Select Press.

_____. (1982). Results of psychological testing on homosexual populations. In W. Paul, J.D. Weinrich, J.C. Gonsiorek, and M.E. Hotvedt (Eds.), *Homosexuality: Social, psychological and biological issues* (pp. 71-88). Beverly Hills, CA: Sage.

_____. (1991). The empirical basis for the demise of the illness model of homosexuality. In J.C. Gonsiorek and J.D. Weinrich (Eds.), *Homosexuality: Research implications for public policy* (pp. 115-136). Newbury Park, CA: Sage.

Gonsiorek, J.C. and Rudolph, J.R. (1991). Homosexual identity: Coming out and other developmental events. In J.C. Gonsiorek and J.D. Weinrich (Eds.), *Homosexuality: Research implications for public policy* (pp. 161-176). Newbury Park, CA: Sage.

Governor's Commission on Gay and Lesbian Youth. (1993). *Making schools safe for gay and lesbian youth: Breaking the silence in schools and in families.* Publication No. 17296-60-500-2/93-C.R. Boston, MA: State House.

Green, R. (1978). Sexual identity of 37 children raised by homosexual or transsexual parents. *American Journal of Psychiatry,* 135, 692-697.

Griffin, C.W., Wirth, M.J., and Wirth, A.G. (1986). *Beyond acceptance: Parents of lesbians and gays talk about their experiences.* New York: St. Martins Press.

Groth, A.N. and Birnbaum, H.J. (1989). *Men who rape: The psychology of the offender.* New York: Plenum.

Haldeman, D.C. (1991). Sexual orientation conversion therapy for gay men and lesbians: A scientific examination. In J.C. Gonsiorek and J.D. Weinrich (Eds.), *Homosexuality: Research implications for public policy* (pp. 149-160). Newbury Park, CA: Sage.

Hamer, D.H., Hu, S., Magnuson, V.L., Hu, N., and Pattatucci, A. (1993). A linkage between DNA markers on the X chromosome and male sexual orientation. *Science,* 261, 321-327.

Hamer, D.H. and Copeland, P. (1994). *The science of desire: The search for the gay gene and the biology of behavior.* New York: Simon & Schuster.

Hooker, E.A. (1957). The adjustment of the overt male homosexual. *Journal of Projective Techniques,* 21, 17-31.

Humphry, D. (1991). *Final exit: The practicalities of self-deliverance and assisted suicide for the dying.* Eugene, OR: The Hemlock Society.

Hunter, J. (1990). Violence against lesbian and gay male youths. *Journal of Interpersonal Violence,* 5, 295-300.

Jenny, C., Roesler, T.A., and Poyer, K.L. (1992). *Assessing the risk that sexually abused children have been molested by recognizably homosexual adults.* Unpublished paper. Denver, CO: The Children's Hospital.

Jenny, C., Roesler, T.A., and Poyer, K.L. (1994). Are children at risk for sexual abuse by homosexuals? *Pediatrics,* 94 (1), 41-44.

Kirkpatrick, M., Smith, C., and Roy, R. (1981). Lesbian mothers and their children: A comparative survey. *Journal of Homosexuality,* 13, 201-211.

Koop, C.E. (1986). *The Surgeon General's report on acquired immune deficiency syndrome.* Washington, DC: U.S. Government Printing Office.

LeVay, S. (1991). A difference in hypothalmic structure between heterosexual and homosexual men. *Science,* 253, 1034-1037.

Money, J. (1987). Sin, sickness or status? Homosexual gender identity and psychoneuroendocrinology. *American Psychologist,* 42, 384-399.

National Commission on Acquired Immune Deficiency Syndrome (1991). *America living with AIDS.* Washington, DC: U.S. Government Printing Office.

Nuland, S.B. (1994). *How we die: Reflections on life's final chapter.* New York: Alfred A. Knopf.

Patterson, C.J. (1992). Children of lesbian and gay parents. *Child Development,* 63, 1025-1042.

Patterson, C.J. (1996). Lesbian and gay parents and their children. In R.C. Savin-Williams and K.M. Cohen (Eds.), *The lives of lesbians, gays, and bisexuals: Children to adults.* Fort Worth, TX: Harcourt Brace College Publishers.

Quill, T.E. (1991). Death and dignity: A case of individualized decision making. *New England Journal of Medicine,* 324 (10), 691-694.

Quill, T. (1993). *Death and dignity: Making choices and taking charge.* New York: W.W. Norton.

Rando, T. (Ed.) (1986). *Parental loss of a child.* Champaign, IL: Research Press.

Reiss, B.F. (1980). Psychological tests in homosexuality. In J. Marmor (Ed.), *Homosexual behavior: A modern reappraisal* (pp. 296-311). New York: Basic Books.

Remafedi, G. (1987). Male homosexuality: The adolescent's perspective. *Pediatrics,* 79, 326-330.

Remafedi, G., Farrow, J.A., and Deisher, R.W. (1991). Risk factors for attempted suicide in gay and bisexual youth. *Pediatrics,* 87, 869-875.

Roesler, T. and Deisher, R. (1972). Youthful male homosexuality: Homosexual experience and the process of developing homosexual identity in males aged 16 to 22 years. *Journal of the American Medical Association,* 219, 1018-1023.

Sacks, O. (1995). *An anthropologist on Mars: Seven paradoxical tales.* New York: Alfred A. Knopf.

Shilts, R. (1987). *And the band played on: Politics, people, and the AIDS epidemic.* New York: St. Martins Press.

Silverstein, C. (1972, October). *Behavior modification and the gay community.* Paper presented at the annual convention of the Association for the Advancement of Behavior Therapy, New York City.

Stroebe, M., Gergen, M.M., Gergen, K.J., and Stroebe, W. (1992). Broken hearts or broken bonds: Love and death in historical perspective. *American Psychologist*, 47, 1205-1212.

Troiden, R.R. (1979). Becoming a homosexual: A model of gay identity acquisition. *Psychiatry*, 42, 362-373.

_____. (1988). Homosexual identity development. *Journal of Adolescent Health Care*, 9, 105-113.

Vidal, G. (1968). *Messiah*. London: Heinemann.

Index

Order Your Own Copy of
This Important Book for Your Personal Library!

FAMILY SECRETS
Gay Sons—A Mother's Story

_____ in hardbound at $39.95 (ISBN: 0-7890-0248-5)

_____ in softbound at $14.95 (ISBN: 1-56023-915-8)

COST OF BOOKS_____

OUTSIDE USA/CANADA/
MEXICO: ADD 20%_____

POSTAGE & HANDLING_____
(US: $3.00 for first book & $1.25
for each additional book)
Outside US: $4.75 for first book
& $1.75 for each additional book)

SUBTOTAL_____

IN CANADA: ADD 7% GST_____

STATE TAX_____
(NY, OH & MN residents, please
add appropriate local sales tax)

FINAL TOTAL_____
(If paying in Canadian funds,
convert using the current
exchange rate. UNESCO
coupons welcome.)

☐ **BILL ME LATER:** ($5 service charge will be added)
(Bill-me option is good on US/Canada/Mexico orders only;
not good to jobbers, wholesalers, or subscription agencies.)

☐ Check here if billing address is different from
shipping address and attach purchase order and
billing address information.

Signature_____

☐ **PAYMENT ENCLOSED: $**_____

☐ **PLEASE CHARGE TO MY CREDIT CARD.**

☐ Visa   ☐ MasterCard   ☐ AmEx   ☐ Discover
☐ Diner's Club

Account # _____

Exp. Date _____

Signature _____

Prices in US dollars and subject to change without notice.

NAME _____

INSTITUTION _____

ADDRESS _____

CITY _____

STATE/ZIP _____

COUNTRY _____ COUNTY (NY residents only) _____

TEL _____ FAX _____

E-MAIL_____
May we use your e-mail address for confirmations and other types of information? ☐ Yes   ☐ No

Order From Your Local Bookstore or Directly From
The Haworth Press, Inc.
10 Alice Street, Binghamton, New York 13904-1580 • USA
TELEPHONE: 1-800-HAWORTH (1-800-429-6784) / Outside US/Canada: (607) 722-5857
FAX: 1-800-895-0582 / Outside US/Canada: (607) 772-6362
E-mail: getinfo@haworth.com
PLEASE PHOTOCOPY THIS FORM FOR YOUR PERSONAL USE.

BOF96